A GHOST IN TRIESTE

a ghost in

TRI

JOSEPH CARY

WITH DRAWINGS BY NICHOLAS READ

THE UNIVERSITY OF CHICAGO PRESS   CHICAGO AND LONDON

Joseph Cary is professor emeritus of English and Comparative Literature at the University of Connecticut, and the author of *Three Modern Italian Poets: Saba, Ungaretti, Montale,* also published by the University of Chicago Press.

The map of Trieste printed on the title page can be found in Alfieri Seri, *Trieste nelle sue stampe,* Edizioni "Italo Svevo" Trieste, 1980 (2d ed.).

The University of Chicago Press, Chicago 60637
The University of Chicago Press, Ltd., London
© 1993 by The University of Chicago
All rights reserved. Published 1993
Printed in the United States of America
01 00 99 98 97 96 95 94 93   1 2 3 4 5 6

ISBN (cloth): 0-226-09528-2

Library of Congress Cataloging-in-Publication Data

Cary, Joseph.
    A ghost in Trieste / Joseph Cary ; with drawings by Nicholas Read.
        p.   cm.
    Includes bibliographical references and index.
    1. Trieste (Italy)—Guidebooks.   2. Literary landmarks—Italy—Trieste—Guide-
books.   3. Cary, Joseph—Journeys—Italy—Trieste.   4. Trieste (Italy) in literature.   5.
Joyce, James, 1882–1941—Homes and haunts—Italy—Trieste.   6. Svevo, Italo, 1861–
1928—Homes and haunts—Italy—Trieste.   7. Saba, Umberto, 1883–1957—Homes
and haunts—Italy—Trieste.   I. Title.
DG975.T825C37   1993
914.5'39304929—dc20   92-37147
                                                                                              CIP

⊗The paper used in this publication meets the minimum requirements of the American National Standard for Information Sciences—Permanence of Paper for Printed Library Materials, ANSI Z39.48-1984.

My animal his sorrafool!
And trieste, ah trieste
ate I my liver! *Se non è*

vero son trovatore.

JAMES JOYCE
Finnegans Wake

tri-es-ti-ni-te (trē-ĕs-tē-nē′tā) n. 1. 'triestinitis,' home-sickness for the city of Trieste, Italy, its people, food, architecture, etc.; being prone to a yearning for same. 2. acute inflammation in response to whatever is Triestine, often transitory. 3. nostalgia for a 'lost' land, compared to a pathological state (cf. Proust, *Sodome et Gomorrhe* II, 4: "It was Trieste, that unknown world in which I felt that Albertine took pleasure, in which were her memories, her friendships, her childhood loves, that gave off that hostile, inexplicable atmosphere. . . . That city was impaled in my heart like a permanent point.")

G. GIOCARE
Vocabolario esoterico

Contents

1   Preliminary

1 1   Some Important Dates

1 5   Miramars

2 7   Up

4 1   Three Triestes

5 1   Joys of Mapwork

6 1   Three Local Martyrs

7 9   Faithfully Waiting

9 5   Tableaux Morts

1 2 1 The Sloblands of Fairview

1 3 9 Trieste Trouvée

1 6 5 The Masters in the Public Garden

1 7 3 Three Farewells

Appendixes

1 8 3   Translations

Nine Trieste Poems from the *Canzoniere*
of Umberto Saba

Two passages from Scipio Slataper,
Il mio Carso

Ettore Schmitz, "Family Chronicle"

Two Trieste poems by James Joyce, with
translations by Eugenio Montale

2 2 3   A Directory of Characters

2 4 7   Literary Trieste: Evidence of Its Existence

2 5 1   Endnotes and Acknowledgments

2 6 9   Bibliography

2 8 1   Index

2 9 1   Personal Acknowledgments

i x

Trieste

Ho attraversata tutta la città.
Poi ho salita un'erta,
popolosa in principio, in là deserta,
chiusa da un muricciolo:
un cantuccio in cui solo
siedo; e mi pare che dove esso termina
termini la città.

Trieste ha una scontrosa
grazia. Se piace,
è come un ragazzaccio aspro e vorace,
con gli occhi azzurri e mani troppo grandi
per regalare un fiore;
come un amore
con gelosia.
Da quest'erta ogni chiesa, ogni sua via
scopro, se mena all'ingombrata spiaggia,
o alla collina cui, sulla sassosa
cima, una casa, l'ultima, s'aggrappa.
Intorno
circola ad ogni cosa
un'aria strana, un'aria tormentosa,
l'aria natia.

La mia città che in ogni parte è viva,
ha il cantuccio a me fatto, alla mia vita
pensosa e schiva.

UMBERTO SABA

Trieste

I have crossed the entire city.
After, I climbed a steep rise
crowded at the start, deserted above
closed off by a low wall,
a place apart in which I sit
alone; and it seems to me that where it ends
the city ends.

Trieste has a prickly
grace. If it pleases,
it pleases like an urchin, rough and greedy,
blue-eyed, with hands too big
to give a flower;
like jealousy
in love.
From here I can discover
each church, each street
whether it lead to the thronged shore
or to that hill on which, at the rocky
top, one house, the very last, clings.
All around
all through everything there turns
a strange air, a tormenting air,
the air of home.

My city, alive in every part,
has the place apart for me alone,
for my moody, secret life.

Preliminary

Trieste.

Ho attraversata tutta la città.

The city has sprawled since 1910 when Saba★ wrote that line: I cannot claim to have walked across it all. I do say that I have climbed half of its ten hills (Roiano, Scorcola, San Giusto, San Vito, and Servola), that I have sat apart in scores of its public places (a stool at the card catalogue in the Biblioteca Civica, a chair in Caffè San Marco, the wind rose at the end of Molo Audace, a shuddering seat in the Opicina tram, and so on), and that I have religiously retraced the poet's hypothetical route that day over eighty years ago past the Distilleria Stock in the north of town by the railroad station, up the increasingly steep mile of Scala Santa—Holy Stairway—to its end beneath the Obelisk at the Carso's lip, the "place apart" of the poem with the marvelous view, where he had his vision of the living whole. *La mia città . . .*

Not, of course, that it could be "mine," a stranger there. The view remained a view, a modern city in economic trouble on a grey sea. No azure-eyed, ham-handed, sexy *ragazzaccio* in sight, as in that poem; no anthropomorphic epiphany. I just sat there, apart. I looked, I narrowed my eyes, I closed them.

But nothing came.

Umberto Saba is certainly not the first to have seen his city as a person. Trieste's earliest historian (Father Ireneo della Croce, *Historia antica e moderna, sacra e profana della città di Trieste,* 1698) mentions a Roman bas-relief once to be found set in the garden wall of the bishop's palace. It

★Signifies that biographical information may be found in A Directory of Characters (see pages 223ff.).

1

pictured Trieste as "a comely youth clad in flowing garments holding in his hands a basket of apples, symbolic of the fertility of the soil." This was good enough for Domenico Rossetti,* city father and philanthropist, who borrowed the Roman image for use in his allegorical play celebrating the return of Trieste to Austria after Napoleon's final defeat in 1814. The basket was replaced by a flowering bough.

Just up the street from my hotel, balanced on the balustrade above the pediment of the old Stock Exchange building and ranged alongside the marble figures of Neptune, Minerva, and Danube, stands Antonio Bosa's 1806 statue of the Genius of Trieste: a tall ephebe with hyacinthine hair, naked with a fig leaf, displays a civic shield embossed with halberd and stares with neoclassically blank eyeballs up the Corso Italia. A little over a century later Scipio Slataper,* Saba's contemporary and rival for Trieste's first poet, likened the city to a clownish and adolescent Parsifal who, awakening one day "between a crate of lemons and a sack of coffee beans," was troubled by his lack of culture and wondered what to do about it.

Others have imagined a *she*. A maiden Trieste sits, for example, just beneath the tip of a pyramid of limestone parcels and barrels and other packaged goods for trade that constitutes the upper portion of the mid-eighteenth-century Fountain of the Four Continents on Piazza dell'Unità d'Italia (Australia was not on the map then). Seated beside her is Commerce, bearded, turbaned, venerable, and distinctly Arabian. They stare at one another with a wild surmise as some sort of Winged Victory at the tip proclaims Trieste's fame by fiat of Maria Theresa, Empress of Austria. (None of this would be intelligible without the help of my dear *Guida di Trieste*.) The breasts of Trieste are bare and well developed. A robe is thrown over her upper legs and thighs.

She is naked in the Public Garden, too, but with a long scarf blown across her lower middle by the force of her belligerent stride. Donated to the city by Milan in 1921, the big bronze honoring the Italian Army rep-

resents Trieste *appassionata* hurling a screaming Austro-Hungarian eagle off her shoulders with one hand, gripping a snapped sword with the other. (Why *snapped?*) Trieste is similarly windblown and athletic and youthful in Carlo Sbisà's 1930s fresco in the Risorgimento Museum. Her blond hair streams in the famous bora as she profiles in her grey toga against a choppy Adriatic with the Cathedral of San Giusto cupped in her left hand, her right arm raised in salute. She is blue eyed. Is it Fascist *Kameradschaft* that makes her wave in that manner?

But at the foot of the spiral staircase in Baron Pasquale Revoltella's *
grand Biedermeier palace, Trieste is in her early forties and much less aggressive: a stately marble matron on the order of Queen Victoria, her contemporary. On the occasion of the completion of the aqueduct bringing water into the city from the underground springs in nearby Duino, she, and the Nymph of the Springs whom she invokes and welcomes, and the two *putti* happily slaking their thirst, are set within an enormous circular conch shell, "symbol of the Adriatic," as Baron Revoltella's press agent points out. He describes her as "majestically covered with a rich robe, a turreted crown—ancient symbol of the city—upon her head, seated upon a cliff washed by the sea, in which she rests her right foot. Beautiful expression of a mercantile city firmly established by seaside . . ."

A motherly Trieste. Lovely still, adorable. Or nubile, beautiful. Or handsome, open, vigorous. All images of promise, of something promising. Trieste.

If I closed my eyes now, what would I see?

I went to Trieste because I hoped to find my business there. A notion for a book, *Literary Trieste,* was in my head, and I felt that going there would translate this notion into a clear and spurring idea. But when I got there I discovered that being in Trieste could be a dismaying experience. Novel and attractive as it certainly was, the city treated me ironically—the actual warm life (*calda vita,* Saba's phrase) that I conscientiously watched flowing by and about me mocked my vague and bookish purposes. Towards the end of my first week I grew quite crestfallen. When time came to leave, I felt less than ever sure about Trieste and what I meant to do about it.

Italo Svevo (dead 1928), James Joyce (dead 1941),* Umberto Saba (dead 1957) . . . by the time I had reached Trieste, of course, they had all been dead for years. My notion had had everything to do with the geographical proximity over the decade 1905–15 of these three writers whose books I admired and owned. Svevo and Saba were natives of Trieste, and spent their lives there. Joyce was, of course, a Dubliner, who earned his living during that decade by teaching English in the Austro-Hungarian port he had come to quite by chance. ("I expound Shakespeare to docile Trieste": he had aimed originally for Paris and, failing Paris, Zurich. Fate gave him Trieste and only later, in reverse order, his cities of preference.) Literary Trieste, then, 1905–15.

Surely—so ran my notion—surely in that time before the schoolboy Princip shot the Archduke Franz Ferdinand in the head in not very distant Sarajevo and World War I broke out (the funeral cortège took place in Trieste); surely, in those final years of Habsburg rule when all three were living and (with the exception of Svevo) writing in that compact entrepôt-emporium between (to quote Saba again) "the rocky highlands and the shining sea"; surely, my notion ran, the lives of these three must have touched in absorbing and unrecorded ways.

I drew a beautiful equilateral triangle in my notebook

and wrote "Trieste 1905–15" beneath it. Trieste was the key. Hitherto a name in a gazetteer, a smallish star on a map, a setting for certain poems and novels, Trieste itself—herself? himself?—would pluck me by the sleeve and show me to my business, which was that undefined but perspicacious view I would go all the way across the sea to seek. It was sufficient to arrive there from the nearby Veneto, wrote Saba, to receive the impression of an horizon opening. Its life was warm, he said. Its air was azure, strange . . .

Once in Trieste I would traverse its hilly blocks and piered portside, its antique center and relatively modern precincts still called, even in the late twentieth-century Republic of Italy, for their Habsburg patrons: Borgo Teresiano, Borgo Giuseppino, Borgo Franceschino. I would comb its libraries and archives and museums. Pilgrimwise, I would contemplate its sacred places, the places I knew already because they had been brushed in one way or another by the wing of literature. The special streets, for example, so familiar from Saba's *Canzoniere:* Via del Lazzaretto Vecchio, Via del Monte, Via Domenico Rossetti. The *cantuccio* (place apart) under the Obelisk at Opicina. The low waterfront bars Joyce frequented in order to drink his favorite Opollo from the isle of Lissa ("treacherous white wine that turns the legs to water without affecting the brain"). San Sabba to the south of the Lloyd Austriaco shipworks where he watched the needleboats and heard the prairie grasses sighing Puccini. Spacious Villa Veneziani beneath the hill of Servola, beside the marine varnish plant that Svevo helped his mother-in-law to run. The public garden where Emilio and Zeno made rendezvous with their respective mistresses. The Canal

Grande, "longest river in the world" according to Joyce, who linked it to Dublin's Anna Liffey, whose waters he adorned with Livia Svevo's glorious golden hair. The "literary" caffès—San Marco, Tommaseo, Stella Polare, Municipio (later Garibaldi)—where surely they met and talked . . .

Literary Trieste. I meant to make a book about it all. If I had thought to close my eyes back then in the beginning, if I could have summoned up a modest vision, I would have seen a city made of books. Of the books, for instance, that had drawn me there in the first place: *Senilità, Trieste e una donna, Giacomo Joyce, Pomes Penyeach, La coscienza di Zeno.* And books about these books. And books I had not read yet by authors with strange names like Benco, Slataper, Bazlen, Michelstaedter, Giotti (born Schönbeck), Stuparich, Marin. . . . And notebooks and albums filled with bits and pieces extracted from other books: the laudatory notices of Baron Revoltella's press agent, an article by Freud* on the gonadal structure of eels, Carducci's ode for Maximilian and Carlota, a rhapsody by Marinetti, hendecasyllables from Montale's extensive gallery of Triestine women (Gerti, Liuba, Dora Markus, Linuccia Saba, Bobi Bazlen's mother). . . . And shimmering in the center of that city made of books would be this one, the book that was to be about it all.

Titles confer a certain provisional reality and this book's name was *Literary Trieste* before I went there. Just how literary it all was it took Trieste to show.

When I got there, *of course,* the streets were jammed with Fiats and mopeds and humans like me only different. The air was not azure but grey and rich with exhaust. (Azure, I might have known, is the color of poetry.) The actual town of the 1980s weighed heavy and unprosperous upon its several hills, an economic casualty of the times. Its creatures moved upon their secret ways through a brimming present, which was "warm" no doubt but exclusive.

The caffès were inevitably empty of that clientele I sought. The old low bars had folded long ago, replaced by others, newly decorated. (One that claimed to remain, across from Scala Joyce where Joyce had begun *Ulysses,* had recently played host to a German television crew making a literary documentary.) Meanwhile, the Canal Grande had been docked of a third of its length and was edged now not with purple-sailed schooners but with parked cars; moored in the dirty waters a step below them were two rows of battered motorboats with Vespa tire fenders. Lyrical San Sabba was an industrial slum and site of the only death camp in Italy, run by the SS in a rice-processing plant from 1943 to 1945. Both Villa Veneziani and the varnish factory had been destroyed in the course of an Allied air raid in 1945. Dead for years. A ghost town. Triste Trieste.

As for my beautiful equilateral triangle, it was hardly worth a paragraph, let alone a book. There were Svevo and Joyce, of course—the English lessons, the reading of "The Dead" and Livia's bouquet in homage,

Joyce's perusal of Svevo's two forgotten novels and his encouragement then ("There are passages in *Senilità* that even Anatole France could not have improved") and practical help much later—but nothing really new. Except for a few letters of the 1920s, their personal relations were quite formal and, as Joyce noted in a letter to his brother Stanislaus* after Svevo's death, class bound: "I never crossed the soglia [the threshold of Villa Veneziani] except as a paid teacher and his wife became longsighted when she met Nora in the street."

Saba, the poet of Trieste, lived abroad in Italy—Florence, Salerno, Bologna, Milan—during most of the decade in question. He and Joyce never met, never mentioned one another. Saba and Svevo, very different personalities from very different social and economic milieux, knew each other only from occasional encounters at the Caffè Garibaldi in the three years before Svevo's death in 1928. Svevo, a self-styled Lazarus just risen from the grave of critical neglect, was basking in his ingenuous glory and delighting in the international attention he was getting. Saba, on the other hand, was in the middle of the psychological crisis that was to lead to psychoanalysis in 1929. Feeling increasingly isolated in (and by) his city, he was a prickly, difficult individual who scorned to talk about literature and preferred to expound the teachings of his master Freud to a captive audience. If he felt an occasional pang of jealousy at Svevo's good fortune, he also felt—but did not say aloud—that Svevo's language lacked formal distinction and that he might have done better to write in German. Novelist and poet, not competitors in any sense, the two egos could sit at the same table on the Piazza Unità for a quarter of an hour each week and, as one witness testifies, "smile at one another without envy."

So much for my beautiful triangle . . . which left me with Trieste. But *their* city was as ghostly as they were.

During my three weeks in Trieste, I shadowed phantom footsteps on selected streets. Sometimes, map in hand, I ended up blankly before a blank facade behind which, perhaps seventy years ago, someone or something had been for a while. I snapped snapshots of certain busts set on pillars in the Public Garden. I mounted and descended some hills, of course, and stared at mostly deserted moles—quays not burrowers—stretched imploringly out towards the grey sea. I contemplated calling all this *Upon a Grey Sea*.

Schoolchildren whispered to each other in the dialect for which my books had not prepared me. They tittered in the reading room of the Biblioteca Civica while I bent blindly, all ears, above a flaking page of the Trieste *Piccolo*—a newspaper so called owing to its modest dimensions—printed years before my birth. Someone's Slovene grandmother did up a parcel with exquisite care as I hung at the counter, trying to think of the Italian for *corkscrew*. Once a tram driver towered in fury above the white face of a stammering woman while I gaped and the others winked or shook their heads. In the Cinema Eden I sat through *101 Dalmatians* wondering what they made of it in Dalmatia. Ghostwise I petered past as a pretty blond peered through a crack in the green canvas at a tennis match on the court behind Villa Necker. For hours and hours, the louvers of my darkened hotel room cut streetlamp light into thin orange stripes across the ceiling. They rippled when a car passed.

This is a book about Trieste: its curious history, some of its residents, some of my stumbling steps to get a view of it. Twenty years ago I wrote, quoting the Touring Club Italiano without a qualm, "One day is sufficient to visit the town." But that was before I went there.

My three weeks in Trieste have been distributed over five years, with long intervals at home. The intervals supplied me with the perspective that the weeks on the spot seemed to baffle. On site in Trieste, more or less alone with my map and senses and faithful *Guida,* I crossed the entire city and watched and listened and sometimes was content and sometimes (as we say) ate my heart out. Only at home, in the bosom of my patient family, did I acquire a point of view.

This is, in fact, a ghost story told by a ghost about a ghost town. It is about seeing the warm life stream by while remembering a past known almost exclusively through books. The mood is phantasmagorical, *ma non troppo*.

Italians call eating one's heart out eating one's liver. *Mi sono mangiato il fegato a Trieste.* I ate my liver (as they say) in Trieste. This is a book about that.

Joyce's occasional drinking partner, Dario di Tuoni, tells how Joyce, en route home after a night on the town, would sometimes pause melo-dramatically in the shadowiest patch of a darkened street and recite, in a voice "mysterious and lamenting," these lines by Paul Verlaine: "ô triste, triste était mon âme / à cause, à cause d'une femme . . ." A quarter of a century later, in one of the two books he didn't work on in Trieste, Joyce jokily echoed such times in a sentence I have used as an epigraph: "And trieste, ah trieste ate I my liver!" *Triste Trieste,* an old joke. But heartening to know that other ghosts have been troubled by Trieste.

And yet Joyce is by no means a "sad" writer, and his punning claim that a book of his was *triste*—if "ate I my liver" is meant to suggest "était mon livre" as it surely does—is mysterious. But perhaps mystery is the right note on which to end the beginning of a ghost story.

This book, at any rate, for reasons that should be clear to anyone who finishes it, is going to have a happy ending.

Some Important Dates

2nd–1st centuries B.C.	Trieste a small fortified trade center inhabited by Japodes, an Illyro-Celtic people.
178 B.C.	Roman military camp established near mouth of Timavo River, 12 mi. NW of T.
c. 60 B.C.	T. a Roman colony, part of Regio X, Venetia et Histria (the 10th Roman Legion consisting of Venetia, Istria, Japodia, and Carnia).
33 B.C.	Walls rebuilt by decree of Octavian Caesar.
394–568 A.D.	Placed slightly south of the main mountain passes from the NE, T. survives various waves of "barbarian" armies (Goth, Hun, Lombard) heading for Italy.
Early 6th century	T. part of Kingdom of Ostrogoths; Slavs appear on Carso.
6th–8th centuries	T. part of Frankish Kingdom; allowed to retain *lex romana* (as opposed to Germanic laws customarily imposed by Franks).
11th century	T. an independent commune, vulnerable.
12th–13th centuries	Intermittent conflict with and domination by Venice.
1382	T., while ostensibly retaining its communal autonomy, places itself under the protection of the House of Austria (Habsburg-to-be).
14th–17th centuries	Period of marginal survival: erosion of municipal autonomy, economic stagnation.

1719	T. declared free port by Charles VI of Austria.
1728	T.-Vienna road.
1748	Beginning of expansion of port facilities and construction of "new town" (Borgo Teresiano) by imperial decree of Maria Theresa.
1797, 1806, 1809–13	Occupations by Napoleonic armies.
1830	Opening of enlarged commercial route linking T. with Laibach (Ljubljana), Graz, and Vienna.
1833	Lloyd Austriaco Insurance Co. founded; expanded to Shipping Co. in 1836.
1857	T.-Vienna railway (Südbahn) opened.
1869	Suez Canal opened: T. as European "eastern gateway."
1882	500th anniversary of Austrian connection; execution of Oberdan.
1918	Collapse of Austro-Hungarian Empire; T. annexed by Kingdom of Italy.
1943–53	German, Yugoslav occupations; postwar creation of "Free Territory of T." under Allied jurisdiction.
1954	T., without most of adjacent territories in Istria and on Carso, returned to Republic of Italy.

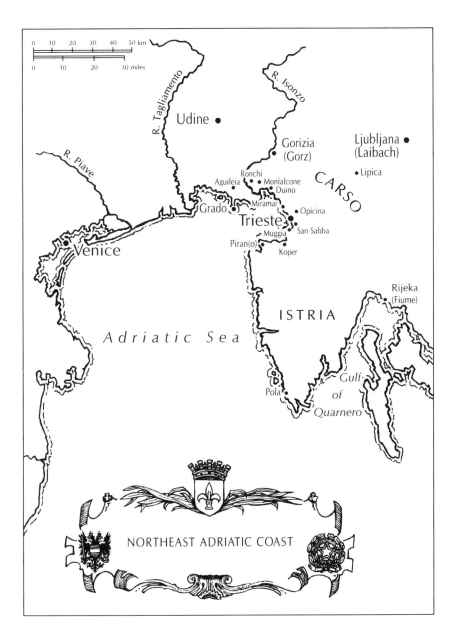

NORTHEAST ADRIATIC COAST

Panoramas are not what they used to be.

Claude has been dead a long time

And apostrophes are forbidden on the funicular . . .

What composition is there in all this:

Stockholm slender in a slender light,

An Adriatic *riva* rising,

Statues and stars,

Without a theme?

The pillars are prostrate, the arches are haggard,

The hotel is boarded and bare.

Yet the panorama of despair

Cannot be the specialty

Of this ecstatic air.

WALLACE STEVENS
"Botanist on Alp (No. 1)"

Right enough the harbours were
there only no ships ever called.

JAMES JOYCE
Ulysses

Miramars

owadays Trieste is an old haven a little less than twice the size of New Haven, Connecticut. Its shrinking population is spread over ten small hills that slope mildly to the sea and a richly piered *riva* and a tripartite port, much of which lies dormant, waiting. It stands at the very edge of Italy upon a slim margin between the northeastern head of the Adriatic Sea and the southeasterly escarpments of the sixty-mile-wide limestone plateau called Karst by the Austrians who once owned all of it, Carso by the Italians who had to cede all but the rim of it to Yugoslavia after World War II, and Krš by the Slovenian Slavs who have been the main ones to live on it.

For them *krš* is first of all the word for craggy stone, a hard row to hoe. For geologists also karst is a common noun, the term for terrain composed of a high degree of water-soluble rock. An occasional secondary feature of karsts are certain subcutaneous marvels: deep-down stalactitic grottoes with intricate drain fields and conduits, sunken rivers like Kubla Khan's Alph. Trieste, too, has its sunken river, once sacred. The Timavo, first arising as the Reka in the Slovenian mountains sixty miles to the east and running underground for nearly half of them, resurfaces as three icy springs in a willow grove near a Gothic church by the autostrada at Duino, about thirteen miles up the coast.

By definition, a port must keep its back to its land and face its main prospects, which will come by sea. And so Trieste, once the great port for Vienna and the Austro-Hungarian Empire, now Italy's so-called Eastern Gate (*porta orientale*) since its "redemption" from the shattered Empire in 1918, looks westward down its gulf, away from its now alien hinterland, towards deep and salty waters over which, nowadays, come fewer and fewer ships.

On the southeast corner of the Piazza dell'Unità d'Italia, behind the back of Emperor Charles VI on his Ionic column, dwarfed by the eclectic and showy nineteenth-century facades of its important neighbors (the Grand Hotel Duchi d'Aosta, the smart Caffè degli Specchi, the various *palazzi* housing the municipal and government authorities as well as the shipping and insurance offices of Lloyd Triestino), stands the small tobacco shop where I bought many of my souvenirs. Postcards, for example: an "I ♡ Trieste" in English; a series of cartoons about the bora—the wild northeast winter wind off the Carso—whistling up ladies' skirts and whisking trolleys out to sea; a historical reissue featuring the two-headed black and yellow eagle of Austria-Hungary above the iconic halberd of Trieste and the motto gratefully bestowed upon the city by the Emperor Franz Josef after the restlessnesses of 1848: TERGESTE URBS FIDELISSIMA, Trieste Faithfulest of Cities.

Here I also bought a combination pen and key ring with—protected by clear plastic—the four conventional local sights: this same Piazza dell'Unità d'Italia; the town set against the Carso as seen from offshore; the top of San Giusto, its main hill (Trieste began as a tiny acropolis there), with its patchwork medieval cathedral and its Renaissance fortified castle; and Miramar. Miramar is out of town, five miles west along the north coast.

Even on a grey day, unless banked entirely in fog, if you stand looking seaward on Piazza Unità you cannot miss Miramar, toy castle with "pearled" turrets—the adjective is the poet Montale's*—posed and profil-

ing on its expensively engi-
neered promontory. Mira-
mar is the "love nest built in
vain"—the epithet is the poet
Carducci's—by Maximilian
of the house of Habsburg,
Franz Josef's gentle and ideal-
istic younger brother, Archduke of Austria and, for the
three last years of his sad
short life, "archdupe" Emperor of Mexico until shot
dead there by firing squad in
1867. For me the ghosts of

Miramar include the stars of the movie *Juarez:* sleepwalking Brian
Aherne; his wide-orbed consort Bette Davis; the great Claude Rains on
his high horse as Louis Napoleon; swart, decent Paul Muni with brillian-
tined hair.

"As well as being one of the symbols of Trieste," writes the president
of the Tourist Bureau in his preface to the official Miramar guidebook,
"Miramar Castle is the city's main tourist attraction." One of my best
souvenirs puts this beautifully. It is a small plastic dome that snows when
you shake it. Flakes float gently down upon a miniature Miramar, soft
green park and pale gold turrets outlined against a sky at least as azure as
Bette Davis's eyes. An unidentified black figure crouches at the tiller of a
sailboat with a red pennant streaming from its mast, running on a baby
blue Adriatic in front of the castle. In block letters nearly obscuring the
hull is the word TRIESTE. Like many of my Trieste souvenirs, it was made
in Hong Kong.

In "Miramar," Carducci's grandiloquent imitation Sapphic ode on
Max and Carlota, the tragic ironies fall pat, especially at that moment in

the spring of 1864 of what turned out to be the couple's final departure from their brand new and, in fact, not quite completed home. *Deh come tutto sorridea . . .*

> Alas, how everything smiled that mild
> April morning, when the blond emperor
> came forth, with his beauteous lady,
> to sail away!

> From his calm features shone
> the virile force of empire; the eye,
> azure, haughty, of his lady
> moved over the sea.

The two are gazing west in the direction of their new life, the crowning reality that is to come. In so doing they enact a perfect *miramar,* since inside this tame name for a million seaside villas is concealed a strong verb: to wonder, entranced, at the sea. If Castle Miramar is one of Trieste's chief symbolic monuments, this way of watching, this miramar, is perhaps the city's characteristic symbolic action. Distinguished local images spring to mind.

There is the tradition—an old irredentist favorite—that seven miles on past Miramar, near the mouth of the Timavo at Duino, the exile Dante Alighieri stood upon the shoal that bears his name and, to use the word provided by the Touring Club Italiano's guide to the region, "meditated." Too good

Miramar Snow Globe

not to be true and sheer miramar: eyes and mind's eye of the supreme poet bending westward towards an Italy and a civil order still to come.

Or, still at Duino, here is Rainer Maria Rilke in the winter of 1912, stopped cold in the midst of his pacing of the icy bastions of the ancient castle—older far than Castle Miramar down the coast towards Trieste—where he is a guest of the Princess von Thurn und Taxis. "What is coming?" whispers Rainer Maria Rilke. Something marvelous is coming, the voice of what he calls "the god," speaking out of the storm that rakes the sea beneath him and bearing him the first words of the first poem of what ten years later he will complete in a Swiss chateau and name, in honor of their provenance, *Duino Elegies. Miramar.*

Just above Trieste, at the very edge of the Carso near the suburban village of Opicina, stands a fat obelisk erected in 1830 to commemorate the opening of the post road linking the port more conveniently than hitherto with Graz, Vienna, and northern Europe in general. At the foot of this obelisk is a belvedere, which offers the classic prospect of Trieste looking out to the western sea as praised and painted by visitors countless times. Here is the eighteen-year-old Maximilian's account of his rapturous first experience of this miramar of miramars in 1850, after a hard journey by carriage from Vienna to watch his older brother lay the foundation stone of the railroad terminal.

> You travel for hours through the stony deserts of the Karst, over which a curse seems to weigh. The rocks form grey masses so that you seem to be seeing ruins of houses and even whole villages. Wretched plants thrust up their desiccated branches. No sign of life to cheer the view—only the greyness of the indefinite and mysterious stretches over the Karst until, after an interminable crossing, the weary eye comes to life again with the appearance of the Obelisk, pointing upward like a symbol of hope . . .
>
> Impatient, you urge your postilion to hurry, you dash up the final little slope to the Obelisk and there, at long last, an infinite azure opens before your

eyes, all the more seemingly miraculous by contrast with the repulsive, stony wastes.

Below, at our feet, spreads the sea, furrowed by white sails as though by swans, edged with a semicircle of richly terraced and well-cultivated hills, with gracious villas scattered here and there. Beneath lies the port city with its waterfront, along which the anchored ships form another floating city, all motion and animation. The panorama from Opicina is truly one of the most marvelous on earth.

Two years later, as naval officer soon to be rear admiral in the Imperial Adriatic Fleet, Maximilian took up residence in Trieste. He became thick with Baron Revoltella, Baron Sartorio, Baron Morpurgo, and other newly titled merchant princes of the city. The lovingly planned construction of promontory and Castle Miramar began in 1856, the year before his marriage to Carlota. How everything smiled, *alas,* for Miramar was only completed in 1871, four years after Max's execution in Mexico, four years before Carlota's permanent removal to her family home in Belgium, where she remained in varying degrees of madness until her death in 1927.

(I remember Bette Davis *sola,* slumped in an armchair staring out the sunny windows . . . Actually, Carlota was bored there, and in this agreed with Nora Joyce who wrote to a friend: "Now I suppose you will think I am very difficult but one cant live only for the sun and the blue Meditarean sea.")

The period of the building of Castle Miramar corresponds exactly with that zenith of Trieste's modern fortunes in which the rapt attentiveness of miramar—the castle is its outward and visible sign—feeds reasonably and contentedly upon its great expectations, which for a time are brilliantly fulfilled. By 1857 the Trieste-Vienna railway (Südbahn) was at last in place, and the port could finally boast efficient access to potential markets in *Mitteleuropa* and the north. (Baron Revoltella and his friends put out a little guidebook in four languages—*Tre giorni a Trieste:* Three

Days in Trieste—to celebrate the event.) With the opening of the Suez Canal in 1869, another one of Baron Revoltella's projects, Trieste found itself truly *porta orientale* for the continent, the nonpareil gateway for passages to and from India. By 1870 Trieste ranked as the seventh largest port in the world, as well as, after Marseilles, second in the Mediterranean, having beaten out Genoa and Barcelona.

Miramar: for Trieste at least the posture is a relatively modern one. The now standard views from the Obelisk, from Piazza Unità, from or of Castle Miramar itself, did not exist at all until the nineteenth century. Almost all pictures of the town up to the close of the eighteenth century show the small walled port beneath the Carso from the gulf side, as from a periplus or offshore sighting angle that might be experienced by a visiting sailor. Such a viewpoint emphasizes Trieste in the context of its terrain—the modest fishery, the salt pans, the hillside vineyards and pastures and woodlots, the several fortresses with cannons trained seaward—and makes it seem comparatively self-contained. And so it was, until the decision had been made and implemented in Vienna to revise Trieste thoroughly into the imperial emporium and port of transit that, in the course of the nineteenth century, it actually became. Even the miramar from Piazza Unità with the castle jutting westward like a prow into the Adriatic was mainly blocked—that is, not deemed necessary or desirable—until 1872. Until then the notorious Grand Hotel where Johann Winckelmann had been sensationally murdered occupied the fourth and seaward side. (As if the miramar, the vision of a working port against its salty context and implicit world horizons, were something that a newborn cosmopolis should conceal.)

The year 1861, when Maximilian and Carlota settled briefly into what had been made ready for them at Castle Miramar, was also the year of the formation of the Kingdom of Italy. And with Italy for the first time a political fact (rather than, as in Metternich's famous phrase, a mere geographical expression), the *risorgimento* dream of an Italian Trieste became a political possibility. Thus the miramar acquired, for some citizens, an anti-Austrian dimension: in fact, the western end of the path, or *passeggiata napoleonica,* along the Carso edge beginning at the Obelisk is still called the *veduta d'Italia,* the view of Italy. And at length, with the crumbling of the Dual Empire in 1918, Trieste became Italian. The great mole—cherished word with its weird insinuation—which stretches seaward just to the right of Piazza Unità, had its name changed from Molo San Carlo, in memory of the Austrian frigate that had foundered on the spot in the middle of the eighteenth century, to Molo Audace, the dashing name of the marine-laden torpedo boat that was first to dock there from Italy in the closing days of World War I.

How everything smiled, *alas* . . . By becoming Italian, Trieste lost both its natural geographical hinterland and its market (since Italy, unlike Trieste, lies mostly on the western Adriatic) as well as its Mediterranean uniqueness. Its history after 1918 is anticlimactic. "Redemption" came

just in time for Mussolini. Fascist nationalism exacerbated the city's problems with its Slav populace, an augmented percentage of largely Slovenian manual laborers who had left their smallholdings above on the Carso in order to find work in the shipyards. After Italy's defeat in World War II, Trieste became a major pawn in the border dispute with Yugoslavia over maritime control of the eastern Adriatic. Not only Marshal Tito but Professor A. J. P. Taylor has argued forcefully that its rightful name should be *Trst* since its current fortunes seem linked both geographically and logically to Central and Eastern Europe. Meanwhile, separated since 1954 from its old adjacencies on the Carso and the Istrian Peninsula (now Yugoslav territory), Trieste has lost out even to its old eastern Adriatic rival Fiume, now Rijeka. "Once the fourth port of the Mediterranean," writes Jan Morris, "now the twelfth port of Italy! No wonder Trieste is sometimes fretful, even bitter." As early as 1922 it was second only to San Francisco in its number of suicides. Surveying its rate of alcoholism and emigration recently, the Italian psychoanalyst E. Jogan has judged that "if by 'neurotic' we mean someone who lives in the uneasiness of a past which conditions his present, then Trieste is neurotic."

Triste Trieste. Even a ghostly visitor can see that the city is a ghost of its former self. Quite deprived of the sparkling "floating city" of hulls and masts and sails that touched young Max to lyricism on the heights of Opicina, the moles along the *rive* at the town center are discernibly of grey concrete, the moorings mainly empty. The souvenir vendors set up their carts as the tourist buses from Yugoslavia come to a halt before the Maritime Museum. Stopwatch in hand, a father clocks how long it takes his sculling son to cross from the bricked-in Lanterna, or lighthouse, to a barren breakwater. On Molo Audace I step around dog droppings and gaze across disconsolate, unworking waters in the direction of Castle Miramar.

Nowadays Castle Miramar is a state museum complete with *son et lumière* and a pageant called *Imperial Dream* given summer nights in three languages. The movie *Juarez* was titled—with who knows how much irony?—*Il conquistatore di Messico* when it was shown out there one evening during my third week. The miramar, symbolic act, is largely retrospective.

My excellent *Guida di Trieste* loses its guide's composure only rarely. It surely does so on the page devoted to the miramar from Piazza Unità, "where the sea's azure dissolution into the infinite opens hearts to dreams and hopes; where the jetties, silent witnesses of a once rich and active port seem to stretch out waiting for new prospects that might erase the nostalgic memory of the lovely, busy ocean liners of once upon a time."

De mortuis nil nisi bonum. So wrote Joyce to Ezra Pound in 1920, alluding to Trieste and his desire to leave it for good. Speak nothing but good of the dead.

"Trouver Trieste" (To Find Trieste) is the name of the ambitious exhibition put on by the city in Paris in 1986 in an effort to attract foreign interest and investors' capital. The French cartoon below, reprinted in the *Piccolo* for January 6 of that year, puts it beautifully.

A PARIS

— Pour Trouver Trieste, s'il vous plait?
— Dans la Rue de la Recherche du Temps Perdu, Madame...

(25 novembre)

She: The way to *Trouver Trieste,* if you please?
He: The street of Remembrance of Things Past, madame . . .

In Trieste the first place to go is up. For a view of the city, if the weather is clear, you take the old-fashioned tram that leaves from Piazza Oberdan and clanks up into the hills toward Villa Opicina. Get off at the stop marked "Obelisco" and go to the belvedere. From there you can see the city below, the Adriatic, the broad setting that invariably dazzled visitors arriving there over the dark hills from the murky north.

WILLIAM WEAVER
"Trieste: Between the Two Europes," *New York Times,*
23 Jan. 1983, Travel section

And the strangers there were sad and double.

ROBERTO BAZLEN*
Il capitano di lungo corso

U p

That first night in Trieste I lay on my narrow bed on the fifth floor of the Hotel Al Teatro propped upon a pillow beneath a dim bulb screwed into a cowl of brown Bakelite. Out beyond the louvers I could hear the yodels and catcalls of my countrymen, gobs on Saturday night liberty off the huge U.S. Navy transport docked in solitary splendor at the foot of Piazza Unità. They were sprawled at the outdoor tables of Bar Rex bargaining with the giggling local trade, cursing and retching. I could also hear Vespas, the strokes of unaccountable bells.

According to William Weaver, the first place to go was up. I had brought his article across the sea with me. My new map showed that it would not be difficult to find Piazza Oberdan. Emerging from the hotel I should turn right into Piazza Borsa. The Borsa was the stock exchange; it was in an office on this piazza that Svevo had clerked for eighteen years at Vienna Unionbank. (Literary Trieste.) Piazza Borsa opened onto a major thoroughfare, the Corso Italia, which in its turn led past a tiny Piazza Silvio Benco*—friend of Svevo, Saba, and Joyce—to Piazza Goldoni, one of whose three sides was the Corso Umberto Saba. A sharp left here onto the broad Via Giosuè Carducci would take me straight to Piazza Oberdan. (Only the *Oberdan* meant nothing to me.) Here a thick dotted line traced the tram route to the Obelisk and miramar of miramars. Svevo had written *La coscienza di Zeno* in an Opicina villa. Obviously the first place to go was up.

Late in the day of my arrival I had come across an auspiciously named bookshop just three blocks up the Corso from the hotel. The shop sign for the Libreria Italo Svevo had a little heart-pink arrow screwed on just beneath the SVEVO that pointed, it said, the way to Cinema Sexy. This had been closed by municipal authority. I bought the map and the first of many Trieste books in the Libreria Italo Svevo that afternoon.

Guida di Trieste by Laura Ruaro Loseri is a fat and formidable "pocket" guide of over five hundred pages with three hundred black-and-white photographs, essays on the city's history and artifacts, eight itineraries, and a bibliography. Dottoressa Ruaro Loseri, whom I shall never meet, was my faithful companion through all my three weeks in Trieste. I seldom did a thing without consulting her. I read her in the streets. I read her over meals. I read her in bed.

That first night she characterized Piazza Oberdan as "one of the focal points of that precise urban plan of the '20s and '30s that was intended, together with the aforementioned main artery Carducci-Sonnino, to link the center with Friuli on the one side and Istria on the other." (I was not clear on the meaning of Istria, let alone Friuli.) She declared that what I was going to undertake was not merely a pleasure but virtually obligatory.

She promised fresh air in summer, bright colors in autumn. She predicted much oak and acacia, sumac afire with red and orange fruit, a romantic twentieth-century *casteletto* erected by a quixotic engineer, plus a passing glance at the university and the "classicistic monumentalism" (read Fascist-imperial style) of its 1940 atheneum.

The tram would proceed first to Piazza Scorcola, at the foot of the hill of that name. Here its motor would be switched off and the car pushed up the steep grade by a cable engine; when the hill modulated into a gentler rise, the engine would be dropped and the tram resume its way under its own electrical power. At the end, signaled by the Obelisk, was the village of Opicina and the beginning of the Carso proper. The Carso edge was lined by a recent plantation of pines in part designed to dissipate the full force of the wintry bora into the town. The Carso itself she called a "green lung," to which Trieste owed the salubriousness of its air. And then there was the view.

I grew sleepy. My initial itinerary in Trieste would be a symbolic one, a *miramar*. I recollected Saba's poem with its steep rise and place apart. *Ho attraversata tutta la città* . . . Pleased with the parallel (although I would be taking the tram) I wrote its name in my notebook. "Trieste": I knew what I meant. The first place to go was up.

I switched off the light and lay there flat, composing my body for its first night's sleep in Trieste. But the high snarl of small-cylinder engines and the crash of glass and metal at Bar Rex filtered through the louvers. For hours to come, the streetlamp light threw thin orange stripes across my darkened ceiling. They rippled when a car passed.

When morning came at last it was grey, inauspicious. Barely visible from the foot of Piazza Unità, what I correctly guessed to be Castle Miramar wavered in and out of focus upon its phantom promontory. The clock on the Borsa pediment was slow, and the almost deserted streets were thoroughly ordinary . . . lined with shut shops such as might be seen on any grey Sunday in Europe. The weather was not clear but I had no other plan. And up was the first place to go.

At the newspaper kiosk beside the tracks on Piazza Oberdan I bought a round-trip ticket to Opicina and waited for the tram. There was a man with grey sideburns in a black raincoat and a checkered cap. There were two old ladies conversing in a tongue I could not follow; it was the dialect of Trieste that I was hearing for the first time. I drew forth Dottoressa Ruaro Loseri from my shoulder bag and began to read about where I was.

The photograph of Piazza Oberdan must have been taken from a point perhaps a hundred yards from where we were waiting. How unremarkable the kiosk looked! In front of it was the tram apparently, a windowed box on wheels with a cluster of rods on top that connected it to the wires. How ordinary were the buildings all around! And when I chanced to look up from the book to the grey features of actual day, how ordinary they really were! Just city buildings of reinforced concrete, fairly new. I felt dispirited.

Others with Sunday business in Opicina had joined us. At length, its wheels agonizing in their grooves, a pear-green trolley clattered out from behind a row of apartment buildings and stopped before us with a brazen shriek. It discharged several passengers. The driver switched the motor off and disappeared into the kiosk. I was the first to climb aboard. I took a window seat in the middle of the slightly ticking interior and looked up "Oberdan, Guglielmo" in my guide. There was a museum about him somewhere in the vicinity. Minutes must have passed.

The others had begun to filter in. The man with grey sideburns had settled across the aisle slightly ahead. The two old ladies, still chattering in *triestino,* had taken seats in the rear. Others as well; the car rocked lightly with their weight. And voices; and then a single voice, male, angry, rising swiftly to such a roar that all the rest but one—softer, female, reasoning—were stilled to thrilled witness.

Our driver was hunched over the entry step at the back of the car yelling down at a woman standing on the curb directly below him. His body shook with rage. She seemed to be trying to get a word in, a smile of entreaty or perhaps embarrassment in course of freezing on her handsome face. The scene was entirely in dialect.

What had she done to provoke him, if provocation was the word? His response, if it was a response, struck me as extravagant, as almost comically overwrought. Perhaps he was crazy. Buried in my guide as I had been, I had missed a clue. I looked about me.

The old ladies had stopped talking and one of them was shaking her head in apparent disbelief. Halfway down the car a man settled back and exchanged a knowing look with his neighbor. The man with the grey sideburns grinned at someone across the aisle. He winked.

I was completely at sea.

As long as our driver stayed stuck in his vein, so long were we marooned in Piazza Oberdan. At length he straightened up and spun upon his heel, stamped muttering up the aisle, entered his stall, and viciously flicked on the motor. His neck was red. The woman climbed aboard and sat whitefaced in the very rear by the two old ladies who leaned toward her and began, I believed, to commiserate. The tram jerked into motion.

She might have been forty. She wore a figured black dress and a dark grey cardigan, possibly a widow. In one hand she carried a straw shopping bag, a cheap telescoping umbrella was in the other. For a few minutes she conversed in murmurs with the ladies. Then she produced a *Piccolo* from her bag and began to read. Except for the fact that as far as I could see she never once looked up but firmly read her paper, it was as if nothing at all had happened to her.

But never for as long as it took us to reach the Obelisk did our driver forget her presence there in the rear. From time to time he ripped his eyes from the track ahead and swung about to glare at her. And when, as my guide had foretold, the pike-snouted yellow cable engine with its own driver took over to push us up steep Scorcola, he made use of his liberty to review in passion whatever his case was with the nearest passenger, the now grave-visaged man with grey sideburns who nodded *già* occasionally with what I read as judicious neutrality.

To be able to scan both ends of the car I had set myself sideways in my seat, caught up almost to the exclusion of the scenery in what seemed—to me alone, perhaps—bewildering. But certain stages of the way were evident.

It was certainly going to rain. We were climbing slowly up through grey ranks of trellised, tiled villas. There was the engineer's tacky miniature castle, the ugly raw concrete structures of the university complex, a brutal pale grey scar, which was perhaps an autostrada on the side of a further hill. And there, down toward the grey sea, was Trieste itself, growing more blank and wraithlike with every foot we rose above sea level. At the top of the rise the cable engine was shunted off to a siding, and our driver, flexing and muttering and glaring still, resumed his testy sway.

I recall a black cat on a picnic table lifting its head and yawning as we passed. A truck backed out of a driveway and maneuvered into another just across the road. A bearded man in a plasterer's paper-bag headgear sprawled on a rooftop scaffold unwrapping a parcel. There were acacia and pine, no doubt, with, in the intervals, beginning glimpses of a grey coast. A drop of something dirty and wet wobbled on the windowpane. And now a stubby pointed shaft disengaged itself from the shrubbery around it while the tracks stretched past onto a wide and level avenue: Opicina. Brakes were applied. I arose, one finger marking the spot in the Dottoressa's guide, and trailed the two old ladies to the midcar exit.

The widow (if she were one) remained wholly engrossed in the *Piccolo*. Could she be shamming? She had not so much as nodded to those I thought of as her comforters when they gathered themselves together and moved up the aisle. *He* had not forgotten, however, shooting her another killing look as the tram came to full halt. I saw that she was starting to fold her paper as the ladies and I descended onto the Opicina road.

I never saw any of them again. The tram with its trivial enigma— would there be a showdown at the line's end?—rocked its way down the avenue toward the center. The ladies moved in its wake, the sound of their tireless commentary in an impossible tongue growing more mockingly audible as the tram's rattle and scrape died off in the distance. They branched off some Opicina path or sidewalk as a van with a ladder roped to its top came toward me up the avenue. It paused to let me cross, then vanished over the brow. It was drizzling lightly.

What William Weaver called a belvedere was a series of concrete blocks set about four feet apart and linked by several rusty iron pipes meant to keep me from foggily falling off the sheer side. I set my shoulder bag on one of them and, guide opened to the seventh itinerary with its photographs of the small inn, Albergo Obelisco, at my back beyond the tram stop and the famous panorama before me—both far clearer than this day!—gave myself over to what I had come for.

Greater Trieste lay muffled in various shades of grey upon its grey sea, *sua grega mare*. Paler to the south, tremulous as a dove grey fata morgana, was the western tip of grey Yugoslavia. (That would be Istria, or was it Illyria?) Blocked by wind-slanted pines and a misty ridge to the right would be Castle Miramar, another place to go. Beyond the slashed hill to my left wavered, almost theoretically, the dim circumflexes of three peaks, bits of grey Yugoslavia, first wan signs of the meridional alps. A wholly hypothetical sixty miles past them would be Fiume, now Rijeka (which probably meant "river" in Serbo-Croatian), where the poet Gabriele D'Annunzio and his legionnaires had had their little one-year fling at a regency a lifetime ago. "This is Illyria, lady," I recollected. Or perhaps it was Istria. What should I do in Illyria?

Maybe this very place I stood was the place apart, *cantuccio,* where Saba had sat before trams were invented and saw his tormenting city whole. I knew the poem by heart. I learned later that the Opicina line commenced operation in 1902. But even when the tram existed he surely would have walked. Perhaps this was not the place.

Perhaps this was the place where, back in 1905, Joyce sat down on a bench miles away from everybody and heard the bora roaring through the tops of the trees and offered up a disconsolate prayer: *O Vague Something behind Everything!* But could you hear that wintry wind in mid-September? Or, seven or so years later, perhaps this was the place on the upland road where he watched Trieste "waking rawly: raw sunshine over its huddled browntiled roofs, testudoform" (transposed, in *Ulysses,* into a memory of Paris) and saw a girl ride by on horseback who reminded him of Hedda Gabler.

Maybe Svevo strolled here from nearby Villa Israeli in 1922, resting from his great novel, to smoke a last cigarette. And then another. Perhaps. It was a long time ago. (Later on, I learned that in the 1880s Sir Richard Burton* had translated most of the *Arabian Nights* just behind my back at the inn across the avenue.)

Literary Trieste. Somewhere in the grey streets down below were Saba's antiquarian bookshop, the auditorium in the Borsa Vecchia where Joyce had given talks in Italian on Irish political and cultural matters—not without their Triestine parallels—to assembled friends and Berlitz students. Somewhere there was Villa Veneziani. But on the belvedere parapet, just beneath my eyes, the pages of my helpful guide open to this very miramar were growing wet. I wiped them off and closed the book.

A stone's throw from my feet was the top of the Scala Santa—Holy Stairway—which I would climb one day. On the hill straight across was a massive grey castle keep with a campanile sticking up behind it. This was San Giusto, another place to go. Way below and to the right was the railroad terminal I had emerged into the sun from, thrilled to be there, nearly twenty-four hours ago. Converging rails helped outline the upper and obviously newer harbor where a clutch of empty docks with aluminum warehouses on them poked out towards a long breakwater. Just above these on a curl of *riva* culminating in a dead grey lighthouse was the edge of the older part of town sprawling down San Giusto hill and ending up in the variously shaped and sized moles I would learn to distinguish. I saw and recognized Molo Audace, however, and beside it, at the broadest mole of all, the huge Navy transport, grey as the day, with all its gobs asleep or passed out cold in their bunks. (The sea was grey and bare of all but water.) Invisible an inch to the left was Piazza Unità and the miramar of Castle Miramar, and at the edge of that my Hotel Al Teatro and the little room at the top in which I fully concurred that up was the first place to go. And here, with the ghosts of Archduke Max and all the other travelers who might have arrived here over the dark hills from the murky north, was I.

What should I do in Illyria? There were other sights to be seen and, diligent, I would see them. All the sacred places. San Giusto. The Borsa. Winckelmann's tomb. The Carso. Maybe even Istria, in grey Yugoslavia.

Somewhere over my shoulder was a man with grey sideburns and a widow, umbrella unfurled, who had bitten her lip not long since. Somewhere was an angry driver. Warm life, with a language I could not comprehend. A hotel clerk. A bookstore proprietor. And up the curved grey cinder pathway to my right, which Dottoressa Ruaro Loseri said was named the *passeggiata napoleonica* since Napoleon and his generals had walked there, came trotting a Scotch terrier at the heels of his mistress jogging in a lavender sweatsuit and listening to whatever she heard in the earphones glittering like a tiara in her damp, ash blond hair.

It was too wet for the *passeggiata napoleonica* today. I moved away from the view towards the Obelisk and the tram stop. MDCCCXXX. FRAN-CISVS·I·P·F·AVGVSTVS·MVTVIS·COMMODIE·ITALIAE·GERMANIAE. Underneath, in spray paint, a cock and balls and the words "Gay's Powder." The Scottie lifted its short hind leg and peed smartly in the light drizzle against the pedestal of the Obelisk. Sheltered below the gleaming sumac his lavender mistress called him ("Rex!") and he came.

Was he named after the bar?

Silly, ghostly, I watch as a little family of three crowded below a black umbrella walks up the road from Opicina and joins us at the stop. I can hear the first peremptory scrape of a tram to come.

I watch the blond pick up her pet and hug it to her, whispering something in his ear. I see Rex begin to wag his tail as the little boy edges closer and holds up one hand. The adults glance at one another and smile. I have my ticket ready.

And now, around the bend of the Opicina road, shiny green with wet and starting to scream, I watch the Trieste tram approaching. And now it stops, with a different driver, ready to take me back down.

Viva San Giusto! la patria storia
Balza dai regni della memoria . . .

[Viva San Giusto! the fatherland's history
springs from the kingdoms of memory . . .]

GIUSEPPE SINICO
Marinella

How therefore did it happen that Trieste and
not Venice became the point of departure for
the flourishing new Adriatic navigation? Venice was a city of memories; Trieste on the
other hand like the United States had the ad-
vantage of not having any past.

KARL MARX
article on the maritime commerce of Austria,
New York Daily Tribune, 1857

[*Synopsis:* Maria, a well-known violinist, comes to Trieste with her uncle to give a concert. An old school friend, Julia, introduces Maria to her brother George.]

Julia: You should know that my brother, besides being a professor, is an artist and an intellectual. His interest is in local history.

Maria: This place has a history?

Uncle: (*interrupting*) What are you saying, Maria? You are being rude to your hosts and, besides, you are quite wrong! This place? Didn't the Romans pass through here?

George: It was a Roman colony.

ITALO SVEVO
L'avventura di Maria

[Although Svevo doesn't indicate it by a stage direction in this unproduced and posthumously published play, there ought to be an icy silence just before Maria's uncle determinedly changes the subject. Maria's tactless tongue has not only embarrassed him, but hurt her friend and infuriated the stuffy George, who is undoubtedly an irredentist. A stage direction ought to read "George: (*coldly*)." Local and more than local, Trieste has a history.]

Three Triestes

Fazio degli Uberti, a fourteenth-century versifier besotted with Dante's divine poem, made a sprawling try at a secular companion to it called *Il Dittamondo*—The World's Description—in which a poet-pilgrim, Fazio himself, travels over the face of the earth guided by the Roman geographer Solinus, reporting on the sights in wooden terza rima. One of their ports of call is Trieste:

> I saw Trieste underneath its heights
> and heard that name on it bestowed
> since it has been uprooted thrice.

Such alertness to the *three* heard in the first syllable of the town's name is a better instance of the medieval mathematico-auditory imagination than of correct etymology, although Fazio is working, in fact, in an old tradition that also found in Trieste's pre-Roman and earliest name, Tergeste, the sense of three times gestated or thrice begotten. (The shift from Venetic *Tergeste* to the neo-Latin or Italian form *Trieste* seems to have happened by the eleventh century at latest.) But false or not, there is a metahistorical suitability in the notion of triplicity preserved in Fazio's monstrous travelogue that makes it useful here.

For, as Silvio Benco noted in 1932, there *have* been three Triestes. There has been, first of all, the small walled acropolis-cum-harbor that managed to persist under all sorts of economic, political, and military pressures from the second century B.C. up to the beginning of the eighteenth century. There has been the great Habsburg port-emporium lasting from the mid-eighteenth to the beginning of the twentieth century, Vienna's warm water window situated at one end of the Adriatic "canal" (with Corfù at the other), the Mediterranean rival to Hamburg on the North Sea. And there has been and still is Italian Trieste, as established first with the dissolution of Austria-Hungary at the end of the First World War, and then as reaffirmed—though now severely shorn of its neighbor territories in Istria and on the Carso—following Italy's defeat in the Second.

Articulated in this way, the history of Trieste over two thousand years would seem to be a matter of two troubled spans (Triestes I and III) arranged on either side of a short-lived economic miracle (Trieste II). Certainly there exists in today's Trieste a detectable strain of sentiment for the dear dead days beyond recall of Trieste II, that *Arabian Nights* world that was supposed to have existed in the period of the great Habsburg bazaar. The record shops display their albums of *gemütlich* Viennese love songs complete with dirndls and accordions; postcards feature double-headed black and yellow eagles, sometimes with a Franz Josef postage stamp reproduced on the message side; romantic-tragic Miramar is the tourist attraction of choice. Some have gone so far as to view the city as created virtually ex nihilo by the economists, planners, and engineers of Enlightment Vienna, analogous in this respect to the St. Petersburg of Dostoevsky's underground man, who saw his city as "the most abstract and premeditated city in the whole world." But Silvio Benco was, among many other things, an irredentist and a man for whom Trieste's history began with the coming of Rome and was thereafter a strand of Roman and then Italian history. For a man of this persuasion—there are, as we shall see, other possibilities—Trieste II was a less than happy interruption.

In 1932, when Benco was writing of the three Triestes, Trieste II had been superseded by Trieste III. This meant that the irredentists' millennium had come, that Trieste was *once again* Italian, and that Benco could be amusing about the psychological adjustments required of elderly *triestini* like himself: "They live in a sort of stupor, since there is no more need to be irredentist. . . . They peer about them. Are there truly no more Austrians to despise?" (In 1932, as Silvio Benco knew very well but could not say in print, the Austrians had been replaced by members of Mussolini's black-shirted legions with their own irredentist notions about Ethiopia also once having been a part of Caesar's empire.)

For Benco, Trieste III had been aspired to in earlier prewar days as a resurgence of Trieste I, and Trieste I, also known as Tergeste for a part of its duration, was wholly Roman. Tergeste was developed as a military outpost during the second and first centuries B.C. Its walls had been built—more probably rebuilt—by Octavian (later Augustus) Caesar in 32 B.C.; Octavian's wife Livia particularly prized for its rejuvenating power the white wine of Prosecco, grown from Duino grapes. Emperor Trajan had had a Roman theater built in Tergeste in the second century A.D.; after more than a millennium of neglect, it was excavated in 1938 by Trieste's Fascist town planners, intent on emphasizing the Roman note. Until the Empire fell to the barbarians beginning in the fifth century, Tergeste was a strategically important military settlement and trade center, second only to Aquileia thirty miles to the northwest. Above all, it was an integral part of Regio X, the Roman Tenth District.

Well before Fazio's Italian-language *Dittamondo,* poets had sung of the city in good Roman Latin. Thus, in the fourth century, before Attila the Hun, observing its storks departing, razed comely Aquileia to the ground, Rufus Festus Avienus wrote:

> Here comely Aquileia thrusts her head amidst the lofty stars
> and nearby Tergeste reclines upon her coast of curving salt,
> where ends the uttermost bay of the Ionian Sea.

Two centuries later, Priscian recalled

> the high walls of the distant Tergestians' land
> where the Ionian bay ends with a languid swirl.

The language of Tergeste was of course Latin, and later "neo-Latin," that is Italian, or a local dialect thereof. Even when the Rome of the Caesars was no more, Trieste's tradition and culture were felt to be Italian. Irredentists always liked to quote the lines from canto IX of Dante's *Inferno* where he mentions the Istrian port of Pola (now Pula) and the Gulf of Quarnero below Fiume (now Rijeka)—both well to the south and east of Trieste— as "closing" Italy and "bathing her borders." The later blurry, and in any case undistinguished, history of Trieste I from the late Middle Ages through the Renaissance was seen correctly as a matter of its stubborn will to survive through dark times by juggling harsh political realities. Hence, for the irredentist, the little port's putting itself under the protection of the House of Austria in 1382—the seed, after all, of Trieste II—meant only that it acknowledged its need for help against the depredations of the powerful and arrogant Venetian Republic a hundred miles due west across the Adriatic. The ancient Roman settlement and ranking municipality of Regio X was simply too weak to help itself. This remained its central problem until the creation of the Kingdom of Italy in the second half of the nineteenth century, which was when irredentists, for any practical and political purposes, became possible.

But it is wrong to think of irredentism as though it represented a single and cohesive attitude: how to interpret the transfer of 1382 is a case in point. Was it a *dedizione,* a "free and spontaneous" gift of itself by the city to a protector, or was it a yielding to main force? A realist like Silvio Benco looks at it as an essentially Machiavellian ploy, a risky gamble in the interests of survival. An "imperial" irredentist like Attilio Tamaro,* on the other hand, who insists in his history on the pure *italianità* of Tergeste-Trieste through recorded time, views 1382 as the dire moment when the city fell easy prey to northern "usurpers." The good Domenico Rossetti, however, second to none in his belief in his city's Italian character although he lived before there was an Italian nation, recognizes Trieste's absolute dependency upon an Austrian hinterland and regards the Austrian assumption of 1382 as a godsend. The comely youth with the flowering apple branch in Rossetti's 1814 allegorical melodrama is rescued by a wise and loving mother named Austria, who is accompanied not only by Neptune, Mercury, and Fortune but by a retinue including Abundance, Industry, Good Counsel, Decorum, Merit, and Virtue. Together they succeed in putting Nemesis, Venice, and eventually Napoleon to flight.

Benco, Tamaro, and Rossetti are intelligent individuals with very different views of the significance of 1382. They are identical, however, in considering Trieste to be pure and singular—a Latin city basically, culturally if not politically Italian.

In book I of the *Aeneid,* the epic of the founding of what at the time of its writing was the Roman Empire, Jupiter prophesies that Aeneas's son will one day acquire the name of Iulus, in anticipatory honor of the Julian dynasty whom Virgil serves and celebrates. The name persists in the modern Italian province of which Trieste III is the major urban center: Friuli is a contraction of Forum Iulii, the Julian Forum, and Venezia Giulia is the Julian Veneto east of Venice. Both names are political, serving as irredentist reminders of the Roman bases of that region the Austrians baldly referred to as mere *Adriatisches Küstenland,* Adriatic coastland or littoral.

But *Iulus,* as Jupiter carefully expounds it, is also meant to recall the great potentate of the East, King Ilus, the founder of Troy or Ilium. His descendant, the displaced person Aeneas, came west from Asia Minor, at last arriving in Italy by way of an Odyssean sea route. Thus the name Iulus may be construed as suggesting two distinct vectors of migration and settlement: one from the seat of empire in the middle of the Italian peninsula moving northeastward, the other from "barbaric" regions to the east moving west and south towards Rome. The first provides the pattern for the varieties of Rome-centered irredentism represented by Benco, Tamaro, and Rossetti. The second is articulated with eloquence by another Triestine writer, Scipio Slataper, who argues that "Trieste is Italian in a different way than other Italian cities are."

In a 1911 essay entitled "Irredentismo," he writes that

there still persists in Italy the ugly belief that Trieste and Trento [a city in the south Tyrol also in Austrian hands until 1918] are Germanic. Yet assuredly there is a significance in this: Trieste and Trento are the points where Roman Italy began to become a Roman colony; points from which the barbarians readied themselves to descend upon Italy proper; in sum, the Italian marches. Hence a mixed and insecure Italianness; an Italianness that must continually Italianize itself, that must render thanks to Venice for having lasted, for staying strong, after the Roman Empire had lost its power to maintain and assimilate the peoples over whom it had dominion. In general, the history of the unredeemed provinces is an Italian history into which have filtered interests and concerns and destinies different from those of Italy.

Trieste, Slataper concludes in a famous formulation, is "a place of transition, which means a place of struggle. Everything in Trieste is double and triple, beginning with its flora and ending with its ethnicity." The very name *Slataper*—Slavic, he was proud to say, meaning "pen of gold"—is a case in point. The Slovenian forebears of this Austrian subject killed on the Carso fighting for Italy arrived in burgeoning Trieste II in the mideighteenth century. He diagnosed his own blood as triple ("*slavo-tedesco-italiano*") and blamed it for his restlessness. Colleagues like the Florentine writer Giuseppe Prezzolini saw him as the "perfect symbol" of Trieste: "tall, blond body from the Slav; sense of duty from the German; poetic soul from the Italian." A human crucible, in effect.

Trieste I's ethnic doubleness and tripleness began well before the transaction of 1382, although Attilio Tamaro predictably dates the coming of the Slavs and Germans to the late Middle Ages, when, in his dramatic words, "a strange, exotic, heterogeneous new world formed itself at the shoulders of the isolated city, pushing two tentacles towards the sea." Tamaro wants his Trieste to be wholly Italian, but the fact is that the Slav presence in what is now Friuli-Venezia Giulia, especially on the Carso, dates from the sixth century. Croat pirates quartered along the Dalmatian coast constituted a serious problem for the Venetian navy from the early ninth century on, and by the time of the so-called *dedizione* much of the Julian countryside was populated by Slav smallholders, hunters, laborers, and subsistence farmers—Croats to the south in Istria and Slovenes from Trieste northward.

Westerly and southwesterly migrations are suggested by other stories as well as the *Aeneid*. The considerably older *Argonautica* of Apollonius of Rhodes, for instance, alludes to the tradition of a southwest passage, a water route linking the Black Sea with the Mediterranean. Jason and his companions are able to sail up the Danube as far as its junction with the Sava River and from there directly into the Adriatic. The coincidence that the ancient name for the Danube was the Ister apparently accounts for this navigational fantasy. The geographer Strabo clearly takes delight in debunking the notion that the Istrian Peninsula and its people, the Istri, take their name from the Pannonia-straddling Ister-Danube. But Pliny the Elder is cagier. Conceding that "the ship Argo came down a river not far from Tergeste," he still holds that part of the transit must have been effected by portage. Since the Argonauts are heroes, this need not necessarily have been over the stony ground of the Carso. A subsequent view assumes that Pliny's river has to have been the mysterious and sacred subterranean Timavo, and that at least sixty miles' worth of the westward odyssey of the *Argo* and its crew was speleological in nature and took place beneath the earth via gloomy vaults and caverns measureless to man if not to heroes.

Routes and passes go in two directions. If one of them was northeasterly and brought the Roman empire-builders, the other, originally milder and less ambitious in scope, was older, in fact, and went in precisely the reverse direction. Might not the Argonauts be considered the epic forerunners of the "barbarians," the Slavs? Even popular traditions surrounding the name *Tergeste* emphasize a sense of the town as a locus of east to west transition.

One folk etymology provided by Dottoressa Ruaro Loseri asserts that Tergeste derives from *Taras,* a fortified city founded by Noah's son Japheth. (Japheth = Japodes?) Another argues that Tergeste is the name of another Trojan warrior-refugee, the eventual founder, like Aeneas (Rome) or Antenor (Padua), of another new Troy in the west. A third says that Tergeste is a corruption of *Tarshish,* "navigator's delight," a fabulous harbor settled by a Phoenician. Does not a Slav resident of Trieste III have his own scriptures to quote in order to prove that he dwells, in fact, in *Trst?*

But the most reputable modern scholarship shows that Tergeste-Trieste derives from the Venetic root *terg,* meaning "market," joined to the terminal *este,* meaning "place." A marketplace. *Trieste:* the name for a function, as Dottoressa Ruaro Loseri comments, "which has been appropriate to the city in every epoch but above all in its moments of greatest splendor."

The irony is, as she certainly knows, that those most splendid moments have been the creation of people whom she and Silvio Benco and Scipio Slataper and many others would at least affect to despise: the Austrian planners, builders, and executives of what Franz Josef regarded as his special city, URBS FIDELISSIMA: Trieste II.

Joys of Mapwork

When supper was through, kind friends who lived near the Public Garden would set out four or five different sorts of grappa to sample before I walked back to the Hotel Al Teatro. One would be crystal clear, the color of gin; another was honey, another cat's-eye green. Several were herb-infused, a delicate sprig afloat within. Grappa Julia—cheap and poor—was distilled at the Stock plant just across town near the railroad station. But most of these came from tiny vineyards and *enotecas* on the Carso, which only my friends knew how to find. I loved the fiery rough taste of it.

I had a small bottle of Friulian grappa, a pale champagne in color, for company in my room. One night during my second week I poured some out in a cup and settled back on the bed to contemplate the maps I had bought that day at the Libreria Italo Svevo. The clock on the nearby city hall struck four and then, after a moment, ten. This meant that the ninth hour had completed all its quarters and the time was ten o'clock. In exactly one minute and forty-five seconds another clock somewhere off to the left in the direction of Palazzo Revoltella would strike ten again. Church bells were still until seven the next morning. Patterns were coming clear.

The first map was a foldout plan of the city in 1890 published in 1981 by Edizioni Tempi Andati ("Times Gone By") of Trieste. The second came in a tube and was very lovely: a full-scale reproduction of the Imperial City and Free Port of Trieste as drawn in 1801, in tan and azure inks, by an artillery corporal in the Imperial Austrian Army, Giovanni Antonio Lechner de Lechfeld. Both maps were very different from the map I used on my walks.

The way to Piazza Oberdan, for instance. A hundred years ago in 1890, Piazza dell'Unità d'Italia was Piazza Grande, the Corso Italia was merely the Corso. Piazza Benco was Piazza Santa Caterina. There was no Corso Saba. Piazza Goldoni was Piazza Legno—Wood or Timber Square—after the market there. Here you turned sharply left onto Via del Torrente rather than Via Carducci, which took you straight to Piazza del Caserma—Barracks Square—where the Austrian troops were lodged. This was where Gugliemo Oberdan had been strung up by the neck shouting *Fuori lo straniero!* Stranger go home! There was no Piazza Oberdan, no kiosk, and, of course, no Opicina tram. It made you think.

I sipped from my cup and thought. In 1890 Joyce was probably being tipped into the square ditch at Clongowes Wood, two hours west of Dublin. Saba (who then was not named Saba but Umberto Poli) was seven years old and suffering ineradicable psychic wounds in a small flat above a secondhand goods shop in the old part of town, *città vecchia,* back of the hotel. Svevo (whose real name was Ettore Schmitz* but who that year signed his first published story "E. Samigli": he hadn't thought of "Italo Svevo" yet) was twenty-nine and clerking at the Vienna Unionbank branch in Palazzo Tergesteo where I had bought the grappa yesterday. All ghosts of times gone by. And what a strange town for one to feel the need of a map of how it was a hundred years ago!

The map I used on my walks was made in Milan and had a circular maze beneath the TRIESTE on its cover. "All towns are labyrinths in which for the townsfolk there are charted fairways; but we are strangers in the town and can find our way only by the exercise of attention and caution."

Thus wrote Joyce's friend, the painter Frank Budgen, referring to Dublin, or rather to Dublin in *Ulysses*. What was clear to me—pouring out another grappa—was that the Milanese cartographer had never meant to imply that Trieste was a labyrinth. Quite the contrary. Or if Trieste *were* somehow a labyrinth, his map would provide a key to the attentive and cautious reader. It was easy enough to find Piazza Oberdan.

Unrolling Artillery Corporal Giovanni Antonio Lechner de Lechfeld's map (Lechfeld was in Swabia, west of Munich), I could see at a glance that in 1801 I might have floated all the way from marketplace to barracks since a rushing stream (the torrent—which was later to be covered over) had run the entire route of Via del Torrente from the hills into the harbor. But how lucid and graspable the Imperial City and Free Port of the Napoleonic era seemed to be! Above and to either side it was edged by graded sepia hills and fields with neatly planted trees, and below by a heavenly azure semicircle of shore and harbor and gulf. Trieste itself folded almost symmetrically into old town and new: the first spilling in jigsaw-puzzle pieces down San Giusto hill toward the little basin or *mandracchio* by the Molo San Carlo at its foot; the second in an enlightened grid of newly cut rectangular blocks bisected by Maria Theresa's Canal Grande, and limited by the lines of a small canal on the left and the obtuse-angled "torrent" on the right. Here in the artillery corporal's world, inked black numbers stood for significant structures—churches of every denomination, *lazaretti,* municipal and imperial offices, forts and factories—all keyed to a scrolled legend inscribed by the artist in his delicate cursive.

Offshore in the gulf at the lower right was another small legend that marked the distances in *Clafter di Vienna,* Viennese fathoms. And almost in the center of the great blue harbor was a large *rosa di venti,* or wind rose, with its lovely litany of Italian wind directions . . . *tramontana, greco, levante, sirocco, ostro, libecchio, ponente, maistro* and, splitting the quarter in the north-northeast, inked with a special dotted line, the famous *bora* . . .

Spiegazioni delli Numeri

Situazione della Città ...

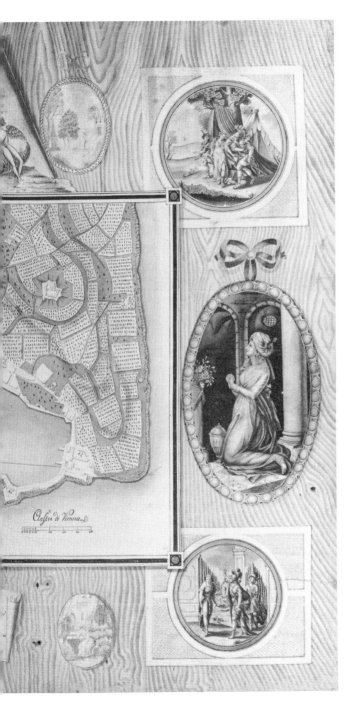

Piazza di Venna

(Yesterday at the end of Molo Audace I had discovered the wind rose, a large iron disk set on a concrete stanchion low enough to sit on. "The pier proffered its bouquet, a wind rose," Saba wrote to his daughter in a heartbroken poem. In the middle were engraved the name, date, and exploit of the torpedo boat *Audace,* first to dock there from Italy at the end of World War I. Around the rim were the winds, a grotesque gale-blasting head for the famous bora . . .)

How beautiful it all was, *azzurra,* in the artillery corporal's world: a vision of serene purpose, of civic, also cosmic, order. So I felt as I sat there contemplating it, sipping grappa. Even my room in the Hotel Al Teatro felt more comfortable, more homelike. But there was more.

For Artillery Corporal Giovanni Antonio Lechner de Lechfeld had imagined his world as though it were mounted upon a wall of grained wood planking, and within the six-inch width of margin this provided he had drawn two sets of what seemed to be depictions of historical events, shaped either as green-rimmed circles set in pink squares or as jeweled oval medallions suspended from green bow ribbons tacked to the wall planks. The effect was brilliantly trompe l'oeil.

A tall, severe woman in a long robe brandishing a smoky torch was drawn in the upper margin of the representation of a curling, slightly torn parchment scroll. A winged cherub was seated beside her on a cornuco-pia. Freedom and Pros-perity, I guessed. She was pointing to a tablet that proclaimed the theme: "Situation of the Imperial City and Free Port of Trieste." A smaller scroll at the bot-tom gave the date ("de-

signed in the month of March, 1801"), name, and rank of the artist. But it was the apparently historical drawings that attracted me the most.

The four circular ones, placed one at each corner of the enclosed map, looked Roman in their reference: filleted hair and plumed gladiatorial helmets, tunics, metal breastplates, robes, and sandals were chief features of the dress code. A young man and woman are emerging from a tent, startled to be met by an armed legionary who is reaching for his sword. A pensive, full-bodied young lady in a formal garden lined with cypress is hailed by two soldiers. Within a palace some laureled Caesar watches coldly as a man with a bleeding face, supported by two matrons, points a finger at him; two other women converse in whispers in the background. A maiden seems to be dying outside the walls of a towered town. Her head is supported by an indignant warrior in rich armor while a garlanded youth in a simple tunic gazes skyward, hands clasped in supplication.

One looked in vain for Octavian decreeing a wall, for the lovely Empress Livia savoring the white wine of Prosecco as one savored one's grappa, for the standards and banners of Regio X, for Alaric or Attila or Alboin reining in at the Carso's edge and choosing to ride on by, to continue to Italy. One looked in vain for the sense of these classical tableaux.

But the two flanking medallions were larger, more emphatic, and even more impressive. They seemed contemporaneous with the artist in costume and decor. On the left, uniformed in boots, tights, swallow-tailed jackets and crested helmets, two dragoons have just burst through a door and down a steep set of stairs into a dark and gloomy chamber where a blond young woman is sleeping—or is she dead?—on the stone floor. Both men have their sabers drawn and raised. One holds a torch to see by. Either they are aghast or they are threatening.

On the right a blond young woman in a turban and flowing robe and cape and sandals kneels praying in what seems to be a chapel. There is an urn at her side and flowers of some sort upon a column by the altar.

No way of telling whether the blond young women were the same. In 1801 Maria Theresa had been dead for twenty years. The troops of General Bonaparte had briefly occupied the town four years earlier—the first of three such disasters—and had just beaten the Austrians at Marengo. In thirteen years Domenico Rossetti would celebrate the end of the Napoleonic menace by writing his stilted melodrama about the comely youth with the apple branch who is rescued from Nemesis and Arrogance and Anxiety and Terror and Excessive Taxation by a wise and loving matron named Austria. Was Austria blond and young? Or were the young women Trieste, Trieste in danger, Trieste in supplication? In any case, these sets of framing images, mysterious and evocative as they were, contrasted powerfully with, and in fact troubled, the luminous bird's-eye view of the mapped tan and azure town upon which they impinged.

I sleepily drained my cup.

And who was Giovanni Antonio Lechner de Lechfeld? I could only say that he was a draughtsman of talent who perhaps squandered that talent as an artillery corporal in the Imperial Austrian Army, then engaged in a series of campaigns against General—then First Consul, then Emperor—Napoleon. He was someone who wrote in Italian, who measured distances in Viennese, who surely felt himself subject and servant of a great Central European empire, and whose name—in some sense analogous to the pen name Italo Svevo ("Italus the Swabian")—perhaps indicated a compound German and Italian ancestry. He had made a beautiful map. How intentional was the enigma? If Lechfeld was a town in the ancient province of Swabia, was that an auspice?

I rolled and replaced his map in its tube and began undressing. The clock struck one, which could mean one o'clock (but only if another clock struck it a minute and forty-five seconds later) or quarter after something. It was late and the streets were comparatively quiet. Bar Rex was closed.

Nearby someone giggled. I heard a flurry of feathers in the eaves above my window. The walking map with the maze insignia on its cover lay folded neatly on the bedstand by my pillow. No further clock struck one so it was quarter after something. The dim bulb waned and waxed above my head.

I lay there and it struck me as auspicious that the Italian for maze was *dedalo,* after Daedalus the maze master of Crete,

> The maze none could untangle, until, touched
> By a great love shown by a royal girl,
> He, Daedalus himself, unravelled all
> The baffling turns and dead ends in the dark
> Guiding the blind way back by a skein unwound.

And also that *Dedalus* was not only the name of the hero of Joyce's *Portrait of the Artist as a Young Man* (written wholly in Trieste) but the exact title of the Italian translation of that great novel: *Dedalo.* That Italo Svevo had been perhaps the very first to read that book as it was being written. And that I had purchased this map beside me with a maze that was floating before my eyes at the Libreria Italo Svevo with the pink arrow pointing. My eyes must have closed.

As always, the thin orange stripes across the ceiling would have rippled when a car passed. But I was enjoying my sleep. My dim bulb waxed and waned until the breakfast knock in the morning, when I awoke to switch it off.

The air of the room chilled his shoulders.
He stretched himself cautiously along under the
sheets and lay down beside his wife. One by
one they were all becoming shades. Better pass
boldly into that other world, in the full glory
of some passion, than fade and wither dismally
with age.

JAMES JOYCE
"The Dead"

Far di sé stesso fiamma. [To make oneself flame.]
CARLO MICHELSTAEDTER*

Three Local Martyrs

Not everybody is going to be edified by the designation I have chosen to link these characters, although two of them elected to die in behalf of what each thought was the highest cause imaginable (very different for each) and the other was slain, scandalously, famously, in the course of what was construed by a number of his admirers as the path of stern duty. Giusto (in English, Justin), thrown tied to a heavy stone into the Gulf of Trieste in 303; Johann Winckelmann, strangled and stabbed in a room of the main inn on what is now Piazza Unità in 1768; Guglielmo Oberdank or Oberdan, hanged by the neck in 1882 on the piazza that now bears his name. A saint, a scholarly aesthete, an irredentist . . . three ill-assorted bodies to be sure, which may suggest something of the variousness of the town in which they met their respective ends. There is no question at all that they are its three most popular municipal ghosts.

San Giusto

On November 2, 1915, James Joyce wrote from Zurich to a Dublin friend that "today is the feast of S. Justin Martyr, patron of Trieste, and I shall perhaps eat a cheap small pudding somewhere in his honour for the many years I have lived in his city." This Justin must not be confused with the much more famous Justin Martyr beheaded in Rome a century and a half earlier for refusing to sacrifice to the gods. Giusto of Trieste will not be found in *The Golden Legend* or Butler's standard *Lives of the Saints* or *The Penguin Dictionary of Saints*. He is a very local martyr indeed.

Until very recently, his right shoulder bone was enclosed in a silver reliquary within the cathedral named for him at the top of the hill named after the cathedral. Before it was the saint's hill, it was a Capitoline hill (as late as a hundred and fifty years ago it was also known as Mount Tiber), and the cathedral was built upon the foundations of a temple that once honored the divinities of empire . . . Minerva, Juno, Jove. Giusto was put to death during the course of the intense persecutions against the sect of Christus carried out under the Emperor Diocletian. The saint's surviving iconography—a twelfth- or thirteenth-century Byzantine statue mounted above the door of the campanile; the late fourteenth-century narrative frescoes inside the church, done by the so-called Master of San Giusto, that dramatize his last days, his death, and its marvelous aftermath; the charming fresco of madonna and child flanked by Saints Giusto and Sergio (perhaps Servolo) done in mid-sixteenth century by the son of the great Vittorio Carpaccio—all this is work done a thousand years or more after the death date recorded on the martyrs' calendar: November 2, 303.

Both the Master of San Giusto and Benedetto Carpaccio testify that Giusto was not much more than a beautiful boy, sixteen years or so, when he was haled up before the Roman prefect Munatius for interrogation. During the reign of Diocletian it was enough to be suspected of membership in the underground church to be condemned to death, and so it was with Giusto. According to the *Acta Sanctorum,* the sentence was appropriately maritime: "to be weighted with lead at the neck and the hands and the feet and to be thrown into the depths of the sea." The frescoes above the altar depict him first incarcerated in a squat tower and managing to pray while his jailers sleep. Then he is shown carrying a heavy boulder— local tradition substituted Carsic limestone for the original lead weight—

Benedetto Carpaccio, *Madonna, Child, and Two Saints*

towards a waiting dory manned by three legionaries. Minutes later, off-shore in the gulf, he is flung overboard. Several fish and one eel gaze raptly upwards from the depths, probably attracted by the bright halo already circling his head. But he does not sink.

Fresco four pans to shore and a room within the walls of Tergeste where a venerable priest, Father Sebastian, beholds in a dream the figure of the expiring youth calling him to the *riva*. When he arrives, there on the sand near the modern lighthouse or Lanterna lies the dead saint, his boulder still hung over the arms crossed peacefully upon his chest, borne there against all the laws of sinking bodies by the pious currents of the northernmost Adriatic. Sebastian throws himself to his knees in astonished prayer. The martyred body is then buried in sacred ground beyond the walls southwest of town, to be transferred centuries later to the new cathedral. Giusto ascends to Paradise.

Pictures of the saint in Paradise endow him with certain symbolic luggage. In Carpaccio's picture he holds in one hand the martyr's conventional frond of palm, while cradled in the other like a baby is a maquette, a large boulder- or egg-shaped golden brown view from the sea, of the medieval town itself: the cathedral with its spacious piazza at the top, the little houses sprawling down the hill towards the unseen harbor, the whole girded by battlement walls punctuated by nine towering gates. San Giusto is Trieste's patron saint, which, given his birth there and the seaside nature of his martyrdom, is as it ought to be.

Not long ago, the reliquary encasing and exhibiting his right shoulder bone was stolen off the altar by unidentified and so far unapprehended thieves. A simulated-gold sunburst frames the ugly cavity where the reliquary once stood. The shoulder bone it held, however, was discarded and left on the spot, sign of either piety or contempt. I have no idea where the shoulder bone is today.

On the other side of the madonna and child in Carpaccio's fresco is San Sergio. Some say that San Sergio is really San Servolo; in any case, neither one was born in Trieste nor died there. Sergio-Servolo is said to have converted to Christianity while on military duty in the town, however, and when this Roman legionnaire was beheaded in Syria for his subversive faith in the same year as Giusto's execution, his gleaming fleur-de-lys-shaped halberd came clattering down out of the sky into the piazza on the hilltop as a sign. Another miracle.

The halberd is the main civic emblem of Trieste and can be seen on its coat of arms. This is perhaps unfair to San Giusto. On the other hand, a big boulder seems to lack iconic flair. In all events, Giusto has the cathedral and the hill, and is unquestionably the main saint.

I went to view the original halberd in the Museum of Civic History and Art on San Giusto hill. Black, perhaps with age, it is set in the top of a large, smooth, ovoid piece of white Istrian stone, which is called "the melon" by *triestini*. An old song in the dialect goes

A Roma i g'ha San Piero,
A Venezia i g'ha el leon;
per noi ghe xe San Giusto
col vecio suo melon.

"In Rome they have Saint Peter's, in Venice there's the lion; for us there is San Giusto with that old melon of his." Vittorio Scussa, a late-seventeenth-century historian, interprets this melon allegorically as a pleasant and morally instructive fruit whose coolness tempers summer heat and reminds us of "civic and patriotic amicability, softening with its

mild influence those oppressive passions that can agitate the breast of one's neighbor." Others, less figurative or more historically oriented, may recognize in this melon a stylization of Giusto's boulder—in which case the halberd finds its heaven-pointing firmness on the basis of that stable and yet uncannily buoyant stone.

Once upon a time both halberd and melon constituted the ornamental cusp of the cathedral's campanile. In 1421 a lightning bolt struck them both—these were difficult times for the town—and for safety's sake they were demoted to a small column on the adjoining piazza. Before they arrived at their current home in the Museum of Civic History and Art, irredentists and the pious could find them among the ruins laid out in the nearby Lapidarium, the city's posthumous homage to the sorry ghost of Winckelmann.

Johann Winckelmann

Somerset Maugham tells the story of a merchant's servant who, having seen Death make a threatening gesture at him in the marketplace, flees from Bagdad to Samarra in order to avoid his fate. When the merchant himself meets Death later on the same day and inquires about that gesture, Death replies that it was not a threat at all but a start of surprise: "I was astonished to see him in Bagdad, for I had an appointment with him tonight in Samarra." Something of this cruelly ironic pattern is discernible in Winckelmann's end in Trieste.

Winckelmann's death there put Trieste on the map of Europe.

That Octavian, later Augustus, Caesar had reinstated its crumbling walls, that there is a picture of Roman troops unloading there somewhere on Trajan's column in Rome, that Dante himself might have slept there or that his epigone Fazio degli Uberti had included it in his medieval Baedeker, were, except perhaps for a few antiquarian irredentists alive a hundred years after Winckelmann's bones had been lost forever in a common grave beside San Giusto Cathedral, matters of remotest history. Nor would many, except scholars of modern mercantilism, be much concerned that in 1719 the Holy Roman Emperor Charles VI of Austria had declared Trieste a free port, or that by the mid-eighteenth century his daughter the Empress Maria Theresa had begun the task of demolishing its ancient protective walls and opening up the town towards the sea, thus initiating its swift transformation into the great world port of the next century. It was under Maria Theresa and her son Joseph II that the center of Trieste moved northwest and downhill away from Piazza San Giusto to Piazza Grande near the water's edge, where the great piers named originally in oblique honor of the empress and her father—Molo Teresiano, Molo San Carlo—were being constructed. But all this was a matter of merely local—at most Viennese—pride.

In 1767, in an area just adjacent to the new governmental and administrative office on Piazza Grande, on a spot fronting on the new port facilities indicated by the pointed index finger of the marble Charles VI high on his Ionic column in midsquare, the imperial architect had just concluded large-scale renovations on the main inn, the Locanda Grande, three stories high with forty rooms, yards, stables, and an all-night caffè. Although the new Locanda was to stand for slightly over a century (it was razed in 1872, yielding, at long last, to the miramar), its unquestionably most famous guest arrived in 1768 during its first full year of operation. His name was only revealed at the inquest.

Johann Winckelmann, esteemed author of *Reflections on the Imitation of Greek Works in Painting and Sculpture* as well as *A History of Ancient Art*, papal antiquary and secretary-librarian in the Roman palace of Cardinal Albani, was fifty years old when, after many hesitations, he decided to revisit his native Germany after an absence in Italy of some thirteen years. His return north was to be a triumphal one, with stops at the homes of admirers in Munich, Dresden, Dessau, and Berlin. The nineteen-year-old Goethe, for example, upon hearing of the great man's projected stay with the enlightened Prince of Anhalt-Dessau, planned a journey there with friends simply to watch and worship. "We made no pretentions of speaking with him but we hoped to see him," Goethe writes in his autobiography. "We thought to lie in wait, now here, now there, in order to see with our own eyes these men so highly exalted above us walking about."

But no sooner had Winckelmann and his companion, the sculptor Bartolommeo Cavaceppi, left Lombardy and begun passage of the Brenner Pass than Winckelmann conceived what Cavaceppi later described as "an incredible aversion" to the height and wildness of the mountain peaks, and even to the steep pitch of the roofs of the Alpine huts along the road. "Look, my friend, look! What a terrible, terrifying landscape!" He saw himself riding in a carriage to his doom. To Cavaceppi's attempts to rally and comfort him, Winckelmann could only reply, over and over, in a monotonous murmur that was half a prayer: *Torniamo a Roma,* let us go back to Rome.

At length the dumbfounded Cavaceppi concluded that his friend had lost his mind. A recent biographer, Wolfgang Leppmann, while noting that at this late date "we cannot psychoanalyze Winckelmann," judges him to have suffered a nervous breakdown en route to his native land. The trip had to be broken off at Ratisbon, north of Munich, where Cavaceppi was at least able to prevail upon him to return to Rome via Vienna, since there were messages from Cardinal Albani to be delivered to the Austrian court. In Vienna Winckelmann was received and fêted by Maria Theresa and her chief minister, Prince Kaunitz. He was awarded two gold and two silver medals by his hosts and then took to bed with a fever. He wrote to Dessau that he was unable to continue his journey owing to its discomfort and his own low spirits, that he was returning to Rome immediately. To Rome he wrote asking that his apartment be readied for him.

There seems to be no appreciable connection between the pitiable creature in a Viennese hospital bed, whom Cavaceppi remembered bidding him farewell "pale and trembling, with eyes as empty as a dead man's," and the distinguished, poised gentleman who registered as Signor Giovanni at the Locanda Grande in Trieste. The four days' trip from Vienna via Laibach (now Ljubljana) over the Carso to Trieste must have seemed a blessed release to the stricken traveler, the first stage of his return to a place where he felt truly at home and free of the menace he had perceived gathering against him in the north. Francesco Angelis, a guest in the next room at the Locanda, who assisted him to locate a boat sailing for Ancona in a few days, reported that he found Signor Giovanni friendly and told police that he believed him to be "some kind of Jew or Lutheran," since he never attended mass and had been reading a large book in a strange language in his room when visited there.

The language was Homeric Greek and the text was the *Odyssey*. Signor Giovanni also showed his new friend a wooden box containing two gold and two silver medals, saying that they were a gift to him from the empress herself. But these were for his visitor's eyes only, he said, since— Signor Giovanni smiled as he said this—"if the innkeeper discovers that I am rich, he will add a guilder to the bill." "Thus," recalls Francesco Angelis, "the idea of robbing him of these medals came to me . . . I decided to kill him."

The next day towards noon Francesco Angelis visited the room next door for the last time. First he attempted to strangle the startled Signor Giovanni with a rope. When the victim resisted, Francesco Angelis drew forth a large black bone-handled butcher's knife and managed to stab him seven times in the breast and belly. ("*Prepare to meet your God,* says he. Chuk!") The sounds of protracted struggle brought a waiter to the door; the assailant fled, leaving the medals behind in his confusion. He was picked up a few days later in Istria.

Francesco Angelis's memories of Signor Giovanni are a part of the confession he made to the Austrian police before he was condemned to death and broken on the wheel in Piazza Grande outside the Locanda. Francesco Angelis was Francesco Arcangeli from Pistoia, cook, pimp, and thief with a criminal record—in any case, an angel of death. The true identity of Signor Giovanni, dead without revealing it six hours after the assault, was discovered on his passport. *Joanni Winckelmann Praefecto Antiquitatum Romae, in almam urbem redit:* Johann Winckelmann, Prefect of Antiquities in Rome, bound home to his city.

The news, when at length it arrived in the north, fell upon Goethe and his friends "like a thunderbolt from a clear sky." There was now no need for them to ride to Dessau. "This monstrous event produced a monstrous effect," Goethe wrote later. "There was a universal mourning and lamentation, and Winckelmann's untimely death sharpened the attention paid to the value of his life." A shocked sense of waste was general and Europe-wide, although the suspect nature of the relations between victim and murderer—they walked the wharves together by day and took supper in the latter's room each evening—during their eight days together in Trieste was also registered, if privately. The facetious tone of the "chronogram" printed in the Jena *Times* (Winckelmann had attended Jena University many years earlier) may suggest something of this:

VVInCkeLManno
tergestI
trVCIDato
salve

("Winckelmann/in Tergeste/hacked to pieces/go in peace": the capitalized letters, also roman numerals, will be found to add up to the year of the crime, MDCCLXVIII.) But Walter Pater's attitude of grave reverence, as recorded in the penultimate chapter of *The Renaissance,* sets the prevailing tone: "it seemed as if the gods, in reward for his devotion to them, had given him a death which, for its swiftness and its opportunity, he might well have desired."

So Winckelmann belongs to Trieste, although in a very different way than he does to Rome, or even to the Athens he never saw. As Hugh Honour points out, he was the poet and visionary of the neoclassic movement; it is only poetic justice that much of the decent architecture left by the Habsburg years in the new town at the base of San Giusto hill is neoclassical in character. The little temple to his memory in the Lapidarium close to the cathedral was sponsored by the civic-minded Domenico Rossetti and is what Silvio Benco called his city's attempt at expiation ("as a defiled temple reconsecrates itself").

I visited it during my last week there. A keeper let me in with a key. Amid the dusty antiquarian hodgepodge is a marble bas-relief executed by a pupil of Canova. An ideal Winckelmann with toga and laurel wreath and torch of enlightenment brandished high displays a heap of classical remains—a bust, an amphora, a tragic mask, and so on—to seven attendant and deeply stirred muses.

(Or so I gathered, trying to piece it out in the gloom. But the keeper behind coughed again and it was time to go. I tipped him for his trouble, and he clanged the vault shut.)

Guglielmo Oberdan

To the ghost or the ghost fancier, to the student of historical timetables and collector of calendar crossroads, the year 1882 is fraught with portent. Item: In the unredeemed British colony of Ireland, in the south Dublin suburb of Rathgard, James Joyce was born. Item: In Trieste, a clerk at the Vienna Unionbank named Ettore Schmitz completed his twenty-first year and published his second article (on the difficulties involved in adapting plays from novels) in the irredentist journal *l'Indipendente*. Item: In Trieste, Schmitz's future wife's grandfather, Giuseppe Moravia, took the gold medal at the Grand International Exposition for his invention of a notable *schmier*, a lubricant made of tallow and various oils devised for the noisy axles of carts and carriages. Item: In Trieste, through the good offices of a marriage broker and in return for four thousand Austrian florins, an elusive character named Ugo Poli changed his Christian name to Abraham, had himself circumcised, and married Rachele Coen, a dealer in second-hand furniture. (Their son, the poet Umberto Saba, was struck to learn much later that the marriage broker's name was Tomba, "Tomb." In point of fact, the marriage fell quickly apart the following year, the year of his birth.)

But 1882 is also portentous on a political level. In 1882 Garibaldi, old hero of a unified Italy, died while the young kingdom he had helped to create signed a triple alliance with a slightly younger Germany and, irony of ironies, the enemy Austria. And the 1882 Grand International Exposition of Trieste was far more than a mere trade fair or sign of the city's considerable stature in the world of European commerce. The exposition had been conceived of and promoted by a consortium of Viennese ministers and Triestine businessmen as a celebration of the five hundredth anniversary of Austria's acquisition of its prime Adriatic outlet.

A half millennium later, the date 1382 remained a vexed one in Trieste. For the prosperous local merchant, it meant the long-ago and rather theoretical beginnings of everything good to come, the auspicious moment when the frail commune, beleaguered by its neighbors in Istria and to the west, and most particularly by the freebooting Venetian Republic, "freely and spontaneously" made its gift of itself to Leopold III, Lord of Carinthia, Carniola, and the Tyrol, effectively to the House of Habsburg. In the fullness of time Austria would become not only Trieste's protector but the creator and architect of its privileged status as a free port, as well as the port's chief customer.

But for the irredentists, drawn primarily from the clerisy and the young with less to lose (as opposed to established businessmen, merchants, and industrialists), 1382 meant the year of usurpation, the year when—according to Attilio Tamaro's metaphor—one of the alien tentacles reached the sea. For such as these, an actual celebration of its anniversary was a bitter pill indeed.

In her life of her husband Sir Richard, British consul at Trieste at the time of the Grand International Exposition, Isabel Burton recalls the August opening.

> The City was illuminated at night almost as brilliantly as Venice had been for the Congress, and Trieste illuminated makes a grand effect with its rising mountain background. The Archduke Charles Louis was there to open it. . . . For months and months endless workmen had been erecting magnificent buildings at the edge of the sea—I should say for a mile in length—all along the fashionable drive called St. Andrea. This great day was devoted to officialdom, and receptions, and bands, and at night Baron Morpurgo [Triestine merchant-prince and friend of the Burtons] had one of his boats out, and supper on board, for his friends to see the illuminations. However, at night there was an *émeute* [riot] in the town, begun by the Italianissimi.

The sudden uproar was caused by an Orsini bomb bursting in air during a torchlight parade of Austrian army veterans in honor of the archduke. Lady Burton's *Italianissimi* alludes to an extremist fraction of irredentists unpopular with the populace at large, irredentist or not. The bomb caused a number of bloody wounds and one youthful bystander was killed.

In the days that followed, the exposition was almost deserted, not so much for political reasons as that it seemed a perilous place to be. "Every night the bands were playing," writes Lady Burton, "and the ices and refreshments always waiting, but nobody ever came." One morning she and a friend ventured down to the grounds and "saw everything most beautifully" since there were not twenty people there.

The bomb had done what it had been meant to do, of course, but there was a swift reaction. A mob of angry citizens stormed the Italian consulate as well as various irredentist meeting places; the police made raids and set up cordons. And then on September 12 authorities announced the arrival in five days' time of Franz Josef, King of Hungary and Emperor of Austria, to honor the demimillennial anniversary with a bold and serenely majestical response to the lunatic act of the month previous.

The perpetrator of the event of August second had been a young Triestine of twenty-four named Guglielmo Oberdan. Standing in the crowd lining the Corso as the veterans marched by, he had tossed his bomb high up in the air to make it seem as if it had been thrown from a window. The resultant bloodshed was an accident.

Prototypical of his city in his mixed Italian and Slav heritage (born Oberdank, he requested friends to drop the final *k* in order to eliminate the Germanic resonance of the original), Oberdan had grown up uncommonly absorbed in two things: mathematics and the redemption by Italy of Trieste. His great heroes were Mazzini and Garibaldi; Scipio Slataper surmises that his mathematical interests worked as a restraining jacket of sorts for the "Byronic nostalgia" of his politics. In 1878, after a year in Vienna studying engineering—despite much agitation, Austrian authorities refused to permit a university in Trieste and degree candidates had to pursue their studies in Vienna, Graz, or Innsbruck—Oberdan fled across the border south to Rome rather than be mobilized into the Imperial Army as part of the Bosnian campaign. In Rome he became one of those exiled young men wondering *How long?* "who but yesterday watched the laughing blue-green Adriatic" in the words of a poem by Carducci.

Oberdan's companions regarded him as shy and almost freakishly studious: a roommate remembers him as regularly laying aside whatever book of poetry he might have been reading at 10 P.M. sharp and doing mathematics until dawn. The sole exception to this pattern of intense withdrawal arose with the topic of Trieste. He became impatient and agitated with irredentist soul-searching as to the proper courses of political action, with meetings and pamphleteering; he was manifestly stirred by stories such as that of the Garibaldian Cairoli brothers ambushed in 1867 while attempting to run guns to the apathetic citizenry of the Papal State of Rome. Once, at a memorial service held for the Cairolis, he suddenly jumped up upon a rock and began to exhort the crowd to take to the barricades. The same roommate remembers one repeated phrase: *Agirò anche se solo,* I shall act even if alone.

The 1882 Grand International Exposition offered Oberdan his opportunity. Risking arrest and execution by the military as a deserter, he made his way back across the frontier and single-handedly carried out his demonstration against the Habsburg presence in his city. Then he returned to Rome. In the weeks that followed, his individualistic brand of irredentism found expression in a new formula: "The cause of Trieste has need of the blood of a Triestine martyr." The announced visit of Franz Josef to the exposition provided the occasion.

Oberdan arrived in Ronchi, a border town twenty miles from the city, on September 16. He was immediately arrested. (The imperial police had not been idle in his absence; there had been informers within the irredentist cell in Rome.) When they kicked open his door in the Ronchi inn, he drew a pistol, fired it into the ceiling, and let himself be captured without a struggle. Several bombs were discovered in his valise. He told the civil and military tribunals repeatedly that the bombs were meant as "a gift for the Emperor."

The legal dilemma for the tribunals was that they had only Oberdan's own word for what he had intended to do; Ronchi was not Trieste, and he had not been taken in flagrante delicto. His friends and his mother urged him to beg for mercy. Carducci wrote to Victor Hugo, who in turn telegraphed the emperor, pressing him to show noblesse oblige by granting Oberdan his life. Neither Oberdan nor Franz Josef complied.

On December 29, 1882, Guglielmo Oberdan was led to the scaffold beside the military barracks on Piazza della Caserma in Trieste. As a reminder of his status as deserter, he was dressed in an Austrian army uniform; even if he could not be executed on the grounds of merely declared intentions, desertion was a crime punishable by death. But Carducci was surely correct when he respectfully criticized Victor Hugo's use of the word *condamné* in his wire to Franz Josef. No, wrote Carducci when it was all over, Oberdan was not a convict but "a martyr to the religion of his fatherland, [who] had come not to kill, I believe, but to be killed."

We are told that the military snare drums rolled from the moment the executioner placed the rope about this martyr's neck, effectively drowning out his last words. Even so, the last words of Oberdan are famous in his city. *Viva l'Italia! Viva Trieste libera! Fuori lo straniero!* Long live Italy! Long live free Trieste! Out with the foreigner! Just over thirty years later, on the anniversary of Oberdan's death, Scipio Slataper wrote a bellicose piece for a Bologna newspaper urging Italy to declare war on the Dual Empire. In conclusion he noted how the action and execution of the student Princip in Sarajevo "reinvokes our purest hero." Now at last, wrote Slataper, "we can speak his name strongly and repeat his will. We want war against Austria."

Oberdan.

If you know where to look, you can see the porticos of the Oberdan shrine from the newspaper kiosk across the piazza. The Austrian barracks were razed in 1927: all that remains are the cell where the prisoner was kept and the exact spot, marked by a bronze statue of him bound and naked and attended by two exuberant angels, where the martyrdom took place. Upstairs in the Risorgimento Museum you can see some personal effects: books and papers, a photo of his mother, a pair of shoes, a white cotton handkerchief with red flowers, a blue and white polka-dot cravat.

as at Pola, close to the Quarnero,

which encloses Italy and bathes her borders,

the sepulchres make all the place uneven

DANTE
Inferno, canto 9, ll. 113–15

Irredentism: the aspiration of an ethnic group
in the possession of a state considered foreign
to rejoin that state to which it feels itself
linked by reasons of history, cultural tradition, and linguistic unity; in particular that
movement of public opinion which in Italy,
between 1866 and 1918, urged the liberation
of those regions inhabited by Italian-speaking
peoples still subject to the Austro-Hungarian
Empire.

Grande dizionario della lingua italiana

Faithfully Waiting

The year 1866, indicated by the *Grande dizionario* as marking the start of the irredentist movement in Italy, helps make the elementary point that there could be no Trieste III, no redeemed city possible, until an actual Italian polity was extant and in a position to act as redeemer. From this point of view, the crucial date is 1861, the year of the creation of the *Regno,* the Kingdom of Italy. ("I was born with Italy," wrote Svevo to his wife on his fiftieth birthday in 1911.)

The year 1866 was a bitter year for the kingdom. Its regular army was routed by the Austrians at Custozza in the Veneto, and even Garibaldi's heroic victory a month later at Bezzecca in the south Tyrol proved indecisive: losses were so heavy that neither side was able to renew fighting the next day. In the Adriatic, near the island of Lissa (now Vis) off the Dalmatian coast, a vast fleet of Italian ironclads was shamefully defeated by a squadron of the Imperial Austrian Navy, as equipped and modernized by the Emperor of Mexico during his stint in Trieste as rear admiral of the fleet. (The battle of Lissa was remembered by his former officers as "the victory of the absent Archduke." Max himself was executed in Mexico the same year.) The frustrating terms of the Peace of Vienna, although they required Austria-Hungary to yield Italy the Veneto, also constrained the new kingdom to accept a northern border well short of what it considered to be its traditional (that is, Roman) cisalpine or natural confines, which should have included not only the south Tyrolean region of the Trentino but Trieste and the Istrian peninsula.

The characteristic Italian irredentist claim in that era charged that Trieste and the Trentino lay within the confines established by Mother Nature herself to designate the Italian peninsula, that high-heeled hip boot surrounded to the west, south, and east by its three seas—Tyrrhenian, Ionian, and Adriatic—and to the north by the broad and sheltering curve made by the Rhaetian, Carnic, and Julian Alps. *Cisalpine* means literally the near or hither side of those peaks, the "naturally Italian" southerly slopes. Until it could include these traditional and legitimate natural confines, then, the Kingdom of Italy as defined by the 1866 treaty was not only incomplete but vulnerable. Thus in the 1880s Giosuè Carducci, a committed irredentist if ever there was one, wrote that with its possession of the Trentino, Austria-Hungary could "penetrate like a wedge directly to the heart of the nation," and that "to the northeast" (that is, in the region of Friuli-Venezia Giulia, of Trieste and Istria as far as Pola and Fiume) the kingdom's frontier was *debolissima:* "the Austro-Hungarian Empire grips her by the throat . . ."

Carducci visited Trieste for the first time in 1878, and his New Year's Day ode to the city, "Saluto italico," was composed just subsequent to that visit. It is written as a kind of outsized envoi, a literary convention according to which the poet addresses—in several senses—his poem and sends it on its way, which in this case (see the map on page 86) extends from Carducci's home in Bologna—San Petronio is the great cathedral at its center—across the unredeemed south Tyrol to, by way of Istria, San Giusto hill in Trieste. Carducci is pleased to call his lines "ancient Italic verses," and in fact in the opening of the ode takes issue with a truculent Venetian critic (Molossus = watchdog) who had commented earlier on the artificiality of the poet's experiments in "barbaric" or classical meters. "Saluto italico" is composed in a modern equivalent of the ancient Archilochian dicolon, and Carducci's riposte to Molossus is that such things come from the feeling heart rather than the head and counting finger. The untranslatable meter is meant to echo the chief point of the poem, which is that there is a Roman tradition in which Trieste is included and which is still alive in modern Italy.

Italic Greeting

Molossus growls, O ancient Italic verses,
that I, marking the beat with my finger, mimic or echo

your scattered numbers—as to the harsh sound
of stricken copper, the buzzing bees swarm.

But you fly forth from my heart as young eagles
fly from their alpine nests at the time of the early zephyrs.

You fly and, troubled, wonder at the murmur which
down through the Julian, down through the Rhaetian Alps,

the rivers, from their green depths, send up to the winds,
laden with epic indignation, proud with heroic song.

It passes like a sigh over silvery Garda,
over Aquileia in mourning for her solitudes.

The dead of Bezzecca hear, and attend;
"How long?" cries Bronzetti, tall phantom, cloud-surrounded.

"How long?" the saddened seniors repeat among themselves
who once upon a time with raven locks bade farewell to you, Trento.

"How long?" fret the youths who but yesterday
watched the laughing blue-green Adriatic.

O, to the beautiful sea of Trieste, to its hills and hearts,
fly with the New Year, my ancient Italic verses;

in the rays of the sun now reddening San Petronio
fly above the Roman ruins upon San Giusto!

Greet Justinopolis upon its gulf,
gem of Istria, and the verdant port and lion of Muggia!

Greet the divine and laughing Adriatic
even unto where Pola displays its temples linking Rome and Caesar!

And then, close to the urn where, still linking two peoples,
Winckelmann watches, herald of arts and of glory,

sing, in the face of the foreigner who, armed, encamps
upon our soil, sing *Italy! Italy! Italy!*

(January 2–3, 1879)

The six strophes of the concluding movement of the ode (now carved on a plaque mounted on the Lapidarium wall in Piazza San Giusto) emphasize by every rhetorical weapon in Carducci's considerable repertory the sheer *romanità* of Trieste and all of Istria. Thus Capodistria (now Koper) is addressed by its ancient name of Justinopolis, Emperor Justinian's city, and the charming little port of Muggia nearby is evoked in terms of its Italian background: it once was a Venetian port and its lion is the lion of St. Mark. Pola (now Pula) proudly shows off its Roman ruins, as does the top of San Giusto hill with its remnants of forum and basilica and the Lapidarium across the way. For all of which the ghost of Johann Winckelmann in his temple, intermediary for ancients and moderns as well as for north and south, provides the ideal witness.

In "Saluto italico," Carducci's eloquence, rather out of fashion in our drier times, is bent to enact a role similar to Winckelmann's for his countrymen on either side of the Austro-Hungarian frontier, reminding them that Trieste II, the flashy product of Habsburg enterprise, is in fact an imposition upon an ancient and perdurable identity. Does poetry make nothing happen? In 1879, the second year of Oberdan's Roman exile, "Saluto italico" was published twice in irredentist papers. Why weren't its last two lines the martyr's cue before the rope began to tighten three years later?

Literary Trieste.

No way of knowing if the points of my beautiful equilateral triangle—Saba and Svevo and Joyce—were united for once on January 12, 1910, in the handsome music hall-cum-theater named for Domenico Rossetti where a notable world premiere took place: the very first of the Futurist "soirées," which were to shock and amuse and polarize much of Europe's literati from Moscow to London over the next decade. A ghostly possibility, nothing more, that they were.

After a rousing discourse on the topic of the stranglehold of the past upon moribund contemporary Italy by the movement's founder, Filippo Tommaso Marinetti (born in Egypt, educated in Paris and in 1910 a resident of Milan); after a stentorian recitation of Marinetti's "Futurist Manifesto" by the bruiser Armando Mazza; after the scandal and cheering and well-orchestrated breakdown of the audience into warring cadres of old and young, bourgeois and bohemian, *austriacanti* and *italianissimi;* after the predictable intervention of the Austrian police and the clearing of the theater and the repairing of the friends of Futurism to the nearby Caffè Milano and a second recitation of the manifesto; after all this and more, at last the respected Triestine lawyer Tebaldi rose dramatically from his seat and, with deep emotion, declaimed Carducci's "Saluto italico," which he knew by heart. It is certain that Marinetti, an irredentist, listened to him courteously and joined the wild applause at the end. It is also very probable that he did so with mixed feelings.

Marinetti had visited Trieste two years earlier, in May 1908, bearing a wreath of flowers to the funeral services for Oberdan's mother and, at the invitation of Silvio Benco and others, reading a selection of his own and French symbolist verse at the Philharmonic. Energetic as always,

Marinetti did much more: he extemporized a prose poem to his irredentist audience in which he celebrated his first view of sunset over the Adriatic as seen from the heights of Opicina.

The skies had been extraordinary, he said, a hectic scarlet, "as though colored by the heroic vapors of a thousand bloody battles." The clouds were puffed out "like the cheeks of archangels sounding the tubas" for Judgment Day. "And the sea? How to describe it? The sea—if you will pardon the boldness of a perhaps too symbolist a metaphor—the sea was a tricolor," and the colors were those of the flag of the Kingdom of Italy.

> I noted areas of silken green, the lovely green of palms swayed by the wind above the white slopes of a city liberated from the foreigner. . . . And there were streaks of red as well, of that voluptuous color that honors the lips of our beautiful Italian women. This beautiful tricolor sea in all its glory flowed into the great port of Trieste and flowed into my heart as well while the sun dissolved its deep red rays into the white candor of the houses and the green of the mountains surrounding.

Marinetti's improvisation is in a partly D'Annunzian, partly Carduccian vein. Futurism, born the following year in 1909, was strongly irredentist in its politics, and from this point of view, Carducci, late bard of the *risorgimento,* was part of the pantheon. Yet the Futurist diagnosis of the trouble with Italy focused less on the foreigner encamped upon its rightful soil than on the young kingdom's cult of the past. From this perspective the poetry of Carducci ("Saluto italico" would be a prime instance) was what Futurists called *passatista,* or passé—nostalgic and retrograde, academic, a dead letter, very much a symptom of the general Italian problem. Marinetti's first manifesto, though it had been published originally in French in the Paris *Figaro,* was targeted home. "It is from Italy that we launch this manifesto of ours . . . because we wish to deliver our land from its fetid gangrene of professors, archaeologists, tourist guides and antiquarians. For too long Italy has been a flea market." Hence the mixed emotions of Marinetti on listening to lawyer Tebaldi recite "Saluto italico" that tumultuous evening of January 1910.

The Futurist solution to the bane of introspection is quite simple: *one must act!* According to Marinetti's memoir of the occasion, the crowd, "goliardically drunken and gaily vandalic," poured out of the Caffè Milano in the direction of the Caffè Eden, "nocturnal lair of Austrian officials," to bait them with a round of catcalls. Then down Indian file to the *riva* and out to the end of Molo San Carlo (eight years must elapse before the *Audace* could dock there) to bellow out welcomes toward the "formidable" Italian fleet of Admiral Bettolo, somewhere in the Adriatic dark. And finally, at midnight, to an ecstatic Futurist epiphany in the southern suburb of Chiarbola, location of the Veneziani marine paint factory and Svevo's home, where the lurid prospect of the great unsleeping port offered an ultimate thrill:

> Cries of victory burst from our breasts. . . . At last the maddest Futurist dreams were being realized: here were fiery structures that moved about, disgorging themselves and pouring their entrails of topaz and ruby upon the ground! . . .
>
> We were surveying amidst the immense incandescent outpour monstrous smokestacks, brutal giants, crested with smoke and unable to hear, passing between their feet, the shrill flight of locomotives, frightened iron mice!
>
> O how we envied those houses perched upon the surrounding hills, those watching houses whose eyes lit up each night with the drunken joy of these fires! How we envied the heated faces of the clouds above and the sea's horizon furrowed with great scarlet reflections!

The romance of the modern! For Marinetti, Trieste had an appeal far beyond its status of political prisoner. In contrast to Rome or Florence or Venice (whose gondolas he wished to feed to a bonfire, whose canals he longed to fill with the rubble of leprous *palazzi* and macadamize into freeways), Trieste was virtually a new town, a town without a past worth

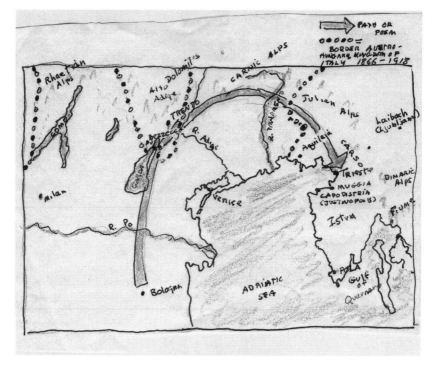

Map of "Saluto Italico"

mentioning, a town equipped and oriented toward the future, a Futurist town in fact. On a par with its swinging cranes and belching smokestacks, dynamic, tough, and as technologically advanced as any Hamburg or New York, Trieste even in its political adversity was what Marinetti inevitably called a *virile* place. "The red shield of Italy" is how he hails it in his memoir of that first soirée, red here signifying not the color of Marx but the furious hue of temper, the color of Mars. From such a perspective,

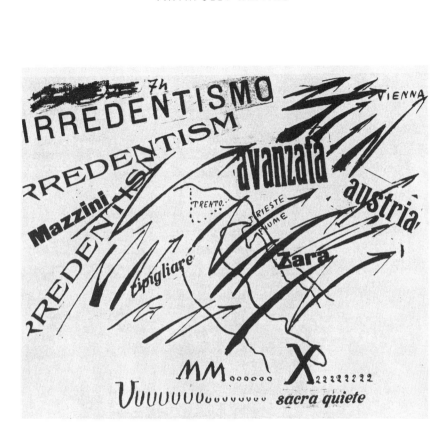

Marinetti, *Words-in-Freedom* (*Irredentismo*)

even the famous Italian hip boot seems like a piece of romantic fancy dress requiring an update. In the book entitled *War Sole Hygiene of the World,* written later that same year, Marinetti concludes by apostrophizing his Trieste as follows:

> You are the scarlet, violent face of Italy, turned toward the enemy! . . . Trieste! you are our sole shield! . . . Do not forget, O Trieste, that the Italian peninsula has the form of a *dreadnought,* with a squadron of torpedo-boat islands!

(Literary Trieste! How the three ectoplasmic faces of my beautiful triad must have looked wry then, and sardonic, if indeed they were there in the flesh seated certainly not together in the orchestra of the Politeama Rossetti that winter evening in 1910. Irredentist themselves in varying intensities of sentiment, they may have been amused but surely not impressed by Marinetti's way with words. But their presence there can only be *entertained,* a ghostly possibility, a purely literary conjecture.)

"He speaks of dreadnoughts in the manner of Byron": thus Jean Cocteau dismissed Marinetti in 1919 on grounds of stylistic mildew. Cocteau has a point, but he is unfair to the author of *Don Juan* in his ascription of lineage. Marinetti's master and model, for whom he had a lifelong cult, was Gabriele D'Annunzio.

(Joyce admired D'Annunzio, his sonorous sentence structures, his rich vocabulary. The adjective *testudoform*—shaped like the segments of a tortoise shell—which Joyce uses to describe the brown tiled roofs of Trieste, is of D'Annunzian derivation, as is his use of the notorious noun *epiphany.* Svevo took issue with Joyce on this and tried—in vain—to argue him out of it. It was about someone very like D'Annunzio that Svevo wrote in his diary: "He is a man who writes too well to be sincere.")

D'Annunzio's dramatic irredentism is most notoriously demonstrated by the episode of his "Regency of Quarnero" (Quarnero is the gulf below Fiume "which encloses Italy and bathes her borders") following World War I, when, in the name of an embarrassed Kingdom of Italy, he and his legionaries seized Fiume from the newly established Kingdom of Serbs, Croats, and Slovenes (i.e., Yugoslavia) and held it in defiance of world opinion for over a year. But over a quarter of a century earlier D'Annunzio was already agitating for a more completely cisalpine Italy based upon the "natural" confines of Caesar's time. One of his several naval odes, "To a Torpedo Boat in the Adriatic" (1892), is not only proto-

Futurist in decor and "superhuman" belligerence (though far above anything Marinetti could manage in this line) but achieves in its ringing conclusion a degree of prophetic accuracy which out-Carduccis Carducci.
The faithful shining city is, of course, Trieste; the voice towards the end
belongs to the tormented shade of Emilio Faa di Bruno, one of the defeated captains at the catastrophe of Lissa.

To a Torpedo Boat in the Adriatic

Steel ship, straight, swift, flashing
beautiful as a naked weapon,
alive, palpitant
as though metal enclosed a terrible heart;

you who on man's cold courage alone are sharpened
like a weapon on whetstone,
and who do not suffer cowards
upon the burning plates of the bridge that throbbing shakes;

first messenger of death on the war-torn sea,
bold vanguard of the sea,
you pass—and your fate
I follow, watching your wake glitter in the flood.

Shaken from the roof of heaven are avalanches of misshapen cloud
between tall columns of rays;
flock after flock wheel by
sea birds skimming with savage cries;

beneath the storm down there towards Ancona
the Adriatic darkens to ash:
if far away it thunders,
the rumble rebounds downward, down through the sullen sultriness.

The clouds make cover. But the soul's eye sees
across the sea in the distance
the city that rises
tall above its gulf, shining to our hope,

from all its towers shining in the sole faith:
"Yours forever! Forever the same!"
since she still believes
our sad, captive sister, in our promise.

And a shadow lengthens, weighs upon the waters (I see it
with a broken shudder
growing, staining
the bruised abyss as with a spot of corrupted blood);

it lengthens from faraway Lissa towards the mother shore.
Now. Here. It is Faa di Bruno.
"Is the shame to be
eternal?" He listens. "Will no one listen? no one?"

You, you, O ship of steel, swift, flashing
beautiful as a naked weapon,
alive, palpitant
as though metal enclosed a terrible heart;

you who on man's cold courage alone are sharpened
like a weapon on whetstone,
and who do not suffer cowards
upon the burning plates of the bridge that throbbing shakes;

first messenger of death on the war-torn sea,
bold vanguard of the sea,
O answer! Fate
is sure; and towards that Day the fires are lit on the altars.

How precisely right and according to prophecy that the first Adriatic torpedo boat from Italy to touch Molo San Carlo before a joyful crowd on November 3, 1918, be called *Audacious!* Had the admirals read D'Annunzio, even as Oberdan had read Carducci? (Literary Trieste.) The Day of Redemption had come, as predicted in some detail over a quarter of a century earlier. It was the beginning of Trieste III.

How everything smiled . . . One witness of that mooring remembered wondering whether it were possible that the future could hold anything equal to it. "Perhaps we all felt indistinctly in our deep-most souls the Faustian *verweile doch, du bist so schön*":

> If ever I say to the passing moment
> 'Linger a while! Thou art so fair!'
> Then you may cast me into fetters,
> I will gladly perish then and there!

The future so far has held chiefly anticlimax and disillusionment: the prompt demotion of a major port to a peripheral one, Mussolini, Fascist nationalism and an exacerbated Slavophobia, the German occupation, the Yugoslav occupation, the Allied occupation and division of the territory into zones A and B, permanent partition in 1954, economic hard times, a shrinking population. Nor has irredentism proved to be a sheerly Italian dream. As with the establishment of the *Regno* in 1861, so with the establishment in 1918 of the Kingdom of the Serbs, Croats, and Slovenes: there is now a nation, Yugoslavia, to which a sizable Slovene minority—about 10 percent of the total population of Trieste—may aspire.† Even the argument for "natural confines" is double edged. A glance at any relief map of the Balkans will show (rather disconcertingly, in my case) that Trst today is Mother Nature's gateway to the *west,* not the other way around.

†Triestine Slavs now [1991] may aspire to the independent republic of Slovenia.

Trieste, which became Austrian in 1382, is essentially a modern city. Destitute of a natural harbor, it owes the beginning of its importance to Emp. Charles VI, who made it a free port in 1719, while its rapid growth in the second half of the 19th cent. is due to the construction of the Semmering Railway, which extended its commercial relations to S.E. Germany. The tendency of the Mediterranean trade to find its outlet in Genoa will, it is hoped, be checked by the opening of the Tauern [transalpine] Railway in 1909. . . . In 1910 the harbor was entered by 11,839 vessels of 4,198,625 tons. The value of the imports in 1909 was 573 million crowns, of the exports 508 millions. The chief imports are coffee, rice, cotton, spices, ore, coal, olive-oil, and fruit (from the Levant); the staple exports are sugar, beer, and manufactured goods.—Sir Richard Burton and Charles Lever both filled the post of British consul at Trieste.

Baedeker's Austria-Hungary with Excursions to Cetinje, Belgrade, and Bucharest (1911)

I feel myself back in that day when my
life was broken. The bright morning sun
was on the quay—it was at Trieste—the
garments of men from all nations shone
like jewels—the boats were pushing off . . .

GEORGE ELIOT
Daniel Deronda, ch. 43

It is snowing pigeons in the squares, amidst
the great blocks of dull and yellow material
of the *palazzi;* and the mix of Italian street
names, Slav shop signs, German inscriptions on
monuments, and Austrian uniforms, intensely
blue in this light, summarizes the political
situation . . . Ah, how far it all is from Bond
Street!

VALERY LARBAUD
Journal intime de A. O. Barnabooth (1913)

Tableaux Morts

ne of the few Habsburgs still on public show in Trieste III is Maria Theresa's father Charles VI, emperor from 1711 to 1740, whose stone effigy stands sceptered, mantled, and bewigged upon a column in Piazza Unità, halfway between the *ingénue* city seated with Commerce near the top of the Fountain of the Four Continents and the tobacco shop with the best souvenirs. He points with pride towards the port.

More precisely, he points with pride towards the *free* port, which in Trieste III no longer exists. The port, of course, still problematically does, as it has for several millennia. But the free port is credited to Charles as his conception. Tradition says that in 1719 he addressed himself to the undistinguished little hill town beneath the Carso on the northernmost Adriatic, with its modest produce of fish, olive oil, salt, and white wine, with its cottage industries of sailcloth and fishing gear, with its salt pans stinking just beyond its mossy walls and its silted-in Roman theater and weedy forum and little boat basin, or *mandracchio,* poking guardedly out towards what was in those days still called the Gulf of Venice, and grandly nominated it *Freihasen, portofranco,* the "Imperial City and Free Port of Trieste" as admiringly depicted by Artillery Corporal Lechner de Lechfeld nearly a century later.

A free port is a port free of the usual protectionist devices (dock restrictions and customs duties; wharfage, portage, and storage charges) by means of which a modern port normally assures itself of order, up-keep, and profit. The aim of a free port policy is, through the offer of optimal trade conditions, to attract an unusually large volume of business, which will outweigh the loss of conventional revenues. Charles dangled other sorts of bait as well: freedom in the conduct of commerce, naval protection for vessels bound in or out of the port, free use of warehouses to be constructed specifically for the storage and display of wares, low-cost property and construction supplies for the raising of trade-related buildings in the town, and—major mark of imperial power—cancellation of all debts that newcomers meaning to stay might have contracted elsewhere.

Precedents for such a policy already existed in the western Mediterranean—in Livorno, Genoa, Marseilles, and Gibraltar—but the main interest of Charles and his advisors was not in competition with the thriving transatlantic trade. In the late seventeenth century the Ottoman Empire at last had been broken as a significant power and threat. Following the War of the Spanish Succession, Austrian Habsburg attention was freed to contemplate Asia Minor and the lucrative territories and continents now accessible without much risk to the south and east. Hence, the *Arabian Nights* note, the jeweled garments and unusual cosmopolitanism of the Imperial Free Port of Trieste as it developed over the decades, its vigorous communities of Greeks and Jews and Levantines, its "open" ghetto and the commercial panache and exotic flavor so noted by travelers there.

What Charles declared by fiat and merely began was implemented in the course of the century by his immediate descendants, Maria Theresa (empress, 1740–80) and her son Joseph II (co-regent and then emperor, 1765–90). Between 1719 and 1800 the population of the city and environs increased fourfold, from seven thousand to twenty-eight thousand. The fortified *mandracchio* gave way to the modern front with its *rive,* its burgeoning moles and breakwaters. The old walls that had defined what still today is called *città vecchia,* the old town jumbled on San Giusto, were razed. Earth scooped from the seaward hills was used to fill in the littoral beyond those walls where for centuries there had been salt pans and where now the districts of the new town—Borgo Teresiano, Borgo Giuseppino—were laid out with their broad, paved avenues and their symmetrical, rectangular blocks. In 1728 a post road was constructed over an ancient bridle path to the northern interior, to Laibach (Ljubljana), Graz, and Vienna . . . the road that Winckelmann would take south. There is a statue of Charles VI, its begetter, at the top of the Semmering Pass; the Obelisk at Opicina commemorates the widening of the road in the 1830s.

In 1799 a municipal committee filed a report urging the speedy construction of a *borsa,* a bourse or stock exchange building, to provide dignified housing for business activity. Modeled upon similar edifices in Brussels, Amsterdam, and Dublin, the neoclassical shape of Palazzo Borsa was in place by 1805, just too late for the artillery corporal's map, just in time for the second Napoleonic occupation. Upon its severe four-pillared facade and above the pediment were mounted an assortment of tall allegorical statues slightly at war with the geometrical rigor below: of Mercury, god of commerce (the town's particular deity); of the inevitable Neptune and Minerva; of the River Danube, helmeted old gentleman with a beard; and of Trieste as virile ephebe. Contemporary judgments of the Borsa building by interested parties, Triestine magnates, are uniformly lyrical. "The facade could not better express the mystical idea of force and vigor of this nascent city, the virility and prudence of its merchants as well as their calmness and solidity." Or: "it seems a magnificent temple destined for the worship of what ought to be inscribed upon its front: TO SPECULATION." Charles VI in eternity can only have been delighted with this handsome monument to his dream of a prosperous port, commissary to Vienna.

One cold grey day in January I walked the little block between the hotel and Palazzo Borsa in order to look at the second-story hall there where Joyce had given his lecture in Italian on "Irlanda, isola dei santi e dei savi" [Ireland, island of saints and sages] under the auspices of the Università popolare, University of the People. Under Austrian

rule, Trieste had no university of its own; the Università popolare had been founded in 1900 to provide adult education and, in the words of one of its organizers (Attilio Tamaro), "to stir things up, to make Trieste's problems known, to feed continuously anti-Austrian feelings." Tamaro took English lessons from Joyce and in 1907 invited him to lecture on Irish matters. Irish history, as Tamaro was aware, had its Triestine parallels: in both cases a subject people, living under foreign domination, claimed a language and a culture different from that of its conquerer. Nor did the teacher disappoint his pupil: the audience, mostly Joyce's students and acquaintances and all irredentist, applauded when he spoke of Ireland's insistence on developing its own culture as "the demand of a very old nation to renew under new forms the glories of a past civilization" or declared, at the end, that tyranny must beget revolution and that "revolution is not made of human breath and compromises."

Beyond the great glass entry doors of Palazzo Borsa, I found a large high-ceilinged room with a modest Christmas tree standing in one of its four corners, colored bulbs still burning (although it was after Epiphany) and a scum of some pale-grey substance, like withered lather from an aerosol can, still decking its brownish boughs. And then something beautiful. Set into the honey-marble floor and extended in a long diagonal from the green blanket bunched about the tree's standard across the entire chamber was an exquisite, inscrutable diagram: a long and narrow, slightly tapering rectangle framed by a band of blond marble; within it three dotted parallel lines of black marble squares accompanied by various numerals suggesting measurements—degrees or distances or days perhaps—of some sort; outside these were ranged the names of the months and, in bronze inlay, the signs of the zodiac. The morning's impresarios and clients, whatever their businesses, tracked brutishly across all this towards the stairs or offices visible in the rear without the least hesitation. I loitered there in vain calculation for several minutes. Then, at length, I followed them.

The auditorium I sought was on the second floor, *piano nobile* the attendant said. He opened a door, switched on the chandeliers, and left me alone by the dais. Rich Palladiana, bronze deities in niches, a lacy fringe of balcony, yellow Corinthian columns gleaming, and four wide rows of empty red plush-bottomed chairs waiting for a word. I cleared my throat and shifted, hung fire, and followed my eyes upward along the thin electrical cord connecting the flashy central chandelier with the precise center of Giuseppe Bernardino Bison's enormous ceiling-spanning fresco, entitled "Charles VI Grants Trieste Its Port Franchise."

Scarred though it has been by the electrical cord unforeseen by the Friulian Bison nearly two hundred years ago, his fresco projects a curiously rakish charm—which is not the expected virtue for such a subject depicted in such a place. Its colors have persisted brilliantly, but the ceiling is very high and the artist's satirical bent is covert unless the viewer bears binoculars or owns, as I do, the Borsa catalogue issued by the Trieste Chamber of Commerce, which provides a color close-up.

Preeminent at picture left on some sort of stone rampart shaded by a festive pavilion (the *Arabian Nights* note) stands Charles himself with members of his entourage. He is suited in white silk and robed with ermine-tippeted orange velvet. He gestures imperially outward with the pointed index finger of his extended left arm—*Fiat portus liber!* must be the silent motto here enacted—towards a small group of astonished individuals, presumably the Trieste delegation, which is placed left center below him at the head of an impossibly precipitous staircase. Charles's thematic and pictorial eminence on the left is counterbalanced on the right by the upper end of an equally impossible bannister, on the top of which, roughly the emperor's scale in size and authority, is set a burly bronze Neptune over whose shoulders floats a pink and white Austrian banner with its double-headed eagle. Observing the transaction is a row of imperial halberdiers as well as—leaning on and over the marble railing around the stair head, which frames three sides of the scene—an assortment of "ordinary" folk, some of whom wear turbans and fezzes and Arabian-looking beards. A sign of the super emporium to come, of course.

Charles is granting Trieste its free port status in no recognizable locale, certainly in neither Trieste nor Vienna. Above Neptune and the Austrian flag soar the columns and entablature of a generic neoclassical pile; above these is a baby blue sky varied with a few nonthreatening cumulus clouds. *We,* of course, stand craning upward from the Borsa floor at the imagined bottom of that impossible staircase. It is a witty variation on Tiepolo—an entrepreneur's Tiepolo executed with a sardonic eye—that we are viewing.

If the vertiginous angle of vision is fantastical—vide the unclimbable stairs, and the acute and gravity-violating angle at which Charles's trim body is made to rake above the delegation—the features of the various faces are not; they are recognizably all too human. (Here the catalogue is essential.) In contrast with his youthful body, Charles's features beneath his powdered peruke are those of a dissolute old man. His chins are multiple, his skin is puffy, and his eyes are trained not on the business at or under hand but—a detail Giuseppe Bison certainly never intended—on the wiring of the electric chandelier to be installed a century later. The big bronze Neptune is gross and running to fat. The Trieste delegation resembles a gang of felons recoiling from a harsh sentencing rather than worthy burghers first hearing of an extraordinary gift. And then there are the smirks and occult grins among the onlookers, whether in the little court group to the rear of Charles or in the motley crew lining the railings. The pair of halberdiers perched right and left at the top of the impossible staircase are going too far in their broad aping of the ceremony going on above!

"Grandpa," asked a little boy one day as he watched two *carabinieri* pass by in their grand cloaks and Napoleonic headgear, "do they know we are not thieves?" And the grandfather, Italo Svevo, answered: "Truly, they cannot know this." Wry and relatively unrecognized high above on the auditorium vault, the target of "Charles VI Grants Trieste Its Port Franchise" is neither universal mendacity (thieves like us) nor Habsburg hubris. It is the spectacle of officialdom, its pomp and pretentious circumstance, its dimly apprehended parody of human intercourse, as seen by the shrewd sharp eye, common sense, and talented hand of a painter from Friuli, for whom the assignment to make such a machine on such a theme in such a place could only mean an enterprise of satire. But only the visitor with binoculars or someone with the catalogue—someone like me—will know this.

Beneath the Bison fresco James Joyce discoursed of Ireland's *savi e santi* to his friends, informing them "of the religious fervour that still prevails in Ireland, of which you, who have been nourished on the food of skepticism in recent years, can hardly form a correct idea." They applaud—his pupil Svevo perhaps among them—and shake his hand, and depart down the stairs; and so did I. On the well-waxed floor of the loggia below, an enigmatic diagram finished under a shabby Christmas tree.

It was a *meridiana* or noon mark, as I found out much later from the catalogue, meant to point out not only the astrological house, the month, and the day, but the five minutes preceding and following the hour of noon in Trieste, the time that the Borsa closes. The diagram itself was a kind of dial. The marker was made by a shaft of sunshine let in through a hole high up and invisible on the chamber wall; but even if I had left at exact noon, I couldn't have seen it on the grey day of my visit.

The catalogue told me more. What I had seen that grey day of my second week in Trieste was not the Borsa at all but the Borsa Vecchia, the old or original temple of specula-tion. In 1844, less than forty years after its completion, the Borsa had moved away into ampler quarters in Palazzo Tergesteo up the block, where, on an upper floor in an of-fice of Vienna Unionbank, Ettore Schmitz would clerk and, as Italo Svevo, would appropriate file cab-inets, desk, and staff—himself in-cluded—for use in his first novel, forgotten by everybody but its au-thor the year after publication. The Borsa moved again in 1928, the year of Svevo's death, this time into a building just across the street from the old Borsa, which is where the Borsa really is today.

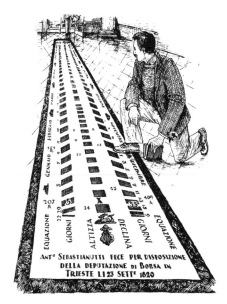

ANT° SEBASTIANUTTI FECE PER DISPOSIZIONE
DELLA DEPUTAZIONE DI BORSA IN
TRIESTE LI 23 SETT^E 1820

What I had visited was not just the Borsa Vecchia but the seat of the Trieste Chamber of Commerce. An anxious place—as I walked right by without sensing—because business these days is very bad indeed.

In 1850 the twenty-year-old Franz Josef wrote his mother of his first visit to Trieste during his second year as emperor.

> Dear Mama,
>
> I've received a magnificent welcome, there's a splendid atmosphere here, shouts of "Long may he live!", enthusiasm, yet everything *comme il faut.* The farther I get from Vienna, the better I find their inner dispositions. At Graz, good tempered and dignified; at Laibach, excellent; and here, enthusiastically Austrian. Everywhere I found the military parades better than I could have hoped for. I saw several today and following lunch a Lloyd steamer was launched. Tomorrow I shall lay the foundation stone for the Southern Line, this evening there is a ball, and so it goes like the Thousand and One Nights.
>
> Your devoted son Franz.

It seems evident from this that the loyalty of Austrian subjects at a certain remove from the Innsbruck court and Vienna is *not* a matter that can be taken for granted; the emperor's letter to the Archduchess Sophie is meant to be reassuring. Franz Josef's allusions to Lloyd Austriaco and the Süd-bahn, to the great steamship line and the railway to come, are also signifi-cant. He has come to Trieste not on a genuine royal "progress"—although he himself may not have seen through the cover—but as star of a parade of symbols keyed to an important commercial venture.

The grey hand behind his throne belonged, in fact, to a Triestine by adoption. The Baron Bruck, Franz Josef's minister of commerce, was a German from Bonn who had come to live and prosper in Trieste in 1821, a self-made man who helped to found Lloyd Austriaco and was later one of its directors. Bruck had a visionary side to match his commercial tal-ents. He dreamed of a *Mitteleuropa,* a Central European "Empire of Sev-

enty Millions" that, chiefly by means of the abolition of internal trade-
and customs-barriers, would mold that vast complex of seething nation-
alities—German, Czech, Polish, Slav, Magyar, Italian—into a peaceful
and prosperous federation under Austrian hegemony. In 1848 the Austrian
Empire (likened by A. J. P. Taylor to "a vast collection of Irelands") had
simmered up into various nationalist uprisings and revolutions. Divided
but in the main docile, Trieste had been laid under blockade for a short
period by a combined fleet of Sardinian, Neapolitan, and Venetian naval
vessels. Trieste's imperial reward for its good behavior, the official epithet
FIDELISSIMA, must have rankled those citizens who had followed events
across the Adriatic and in the Piedmont with sympathy and quickening
hopes.

A major priority for Bruck in the development of his regional
schemes was an efficient and accessible port-entrepôt-emporium for Vienna, and this—completing what had been begun over a century earlier
by Charles VI—was meant to be Trieste. The august presence of Franz
Josef laying the foundation stone for the terminal that May afternoon in
1850 placed a ceremonial seal upon a key policy feature: fast, up-to-date
transit between the capital and its Mediterranean access by way of Laibach, Graz, and—extraordinary feat of early industrial age engineering—
the Alpine rail route over the Semmering just south of Vienna.

There is a tableau in honor of it all in definitely the most burden-
some of all the souvenirs of my first week in Trieste. It took both arms to
hump the duffel bag containing it up onto the station bus the day I left; I
then had to drag it over the dirty marble floors to the platform where my
train was waiting; someone or something had broken its spine by the time
I was required to display it as evidence of my scholarly intent to the skeptical customs officer at Kennedy Airport.

The tome *Trieste nelle sue stampe* [Trieste as seen in its engravings]
was found remaindered in the stalls of the Libreria Italo Svevo, and I
bought it with misgivings not only on account of its weight and size.

What in my future plans could justify its nostalgic focus on a picturesque and prephotographic world? What had it to do with whatever remained of my beautiful triangle? (Only later did it help me to recognize that I was meant to write a ghost story.)

Spread across two pages of *Trieste nelle sue stampe* is a commemorative engraving of Franz Josef's visit to Trieste done for the occasion by someone who signed himself "F. Faltus." Of F. Faltus himself there is not much more to be said than there is of Artillery Corporal Giovanni Antonio Lechner de Lechfeld. He was a technically competent engraver who managed to get the lie of the hills around the harbor quite wrong and also someone whom Franz Josef's grandfather would certainly have called "a patriot for me." His tableau is dedicated to the *fidelissimi triestini* and is designed to illustrate the justice of the adjective. Its centerpiece shows the twenty-one-gun salute offered by the imperial frigates in Trieste harbor to the youthful emperor waving back from the stern of his expertly manned cockle boat. Riggings are streaming with bunting and crawling with sailors huzzahing, dinghies filled to the gunnels with the most faithful Triestines waving their caps bob respectfully downwind of the grand flotilla.

In the top and bottom margins F. Faltus has provided six smaller vignettes depicting ordeal and reward. Three focus on the recent Sardinian-Neapolitan-Venetian blockade: the ordeal. Grim harbinger of looming irredentism, the fleet of "Italian" warships construes itself as an offshore wall while meantime, in Piazza Borsa, imperial troops and cheering citizens prepare to resist if necessary; elsewhere there is a blessing of the imperial banners in the same piazza.

After ordeal comes reward. Reward means the advent of Franz Josef and his retinue, and the ecstasy engendered by his three-day visit. F. Faltus depicts the majestic arrival at the twenty-year-old Obelisk at Opicina described so rapturously by the emperor's younger brother Max. The steam paddle wheeler *Dalmatia* is royally launched at the Lloyd Austriaco shipyards. Franz Josef lays the foundation stone for the Südbahn terminal. In

TRIESTE

AI FEDELISSIMI TRIESTI

LE FESTE TRIESTINE AL VARAMENTO DEL VAPORE "DALMATA" DEL 3° MAGGIO 1856

I TRIESTINI ALL'APPARIRE DELLA FLOTTA SARDO-NAPOLETANA DEL 29 MAGGIO 1848

T. di Piolti disi.

F. FALTUS DEDICA

effect, the artist shows that the political revolution—1848 and all that—apparently has been supplanted, or obscured, by the industrial one.

And counterpointing the grand themes of renewed political stability and free but prudent enterprise as shown by the combined power of emperor and court and merchant princes and gleaming locomotives and plumed steamers, there is also, throughout the tableau, the Arabian note: tossed hats of an enchanted citizenry; snapping pennants and flags everywhere on masts and poles; everywhere the rich, carpeted, silken pavilions erected—at the Obelisk, at the Lloyd Austriaco dry docks, in front of the phantom railroad—to ward off the smiling sun from Sultan Franz Josef and his jeweled entourage.

The Arabian note: "Jinns and Jinniyahs . . . demons and fairies . . . flying horses, talking animals and reasoning elephants . . . magic rings and . . . talismanic couches which rival the carpet of Solomon," as Sir Richard Burton was to describe it several decades later in his Opicina inn across the way from the Obelisk. And so it went, as the emperor himself remarked, "like the Thousand and One Nights."

Professor Taylor believes that the two chief legacies of the Habsburg monarchy to *Mitteleuropa* have been its railway system and the port of Trieste ("Correct name: Trst"). He calls Trieste "a project inconceivable before the age of railways." He thus emphasizes access to hinterlands at the expense of the notable port developments begun the previous century, and so expresses a half-truth. But the great railroad decade of 1850–60 surely marks the high tide of Triestine self-confidence.

Six years after the foundation stone was laid for the station, work was begun on Castle Miramar. The year after that, Maximilian married Carlota and Franz Josef returned to Trieste for the solemn opening of the completed Südbahn. In 1858, the Congress of the International Society of Railroads was held there; the little guidebook *Tre giorni a Trieste* [Three days in Trieste] was issued by Max's friend, the Baron Revoltella, in honor of that occasion. Everything smiled . . .

There is a magnificent paragraph on this period in another guide to Trieste, written with ironizing hindsight in 1910 by Silvio Benco.

> Through every Trieste street is now diffused the effluvia of cinnamon and pepper, of orange, of camphor and chrysanthemum. Commerce glitters at its apogee. The city's bankers haul buckets of napoleons up to their windows by means of ropes; the populace, in effect no better off than in our day, deludes itself with imagining life as a lottery where anyone may be touched by a lucky draw; youth sows its wild oats with the sylphides of the ballet, all the more thoughtless since one last freedom that absolutist Austria has granted its emporium is a dispensation from military service. All those for whom the liberty to enjoy and to amass precludes any desire for other liberties renounced or canceled live in a great blare of optimism and faith—ignorant of the city's decline, which was already virtually begun the day the other ports, major or minor, started to radiate outward in railroad lines towards the continental countries of consumption and outlet; while the Viennese government, intent on spying out whether uprisings were afoot in Hungary or Italy, delayed putting Trieste on the railroad map of Europe. But the railroads will be Trieste's ruin, even as the steamships with which it had provided itself at the dawning of their era had been, at least in part, its exaltation.

In fact 1857, the year the Trieste-Vienna line was completed, is, economically considered, a shamefully late date. The nearby smaller and far less elaborated Austrian port of Venice already had a considerable network of rails linking it with its hinterland by that time. Hamburg, Trieste's chief shipping rival on the North Sea, had its rail connection with Vienna in place by 1851 and profited enormously by the earlier access. Trieste did not even get its local line to Istria until 1887. Even in its heyday, then, the empire was—as Joyce put it later—"ramshackle" and sluggish to act. The great Austrian novelist Robert Musil writes of the "magic formula:

'*Ass.*' " as typifying the civil service of Kakania (his parody name for late Habsburg Austria) before its demise. *Ass.* is short for *Asserviert,* "which means as much as *Awaiting further consideration . . .*an example of the circumspection that does not lose sight of anything and does not try to rush anything." (Something of the same bureaucratic adagio may be found in the fiction of another Kakanian author, Franz Kafka, who was employed at the Prague branch of Assicurazioni Generali, a Trieste-based private insurance company, from October 1907 to July 1908.)

But such is the illumination of hindsight: at the time, of course, it is never so clear. Trieste's population sextupled over the course of the nineteenth century, from about 30,000 in 1800 to close to 180,000 at the start of the twentieth. The magnificent Palazzo Borsa of 1806, as we have seen, quickly became Borsa Vecchia—which is as much as to say too small for its job. Even the railroad terminal symbolically instigated by Franz Josef turned out to be provisional; destroyed by fire in 1878, it was replaced by a building in which Silvio Benco could take an undilutedly solid, civic, and somewhat Marinettian satisfaction:

> A most elegant Renaissance facade: one hundred meters of vaulted platforms for train service, colossal metal ribbings smoked with glorious soot. The iron architecture has an athlete's robust movement and visible musculature; the stone preserves his poised nobility and gracious expressiveness.

(But Benco omits the sun and how it penetrates this structure—and did so in the hour of my first arrival in Trieste. He leaves out the glass galleria above the platforms. He forgets the stone- and iron-cancelling clerestories that allowed bright lances of meridianal light to transmogrify me moving with my two buoyant bags from the loudly ticking Milan coach—sloughed like a former life—toward the splendid brass and oak door opening out onto Piazza Libertà and my chosen city with its warm life and azure air that I had come all the way across the sea to seek. My hour of entry was my happiest hour in Trieste.)

In 1893 a series of oil paintings devoted to the Triumph of Progress was installed on the walls of the station caffè. Two of these, the largest and the most ambitious, provide a final *tableau mort* of Trieste II: the allegories of Commerce and Industry composed by the Triestine painter Eugenio Scomparini.

Both of them occur in the definitely unazure skies above town, turbulently clouded in the lower halves—the mood is indigo there, with what D'Annunzio or Benco would call the *effluvia* of smokestacks—and lightening in the upper, which are rayed with cloud-piercing sun and pale blue interstices: here is where the artist has set his theophanies, the fabulous manifestings of the high destiny of his birthplace. In "Commerce" the god is, inevitably, Mercury, patron of commerce and streamlined exchange, here surprisingly mounted upon the winged horse Pegasus—perhaps suggesting the poetry of business. In "Industry" divinity is double. Glory leans back against a blond cloud and extends undying laurels towards the heavens above, while the fate Clotho sits with her spindle winding the thread of life and reminding the traveler sipping *limonata* at a table underneath that permanence is a communal rather than an individual possibility. But such high matters are rather conventionally handled in pale hues in the upper distances of both allegories. Scomparini's distinctive skills and interests declare themselves in the foregrounds below.

He considered himself, surely, to be a "realist": a painter (and a teacher of painting—Svevo's sister Paola took lessons from him) who strove to present things *as they really are*. The foreground figures of both oils (Richness and Abundance in "Commerce," Industry in "Industry") are personified ideas, but these ideas are impersonated by flesh and blood, earthy females, bare breasted and scantily draped about the lower regions with brocade or gauze. All of them loll in the realistically polluted atmosphere without discernible means of support, gazing or pointing upwards towards their respective deities.

Commerce

Industry

Richness and Abundance are distinctly sexy, a bit overblown and slightly raddled, "commercially viable" as a connoisseur of such things might say. Abundance, so designated by her attendant *putto* with his cornucopia of roses, lies back supine upon a smutty cloud, eyes half shut in a suggestive ecstasy. Richness, on the other hand, is more vertical. She holds an overflowing jewelbox, a string of pearls is wound about her arm. The connoisseur might be reminded of the more or less contemporaneous *tableaux vivants* staged by Émile Zola's Nana for an audience of discerning males of a certain class, an *Arabian Nights* entertainment quite within the reach of the entrepreneur's plump wallet.

"Industry" focuses several degrees lower on the social scale and exalts the tough underpinnings of sexy commercial success. Like Svevo and like much of the fin-de-siècle intelligentsia, Scomparini acknowledged a comfortable "humanitarian socialism" in his politics. Here a southern-looking Industry, faint mustache upon her upper lip, half turns her muscled back to us and, profiling one large and slightly sagging breast, addresses a member of the Trieste working class. His gross feet are bare, and he is naked except for his long black apron and an enormous sledgehammer. She is directing his vision upwards towards the paired apparition of *vita brevis* (Clotho) and civic perpetuity (Gloria). He appears attentive, even rapt, but his eyes are fixed on her front. Below them is a panorama of industrial Trieste, probably the newly developed yards and factories beneath the hill of Chiarbola to the south where Svevo lived and worked. Six stacks belch forth the black smoke upon which the worker is seated. It is the sort of "futurist" cityscape that in a few years' time will drive Marinetti to rhapsody.

If an absence of loyal acknowledgment of the patronage of Austria-Hungary is a sign of irredentism, then Scomparini's oils are irredentist; in life he was considered one. But his "Commerce" and "Industry" are, in fact, boosterish products that seem quite indifferent to the Kingdom of Italy. The point seems to be that in Habsburg Trieste things as they really are will get better and better with energy, application, and—for some of our blue-collared brothers—a bit of self-sacrifice. Even the fact that in 1891 the *portofranco* had been drastically reduced to a *puntofranco*—a free *point* or dock area, only without many of the old participatory privileges—cannot curb Scomparini's florid exuberance. Business is still business, after all. Probably business, or, in the allegory, Mercury, the patron god of business, is (realistically speaking) still the real emperor.

Of course I never missed them in the hour of the glory of my first coming, but the truth is that the Scomparini murals are not to be found in today's station caffè. Neither, in fact, can one find the caffè—once, fifty years ago, a "literary" one where writers like Virgilio Giotti* and Giani Stuparich* and Pierantonio Quarantotti Gambini* met and conversed beneath the Triumph of Progress. It has been shut up tight since 1955; the new caffè is a cafeteria where you eat your microwaved pizza beneath blank walls of institutional yellow. As I learned quite by chance in the course of my third week in Trieste, the entire Triumph—Commerce and Industry and smaller panels like Mechanics and Electricity and Transportation—has been moved across the street to the *piano nobile* of an old *palazzo* now operated by the Office of Archaeology of Friuli-Venezia Giulia as a gallery of ancient art. It hangs amidst the bleeding Christs and Acteons, an allegory of Progress subverted by the more telling progress of Time itself.

Tableaux morts. You pay your money and the bored attendant hands you your ticket and returns to her novel. You have all the time and space you need for a really good look. Your heels click upon the marble in a ghostly way. Nobody comes here but you.

This new Trieste, rather than neglect the
fine arts, has turned her friendly smile and
animating hand towards them, and has promoted
works of various sorts that attest to the refined
customs of this cosmopolite colony and
put young Trieste in line with other cities
in which the stranger will discover not a
few means of nourishing his spirit, desirous
of both the beautiful and the useful, in
nature, in the sciences, and in the arts.

Tre giorni a Trieste (1858)

In this city there shall dominate perhaps a
greater liveliness than today, although there
shall be less movement in the streets and
less clanking of wagons. Commerce shall flourish
discretely, but it shall not overrule,
nor overpower, nor exclude all the rest. Mercury
shall rank alongside all the other gods,
not above them as he does today. . . . Trieste
shall not live by commerce alone and commerce
shall not sully everything else. . . . Our sea shall
be limpid, beautiful, poetic . . .

letter from ELIO SCHMITZ
to Ettore Schmitz (June 1882)

The songs of Apollo are harsh after the words
of Mercury.

SHAKESPEARE
Love's Labour's Lost, act 5, sc. 2, ll. 924–25 (misquoted)

Palm trees don't grow on ice.

UMBERTO VERUDA
(c. 1890)

TRIESTE DOES NOT HAVE TRADITIONS OF CULTURE.

SCIPIO SLATAPER
Triestine letter 1 (February 1909)

The Sloblands of Fairview

This book's dwarf ancestor, *Tre giorni a Trieste,* was commissioned by Baron Revoltella and his associates in order to persuade delegates to the Congress of the International Society of Railroads of Trieste's virtues as a culture center. It recommends the view from Castle Miramar (in 1858 still under construction) and the way it transforms the northern coastline "a German league from Trieste" into something "truly magical, thanks to the exquisite taste" of His Most Serene Highness, the Archduke Max. It is enthusiastic about the town's recent rich revivalist buildings: the Borsa Vecchia of course, the latest Borsa beneath the glass roof of the Tergesteo, the "grandiosa" railway terminal. It evokes the large collections on view of various fine or applied arts, all imported from elsewhere: the cases of medals and coins, the salons full of bronzes and marbles and oils adorning the *palazzi* of local oligarchs like the Morpurgos, the Sartorios, the Revoltellas. (Three pages are devoted to the marble matron Trieste at the foot of the Baron's staircase, two to his other holdings. Not even Castle Miramar gets so much space.) It recommends the exotic *orientalia* for sale at Wünch's Chinese Cabinet, Trieste's own Gump's. It points with pride to the city's several theaters, its handsome opera house inaugurated in 1801 with a performance of Salieri's *Hannabel in Capua.* (Understandably, it does not mention two disastrous world-premiere failures—*Il Corsaro* in 1848 and *Stiffelio* in 1850—composed by the relatively unknown Giuseppe Verdi.) But the select group of local magnates responsible for *Tre giorni a Trieste* is reticent, has nothing much to say, in fact, when it comes to literary Trieste.

There was, to be sure, a public library, with rich collections of Petrarch and the *opera omnia* of Enea Silvio Piccolomini (bishop of Trieste from 1447 to 1450 and later Pope Pius II) bequeathed it by the scholar-philanthropist Domenico Rossetti. There was a busy printing press run by Lloyd Austriaco (publisher in four languages of *Tre giorni a Trieste*), which turned out handsome editions of Italian classics from Ariosto to Alfieri. There was even a literary society, the Gabinetto Minerva, founded by Domenico Rossetti in 1810, when Trieste was under occupation by French troops, as a meeting place where local essays on Italian culture and Trieste's relation to it might be read and discussed. But the 1858 booklet made no reference at all to contemporary Triestine writers for the simple and sufficient reason that there were none worth mentioning to an extramural, European clientele. A literary Trieste did not exist. The Baron Revoltella's emphasis on conspicuous consumption and collectibles indicates that Mercury was still the deity to be propitiated. And, as Shakespeare actually does not say, Mercury's dominance is apt to put off Apollo entirely.

The novelist Stendhal, French consul in Trieste in 1830–31, hated the city and thought himself to be upon a desert island, "among barbarians." If the effusive Isabel Burton often refers to Trieste as "our beloved," her husband Sir Richard chiefly found it wearisome. "This day eleven years I came here," he wrote in his diary in 1883. "*What a shame!*" During much of his 1872–90 tenure as British consul he holed up in the inn by the Obelisk at Opicina and got on with his "plain and literal translation" of the *Arabian Nights* in which he found, although plagued by excruciating gout and angina and the exasperations attendant upon old age, an exotic asylum from his appointed town.

"Trieste shall not live by commerce alone . . .": poor Elio Schmitz's*
little utopia is, after all, only a utopia. Although wistfully imagined, it is
meant mainly as an amusement for his worshipped older brother. He
notes in his diary how Ettore's clerkship at the Vienna Unionbank branch
on the second floor of Palazzo Tergesteo seems to eat away at his literary
ambitions, how he writes less and less, how he reads far more than he
writes and may soon give up even that, "losing any hope of overcoming
all those difficulties standing in his way." In his own diary for 1889 Ettore
seems very close to despair. He judges his own first novel in progress "a
foul mess I shall never be able to cough up. My strength was always hope
and the trouble is that even that is growing weaker." Elio is dead, and there
is no one left to take any interest in what he thinks or does.

The case of Ettore Schmitz* (*il caso Svevo* as it has been known in
Italy for over sixty years) is, in this respect, exemplary. His recalcitrant
first novel, *Una vita* [A life], tells of the last year in the life of a poor young
man from the country who has come to Mercury's city to seek his fortune. Callow, ingrown, and bookish, he works as a minor clerk in a Trieste bank but "wants to write." He collaborates on a novel with the supremely self-centered daughter of his employer (subject: "Clara, a young
countess, learns that the duke is marrying a shopkeeper's daughter; her
desperation"), but the project founders when she judges his first chapter
draft too grey, "grey, very grey." He withdraws to the loftier realm of
pure and solitary thought, intending to "lay the foundations of modern
Italian philosophy by translating a good German work and at the same
time writing an original work of his own," but a title (*The Moral Idea in
the Modern World*), a sketch for a table of contents, and three pages of preface are as far as he gets. The rest of *Una vita* deals with the pathetic Alfonso's increasingly successful efforts to persuade himself that his lack of progress in the office, in society, and in his writing is due not to personal
incompetence—although Svevo's main aim is to show that it is—but to a

systematic program of philosophical renunciation. His death, an unchar-acteristically efficient suicide by gas inhalation, is, according to a com-ment made by the author many years later, meant to be a Schopenhauerian Q.E.D., "as dry and abrupt as part of a syllogism."

Until his local publisher advised him that the reading public would never buy a book so glumly named, Svevo had entitled his novel *Un inetto*—"an inept one," a bungler or misfit. In fact *Una vita* is a cool and consciously "grey" study of a specific "case," a young man's abulia and want of aptitude. Alfonso Nitti lacks all flair or talent—this is his fate as demonstrated—and is no more a portrait of the young bank clerk who "wants to write" named Ettore Schmitz (who signs himself Italo Svevo mainly for business reasons) than Emma Bovary is a portrait of Flaubert. Nor can the ambiance of Trieste be held accountable for Alfonso's failure: it is made very clear that he would fail anywhere. (This a priori iron fatal-ism as regards its main character is one of the flaws of the novel.) Yet, besides psychological analysis, *Una vita* provides a shrewd and sardonic appraisal of a particular milieu—mercantile Trieste at work and at lei-sure—and the fact that Alfonso is hopelessly inept at dealing with it in no way diminishes the chilly brilliance of Svevo's scrutiny. The scenes of after-business hours in banker Maller's house on Via Forni in the Borgo Teresiano, a block away from the Canal Grande, offer an album of ironic drypoints on the state of Triestine culture in the 1880s. The bluestocking Annetta's reception room is crammed with tiny pieces of furniture "made for creatures who never existed"; the tabletops display chinoiserie from Wünch's. In the drawing room, photographs have been arranged like open fans upon the walls above the piano. Bric-à-brac and complete sets of the classics are loaded in the cabinets and cases of such a height as to make the oil paintings crowded above them difficult to see in any detail. The *casa Maller* aspires to the condition of Palazzo Revoltella: the measure is costly quantity; the effect aimed at is opulent plenitude. Svevo notes dryly that an eye more trained than Alfonso's might have noticed "something excessive" in the decor, but in fact the young man is just as dazzled as he is meant to be.

So far as literature is concerned (beyond the matched sets from the Lloyd presses) "it was the era in which, when literature was mentioned, one inevitably debated the merits of realism and romanticism, a convenient literary topic in which all could take part." Signor Maller roguishly confesses that, as a man, he prefers realism because of its immorality, but adds more seriously that he feels a certain scorn for its "popular" methods. His daughter Annetta (and therefore, perforce, her accommodating collaborator Alfonso) insists upon a star- or class-crossed love interest as the focus of her projected fictions, which, if finished, would conform perfectly to the specifications of kitsch or today's "regency" novel. In Svevo's Trieste II, literature can be one of three things: a manifestation of "operetta wisdom" or the Biedermeier spirit (defined by Milan Kundera as "the veil of the idyllic draped over the real"), a vehicle for sprightly salon discourse as well as proof that one has read the right gazettes from Rome or Paris, or a respectable massed presence on the bookshelf yonder, splendidly gold tooled with morocco leather spines uncreased.

Of course Svevo's Trieste II also must include the publication and failure of *Una vita* in 1892 and *Senilità* in 1898, both in editions of one thousand copies printed by a local bookseller at the author's own expense. Copies were given to friends, were up for sale in local bookshops, were sent to newspapers and journals at home and abroad, above all Italy. In the third-person autobiographical sketch composed just before his death in 1928, Svevo explained his turn–of–the–century "iron resolution" to abstain from "that ridiculous and harmful thing called literature" as ensuing from a lack of any critical response: "The silence that his work received was all too eloquent." But silence is relative. The local press, while noting the author's cumbersome Italian and the meticulousness of his analytical approach ("grey, very grey"), in general not only "noticed" but welcomed both novels. Svevo's friend Silvio Benco gave *Senilità* the longest and most intelligent assessment that Svevo was to have until Benco's review of *La coscienza di Zeno* a quarter of a century later. Still, such praise came from friends and fellow citizens: that Italo Svevo was really "Signor Ettore Schmitz, a cultured young Triestine" was an open secret in the city. One can understand that, for an ambitious young writer wanting to have his work appraised—and praised—objectively by genuine Italian literary critics on the peninsula, kind words from home might not really count.

Una vita was reviewed, in fact, by the literary editor of the widely read *Corriere della Sera* of Milan, who arrived in 350 words at an even-handed estimate: "At any rate, although of minor interest, although of a rather limited technical worth, this novel reveals an artistic conscience and a clear-eyed observer. . . . With all its faults, it is not the work of a novice." Such words "heartened" Svevo—the verb is his—for the writing and eventual publication of *Senilità,* for which he hoped much better things. But this time he was crushingly disappointed: outside of Friuli-Venezia Giulia, the book was hardly noticed at all.

Prophetically enough, the hero of *Senilità* is a thirty-five-year-old insurance agent who has written one novel. That novel, about which Emilio has few illusions,

> had turned yellow on the shelves of the bookshops, but Emilio, who at the time of its publication had been spoken of as a great hope for the future, was now thought of as a species of literary respectability who had some weight in the small artistic scales of his city.

Cold comfort, if even that were true for Svevo. Silvio Benco's acute and thorough estimate of *Senilità* was for home consumption only, quickly skimmed and soon forgotten. We are told that the bookseller Vram, who had printed both of Svevo's novels for a price, in a few years' time was unable to remember that he had published them.

Benco had concluded that even the awkwardness of Svevo's prose could lead at times to a certain freshness and *modernità* in expressivity, "so true is it that, more than the most knowing artificer, sometimes the naive one [*l'ingenuo*] succeeds in saying precisely what he means to say and stamping this with an imprimatur equal to life itself." Italo Svevo might be occasionally ingenuous, even crude in his diction, syntax, and construction, but he also had "a cultured and impressive spirit . . . the spirit of an artist."

If such words had been written by a reviewer of stature in Milan or Florence rather than in Trieste by a twenty-four-year-old unknown named Silvio Benco, how altered the history of Italo Svevo might have been! He might have taken—as his wife says he had thought of doing earlier—a writer's sabbatical in Florence as Manzoni had done in order to educate himself in Italian language and literature. (But a Tuscan or magniloquent or "literary" Svevo could not be a Svevo at all.) He might have continued on as he conceivably could have been, a provincial novelist who, with hard work, might one day turn out to be the Giovanni Verga of Friuli-Venezia Giulia. Instead, deeply hurt but also pragmatic and resourceful, devoted husband and father and wage earner that he also was, he bit his bullet, made his iron resolution, and with his stoic's shrug accepted the part fate apparently meant for him: to be Ettore Schmitz, executive in a marine varnish plant owned and run by his mother-in-law, amateur violinist and writer on the side (though never, nevermore, for publication). And so, for roughly twenty-five years, "Italo Svevo" vanished from the mortal memory of practically everyone but Ettore Schmitz, members of his family circle, James and Stanislaus Joyce,* and perhaps a dozen Triestine friends.

Literary Trieste.

In 1910, just over ten years after his review of *Senilità,* Benco could give little more than a passing paragraph to his city's literary performance.

Trieste's urban life has not been documented in the modern analytic novel. There are, however, a few traces of it in the books of Alberto Boccardi, in the stories of Haydèe and Willy Dias, in the two novels published years ago under the pseudonym of Italo Svevo, in the lively pages of Emma Luzzato.

Period, so far as Svevo is concerned. And yet what strange company for Benco's unlamented friend, whose books surely do "document" life in contemporary Trieste in a detailed and veristic manner very different from the light and forgettable confections served up by the other four! But Benco devotes the remainder of this paragraph to brief considerations of the nugatory Boccardi, Haydèe, and Willy Dias, and how their work conforms to "the literary currents of Italian life." (His correct critical point is that they are mainly derivative, *italianate* in more than just their choice of language; they all follow, with varying success, peninsular literary models then à la mode. Benco's own first two novels, published in Milan in 1904 and 1906 and not mentioned in his *Trieste,* are further cases in point. Both are skillful exercises in the overwrought manner of Gabriele D'Annunzio, who in fact had helped them find a publisher.) In Benco's comprehensive overview of Trieste II in 1910, Italo Svevo is a closed book, and the few other local authors worth mentioning are accorded decidedly satellite status. In Mercury's city the songs of Apollo are less "harsh" than utterly inaudible.

To put it another way, "while Carducci was alive, art, for our poets, was incarnate in Carducci." (Carducci died in 1907.) The speaker here is Professor Baccio Ziliotto of the newly established University of Trieste who issued his diligent *Storia letteraria di Trieste e dell'Istria* (Literary history of Trieste and Istria) in 1924. In 1924, the year following the publication of *La coscienza di Zeno* and the year before the *caso Svevo* reached its happy ending, Professor Ziliotto saw no reason to discuss Svevo at all in his survey of modern developments in Friuli-Venezia Giulia. He mentions just four recent Triestine writers: Riccardo Pitteri (patriotic poet, "a Carduccian with Virgilian soul"), the historical novelist Tito Dellaberrenga ("a modest example"), Scipio Slataper (whose *Il mio Carso* he rightly sees as "representative of the tormented Triestine soul" in the years prior to redemption), and—the one name also on Benco's list—Alberto Boccardi ("who enjoyed the clear narration of not very complex cases from which he could draw a moral lesson").

All in all, the good professor observes, if literary Trieste were to be "considered solely from the aesthetic point of view it must be confessed that it has created nothing of permanent artistic worth, that it has left no decisive mark on Italian literature." But there is another viewpoint possible, one closer to Professor Ziliotto's own, and his conclusion here is far more positive. "The literature of the borderland, embittered over the centuries by the clash of foreign peoples and by the policies, both subtle and violent, of its rulers, was essentially one of national affirmation; and with this—let us not forget it—it has carried out a most noble task." Carducci, after all, was not just master of the aureate style, he was also the poet of irredentism. As Benco put it earlier with considerably more misgiving, what distinguished "all of modern Triestine literature" was its *anima patria,* its fatherland-focused spirit: "first *la patria,* then poetry; and in the poetry still the voice of *la patria.*" By *patria* Benco of course meant the Kingdom of Italy, not Franz Josef's Austria-Hungary. In Trieste II it was impossible to be more explicit.

By 1924 Professor Ziliotto was writing as a proud and jubilant scholar of Trieste III, a *finally* Italian Trieste and Istria. His slender history ends with a list of local authors dead in the late war and an epiphany of their final passing: "into the consecrated tomb they descended comforted by the vision of a radiant future." For these glad ghosts as for their historian, the real Literary Trieste was still to come.

(While for me, frowning over my impossible equilateral triangle some sixty years later, it was possible to argue that in 1924 it was beginning to wind to its close.)

Saba

Svevo   Joyce

Trieste 1905–15

Originally that triangle had aspired to the condition of a *circle* signifying the personal relations that linked those three oddly assorted writers living in the same small place over the same period of time . . . until a modest investigation showed me there was nothing much in it, nothing new at any rate. Yet insofar as a literary city is a city made of books (the books produced by inhabitants of that city, the books in which the city itself is a condition of the story told), in Trieste in 1924 the basic books were virtually already there. Who could quarrel with the following schedule?†

> 1892 Svevo, *Una vita* (Vram, Trieste)
>
> 1898 Svevo, *Senilità* (Vram, Trieste)
>
> 1910 Saba, *Poesie,* preface by Benco (Casa editrice italiana, Florence)
>
> 1912 Slataper, *Il mio Carso* (Libreria della Voce, Florence)
>
> 1912 Saba, *Coi miei occhi: il mio secondo libro di versi* (Libreria della Voce, Florence)

---

†I have set Joyce aside here as being an exotic, extraneous to Professor Ziliotto's Italian purview. I have left out also the dialect poetry of Biagio Marin and Virgilio Giotti (as being, according to the same purview, "too local" and thereby esoteric) as well as important but relatively minor items by Saba, Slataper, and Benco. A complete listing of the essential books of literary Trieste will be found in the appendix Literary Trieste: Evidence of Its Existence (see pages 247ff.).

1921 Saba, *Il canzoniere 1900–1921* (Libreria antica e moderna, Trieste)

1924 Svevo, *La coscienza di Zeno* (Capelli, Bologna)

But what was there about all of these books (except one, by a Slataper I had not read when I first came to Trieste) that in 1924 made them invisible or negligible to Trieste's literary historian, a man who I am certain read everything having to do with his subject?

The exceptional *Il mio Carso* suggests an answer. Scipio Slataper was not only a passionate irredentist, a citizen of Austro-Hungarian Trieste who died fighting for Italy early in the war, but the author of the first *self-consciously Triestine* book ever written. *Il mio Carso* constitutes his lyric autobiography, tracing "the growth of a soul in Trieste" from early childhood to the age of twenty-three when it was written. And it dramatizes a peculiarly Triestine division: the clash of Slovene and Italian components not on the historic, economic, civic, or political plane but within the inwardness of Scipio Slataper (whose name itself recapitulates the problem, the nobly Roman first versus the "pure Slav" last).

This division is projected not only in topographical and even Zarathustrian terms—the healthful, nature-nurtured solitude of the Carsic heights ("my Carso" but also, since Slataper occasionally wrote the second word with a small *c,* "my karst"—thus emphasizing its sheer physical presence) as against the harsh but invigorating struggle for social and personal identity in the city on the gulf below—but also by means of the two alternative names the author bestows upon himself: Alboin and Pennadoro. The first refers to the barbarian king who in the mid-sixth century led his Lombards down off the Alps onto the plains of Lombardy and what is known today as Friuli-Venezia Giulia. *Pennadoro* means "pen of gold" and is in fact the Italian translation of "Slataper," although only a very particular sort of Triestine would be liable to know that. The barbarian invader connotes the writer's Dionysian aspect, his wild and earthy and "Slavic" side, while Pennadoro suggests his Apollonian or "Italian" impulse, "seeking"—as Slataper put it in a contemporaneous letter—"to harmonize [disparities], to equilibrate them, to make me 'classical' and *formed,* a hendecasyllable rather than free verse." It is in fact by means of Pennadoro's enraptured prose—far less classical really than feverishly Nietzschean—that Slataper is able to express his hot desire and pursuit and, at the close, at least momentary capture of a certain wholeness and well-being. Which is to say that the wild Carso child can see himself as citizen of his conflicted city and also, although "in a different way" from Italians of the Kingdom, an Italian nevertheless.

For *Il mio Carso* is really about being Triestine and different: the health brought about through Slataper's introspection means that he is in the end able to view this state of difference with a measured pride rather than with shame. From time to time throughout the book, but especially at the very beginning, the author's divided "I" addresses a *voi,* a plural "you," which signifies not merely the general reader but the Italian intelligentsia at whom the book is aimed. *Vorrei dirvi:* "I would like to tell you," he begins, all sorts of stories about who I am and where I come from, but I am afraid to, you would see through me, "I feel myself timid before your culture and your reasoning." (See appendix entitled Translations below for the opening and close of the first part of *Il mio Carso.*) The Triestine's inferiority complex vis-à-vis his elder brothers on the peninsula stems from his sense that he is of the marches, of a "mixed and insecure Italianness," that his background and upbringing are marginal. (Hence the compensatory primitivism adopted by Slataper in his Alboin mode, or the equally compensatory insistence, by the historian Tamaro for example, on his city's *romanità.*) Relief of some sort becomes possible only when this Triestine can recognize that fraternity does not mean identity, that brothers can indeed be different.

But brothers even so, and above all. In its uneven, prickly, mettlesome way, the solo voice of *Il mio Carso*—never a soliloquy, always a mon-

ologue dramatically turned towards *you*, Florentine friends, citizens of the
Kingdom of Italy—is infused with *anima patria*, with the need to affirm its
participation, cultural if not as yet political *and on its own terms*, in that
kingdom. It is precisely this note of poignantly complex "national affirmation" that recommends the book to Professor Ziliotto's scholarly and
patriotic attention in Trieste III.

For Svevo and Saba, on the other hand, "Trieste" is the place where
one lives, a fact of life like any other; like being born Jewish, for example,
or poor. When Saba says *la mia città* towards the close of his poem, he
means that this is where he lives and breathes, his home. There is no need
to comment, to compensate, justify, or explain. It is the total absence of
anima patria in the novels of Svevo (whose Italian, furthermore, was technically atrocious) and in the poetry of Saba (whose solitary study of what
he called "the golden thread of the Italian [literary] tradition" from Dante
and Petrarch to Leopardi furthermore exposed him to the charge of being
"timid"—Slataper's adjective—and derivative) that accounts for their absence from the pages of *Storia letteraria di Trieste e dell'Istria*.

A city made of books: literary Trieste. And also, for me, a city
soaked and permeated with literary associations.

In Joyce's *A Portrait of the Artist as a Young Man* ("born in the shadow
of San Giusto" in Svevo's phrase) Stephen Dedalus leaves his home at
Drumcondra on the outskirts of Dublin and makes his way across the city
towards University College. The sordor of his family circumstances fills
him with "loathing and bitterness," but as his attention falls away from
that towards the sensorial details of his immediate passage, a transformation occurs.

> His morning walk across the city had begun, and he foreknew that as he passed
> the sloblands of Fairview he would think of the cloistral silver-veined prose of
> Newman, that as he walked along the North Strand Road, glancing idly at the
> windows of the provision shops, he would recall the dark humor of Guido

Cavalcanti and smile, that as he went by Bair's stone-cutting works in Talbot
Place the spirit of Ibsen would blow through him like a keen wind, a spirit of
wayward boyish beauty . . .

Now through this chain of subjective correspondences, Dublin has become "literary." Its actual sites (such as the sloblands of Fairview, that
muddy dumping ground between the North Strand Road and Ballybough
Road near the vitriol works on the River Tolka, "the dingy way past Mud
Island" that Father Conmee declines to traverse on foot in *Ulysses*) are
occasions of energy for the various associational flights that lift Stephen
up out of his nightmare labyrinth, his particular oppression as citizen and
son, into the free air of human spirit, the transcendent world of the artifi-
cers. For the time being, historical daily dirty Dublin has been left below
and lost from sight.

In this way, the *literary* functions as an escape hatch. More or less
concurrently with Stephen's walk by Fairview, James Joyce, expatriate
writer and English tutor more or less unhappy in Trieste, watches a young
woman ride *apace apace* on horseback on the upland road near Opicina and
thinks of Hedda Gabler. ("Easy now, Jamesy! Did you never walk the
streets of Dublin sobbing another name?") The thought makes him
happy, makes even the upland road possible. The sloblands—that is,
wherever here and now is—dwindle or coruscate with another light, the
light of imagination. For the time being he is elsewhere, some Trieste-
cum-Oslo of the mind, and slightly more free. "He walks in order to be
left to himself," as Svevo observed.

In my own case, as I unhappily discovered my first week in Trieste,
the function of the literary was not very different. The Trieste that drew
me over the sea in the beginning was a Trieste I had encountered in its
literature, a city made of books in my mind. The Irishman Joyce apart, I
was coming to the town of Svevo and of Saba. Before I had so much as set
foot outside of the radiant railroad station that first day, Via Forni was
already where the Maller family lived, the Public Garden was already

where Emilio, then Zeno, met their mistresses, Via Domenico Rossetti was already the "street of joy and love" where Saba first saw his future wife Lina in 1905. (In my mind literary fact and fiction mingled easily.) In the days that followed I worked out my walks by reference not only to the labyrinth map and Dottoressa Ruaro Loseri but to Svevo's novels and Saba's *Canzoniere*. One awful moment in the once rural section of Montebello where now the autostrada arcs up onto the Carso towards the Yugoslav tollgates, I was sitting in a littered field beside a shattered toilet bowl when I suddenly awoke. Crouched in that dismal spot, I found myself attempting to conjure up Saba's noisy scapegoat with its famous Semitic features that once upon a time—I hoped so hard that I half believed it—must have been tethered there.

Why was I so unhappy that first week? Because unlike the artists Dedalus and Joyce, I could never be carried away entirely. Two worlds—literary Trieste and the sloblands of the Trieste I was actually visiting—coexisted in an unreliable symbiosis, a mocking palimpsest, in my mind and occasionally through my eyes. They brushed or washed against one another, seldom mixing, and they undercut. And in the end, because my reading and memory were limited, because the Trieste of my first week's visit in 1985 was unremittingly and fundamentally *there* all the time (because Via Forni was nowadays Via Macchiavelli and *casa Maller,* if ever it had existed, was long gone; because 29 Via Rossetti where Lina had bent watering the geraniums was now a mustard-colored apartment house; because the sound of the tandem trailers hurtling through the air en route to Yugoslavia drowned out the bleating of a rain-soaked goat; because . . .), because the world I had borne across the sea in my mind was only in my mind, the sloblands won. There was no actual literary Trieste.

It was dead and gone. It was merely myself, poor ghost, who was literary.

Trieste has a Triestine type; this ought to
necessitate a Triestine art.

SCIPIO SLATAPER
Triestine letter 4, March 1909

A melting pot is a utensil into which are put
the most disparate elements, which are then
melted; what is produced is a homogenous
fusion, with all its elements proportionately
distributed, with constant characteristics.
But in Trieste as I know it, a fused type has
never been produced, nor any type with stable
characteristics (in the sense that a Roman, a
Milanese, a Sicilian, if typical, is recognizable
the moment he enters a caffè; but try to
identify a Triestine when he enters, unless he
opens his mouth . . .) And since a unique Triestine
type does not exist, so a Triestine creative
culture does not exist either.

ROBERTO BAZLEN
"Intervista su Trieste" (c. 1946)

There is something in this city of mine that
blocks any initiative designed to give it a
cultural character or physiognomy, not only in
its disintegrative atmosphere but in its individuals,
who willingly isolate themselves or
go elsewhere. It has a bitter air . . .

GIANI STUPARICH
Trieste nei miei ricordi (1948)

Trieste is perhaps the sole Italian city that
derives its glory from its writers, even if in
certain cases (one thinks of Virgilio Giotti)
it remembers them too late. The fact is undeniable
and the reasons for it obvious.

EUGENIO MONTALE
"Italo Svevo nel centenario della nascita" (1963)

Trieste Trouvée

Giuseppe Prezzolini considered Scipio Slataper, his youthful Triestine colleague, to be the very incarnation of his complicated birthplace: Slovene height and blondness, German punctilio, Italian sensibility—"the perfect symbol, in short, of that Trieste of his where three races mingle." With Giovanni Papini and a cadre of bright young Italians, Giuseppe Prezzolini was the founder in 1908 of a new Florentine weekly called *La Voce: The Voice.* Its emblem, designed by the Futurist poet Ardengo Soffici, likened its practical goal of disseminating culture to the work of a man with a hoe cultivating his ground. The voice of its title was meant by Prezzolini to suggest "that poetical or philosophical inspiration which is an inconvenient companion for those men singled out by destiny to suffer torments on behalf of liberty, dreams, battle, glory, the inward search . . ." *La Voce,* in short, was to act as the voice of *coscienza* (consciousness and conscience are the same word in Italian) arousing a drowsy Italy lulled by its famous past and recent nationhood to new developments in contemporary political, philosophical, and artistic affairs both at home and abroad. Among other things, *La Voce* ran a series on the cultural conditions of the various regions of Italy, including the several "unredeemed" territories. Both articles on the Trentino, for instance, were written by a young socialist newspaperman named Benito Mussolini.

A number of *triestini* had been drawn to Florence in the early years of the twentieth century, either because of its university—there was none at home—or because of its reputation as the cultural center of Italy. Umberto Saba lived there off and on from 1905 to 1908, giving poetry readings under the exotically D'Annunzian name of Umberto da Montereale. Virgilio Giotti first began to write his poems in Triestine dialect in Florence; he settled there from 1907 to 1919, married and raised a family. Biagio Marin* studied at the University of Florence from 1911 to 1912, as did Carlo Stuparich and his brother Giani, who received his doctorate in 1915 with a thesis on Machiavelli in Germany.

Slataper, aged twenty-one, arrived in Florence in 1908, the winner of a study grant at the Institute for Higher Studies. He picked up a copy of the brand new *La Voce* in a local bookshop, admired it, and in his impetuous way immediately conceived of writing for it. He sent his subscription to Prezzolini and added this note:

> I am from Trieste: what bookstore sells your paper there? Perhaps a little personal propaganda up there might be useful to you? It would please me if my city—cut off as it is from the intellectual life of the Kingdom—became aware of *La Voce*. And maybe you yourselves might not be averse to an exposition of our special conditions as they relate to art and science. What do you think?

Prezzolini invited him over for a talk. The result was Slataper's five "letters" to *La Voce* on the subject of his city [*Lettere triestine*], published between February and April 1909, the first invitation to *trouver Trieste* (see page 24) directed "abroad" since *Tre giorni a Trieste* put out in the halcyon days of a half century earlier. But the mood is very different.

The first letter begins notoriously with its aggressive banner title: TRIESTE NON HA TRADIZIONI DI CULTURA—Trieste, city of Mercury, does not have traditions of culture. There follows, brilliantly conveyed in Slataper's colloquial, impertinent prose, the sardonic image of an *ingenuo,* a young Parsifal ill educated and clownishly dressed (deliberately so by his anxious mama, Austria, to keep him from wandering off in search of adventure and glory), who "awakened one day between a crate of lemons and a sack of coffee beans thinking that, for his own good, he ought to modulate his life to another rhythm than that of a snorting or puffing engine, treat it to another melody than that of silver clinking in the pockets of some capacious waistcoat." This youthful giant troubled by his lack of culture is, of course, Trieste, who sometimes dreams of being like other commercial cities he has heard of, like Venice or Genoa, for example, or even—*perbacco!*—like Florence "in the times of Dante and Poliziano." The trouble is he doesn't know the way; his spirit is willing but weak; he wanders through the woods and bumps his nose on trees and then, once out of the woods, finds a dumbfounding multiplicity of paths that might or might not lead to the court of King Arthur. "But, once upon a time . . . but that was then, in the times of once upon a time . . . " Nowadays good intentions, unfueled by discipline and informed study, are ineffectual.

Letters two, three, and five get down to specific cases: Trieste's several shabby museums, its ineffectual Gabinetto Minerva, its lack of a university, its provincial newspapers. Apropos of newspapers, Silvio Benco is singled out as "our strongest writer" (Slataper seems not to have read Svevo) but is treated diagnostically as a writer torn between the claims of his art—Benco the novelist à la D'Annunzio, the superb art and music critic, the elegant essayist soon-to-be of *Trieste*—and the requirements of daily journalism—Benco the feuilletonist, the publicist, the editor of the *Piccolo.* Mention of the *Piccolo* permits him to be ironic at the expense of that paper's "stylistic *triestinità,*" which lacks, "like all of us, that nonchalant ease in writing that is the lifeblood of Italian literature and that no loving study of the classics can purvey. Almost always, even if we try to break it up in the snorting periods of an Alpine locomotive (I'm speaking of myself), our style is heavy handed [*peso*]. It is shaped by literary convention, not animated by life."

Letter four, on "the life of the spirit," is less abrasive and glittering, quieter and more intimate, than the others. Its great theme is that "Trieste is Italian in a different way than other Italian cities are." There are its famous three races that irredentists like Attilio Tamaro would deny. There is its vocational schizophrenia, "the two natures that clash and cancel one another out: the commercial and the Italian . . . they are its double soul." For Slataper, Trieste is a tragically divided town. "It longs for Rome but must address itself to Vienna. From Vienna it gets nothing, so it pines away and must try to feed itself." And here is the strong conclusion that makes this fourth letter his manifesto for a literary Trieste.

> Our spirit is different . . . it cannot with all its conflicts be confined within the formulae of a mode of thinking born under simple conditions. Trieste has a Triestine type; this ought to necessitate a Triestine art. Which would recreate in the joy of clear expression this convulsed and difficult life of ours. And I, thinking of all this, feel the inanity of these my frigid elucidations. I should throw down my pen. But no . . . the crows must finish croaking before the nightingale can sing.

Certainly this last is a merely rhetorical flourish: Slataper has just been urging that a classical, Ovidian fowl like the nightingale cannot possibly articulate his drastically divided city, "where everything . . . is double or triple." (This is one reason he will soon feel free to dismiss scornfully the poetry of his slightly older contemporary, Umberto Saba, "lovingly" saturated as it is in Petrarch and Leopardi.) He himself is a crow—a tough bird—and proud of it.

The *Letters,* then, are "Triestine" especially in their multiple motivation. In the first place they are what Slataper called an "exposition" of a certain city's "special" cultural circumstances to a sophisticated Italian readership. But insofar as they are simultaneously an *exposure* of cultural poverty—and of the Biedermeier boosterism attempting to mask it—they constitute a deliberate scandal to that city's citizens, those who read *La Voce* at any rate, who indeed regarded the letter writer as a cad, a turncoat, a show-off, an egotistic adolescent. The *Letters* also mark a distinct cultural novelty since, within an Italian context, they provide a vehicle for the self-examination of a Triestine "type" who, very unlike Carducci's fretting youths wondering "How long?" beside the blue-green Adriatic, insists upon his awkward difference and has much more than the usual irredentist *anima patria* in his head. Finally and above all, the *Letters* amount to an informal historical-sociological preface to a Triestine work of art in progress: for Scipio Slataper had a very clear picture of who his city's premier artist was going to be.

Variously entitled *Carsina* (his name for a *spiritus loci* taking the form of a Slovenian peasant girl-cum-oread), *Vita e sentimenti di Giusto da Trieste* (Life and feelings of Giusto from Trieste), and *Il mio Carso e la mia città* (My Carso and my city); variously projected as a pastoral novella, an epic drama, a "scientific-artistic double volume" with certain parts written in dialect, a poem, and an autobiographical prose poem, Slataper's book is not merely about Trieste but directly expresses "the growth of a soul" that had been in gestation ever since his arrival in Italy in 1908. Actually drafted between January 1910 and May 1912 (when it was published by *La Voce* as one of its series of books called the Libreria della Voce), that book was, of course, *Il mio Carso*. In every number of *La Voce* for the rest of that year a small paragraph was inserted, declaring: "Read *Il mio Carso,* the first book of poems written by a Triestine."

Ten years later, another Triestine poet, Umberto Saba, whose first book had been published in Florence in 1910, recorded his own Florentine period—and the bitter mockery of that insert—in the final tercet of an autobiographical sonnet:

A Giovanni Papini, alla famiglia
che fu poi della «Voce», io appena o mai
non piacqui. Ero fra lor di un'altra spece.

"With Giovanni Papini and the *Voce* family of those days I found scant favor, or none at all. Among them, I was of another species." Also "among them," though never named, was a member of the same species, his townsman Scipio Slataper, who in fact was, at Prezzolini's request, acting editor of *La Voce* from late 1911 until the spring of the next year (when he was succeeded by Papini).

Six months after it had published *Il mio Carso,* the Libreria della Voce brought out Saba's *Coi miei occhi: il mio secondo libro di versi* [With my own eyes: my second book of verse]. Unlike *Il mio Carso,* it was barely noticed. Letters exist from Saba to Prezzolini and Papini (though never—I think significantly—to Slataper; as if reproaches would be wasted on him) complaining of *La Voce's* handling of his book: it had not been promoted, no review copies had been sent out, no copies of the book itself could be found in the shops that Saba visited. The editors "forgot," he wrote sarcastically much later. In fact Saba was convinced that *Coi miei occhi* had been deliberately sabotaged.

And then there was that taunting little paragraph: "Read *Il mio Carso,* the first book of poems written by a Triestine." Isn't Saba's subtitle, "my second book," a response to this, even to the double echoing of the first-person possessive? It is difficult to believe that he didn't hold Slataper responsible.

From the same city, the two men had had a critical relationship prior to 1912. Even "abroad," in Florence, Italy, the bitter air of home . . .

The ubiquitous Benco has left a charming portrait of the young Saba just returned to Trieste from his *vagabondaggio* in Italy and who had yet to discover his voice and his pseudonym.

Roughly twenty years ago [i.e., in 1908 or 1909] there roamed the streets of Trieste with the springy step of a *flâneur* which life since then has made him lose, a young man who had patched together for himself a rather bizarre persona: a blond and D'Annunzian goatee, a precocious baldness, a large thorax slouched down as from the habit of talking to shorter companions; a crooning, nasal way of speaking manufactured in Florence in which were jostled together seraphic courtlinesses and savage sincerities, a pimp's obscenities and Venetian sweet talk, neurotic outbursts and priestly suavities; with hands dressed in white wool gloves that could be spotted a mile off, and a rhinestone literary moniker whose cut-rate value fooled nobody: Umberto da Montereale. This was the phantom of Umberto Saba before life remade him, and Trieste, desperately loved by him, immediately and instinctively dedicated to him an aversion, an incredulity, an insider's mockery that only fame and certain flattering murmurs in the great world's ear have succeeded in softening over the years.

A year later, this derivative and weirdly Italianate creature—so different from the wild Carso child, from the rhapsodizing Pennadoro—published, in Florence at his own expense, a first book entitled *Poesie di Umberto Saba,* with a preface by Silvio Benco.

As one would expect, Benco's remarks are free of any specifically civic vibrato—Umberto Saba is judged as a young Italian poet—and are both perceptive and constructive. He notes the frequent prosodic awkwardness of the poems, their straining for rhetorical effect, their occasional flatness. He acutely remarks the importance of Leopardi as a presence accounting for a few of the poems' "almost Biblical gravity," the "robust and compact realism" of the sonnets dealing with Saba's military service in Italy (the poems, in fact, in which "life" began to remake him), and the evidence that prosaism may give of a disposition against "literature" and for "expressive sincerity." He brilliantly articulates the novice's emergent *ars poetica* at the moment it barely begins to declare itself: "good literature is entirely autobiographical; any other literature is not a good one." As with his review of *Senilità* a decade earlier, Benco shows himself as virtually one of a kind, a judicious and attentive reader of the work of his townsmen.

The reviewer of *Poesie di Umberto Saba* for *La Voce* in January 1911 was another townsman, Scipio Slataper. Like Benco, he omits any note of civic recognition but focuses upon what he conceives to be Saba's "Jewish" passivity: "he lives on uncertain and nostalgic memories, since behind him there lies an abandoned homeland and thousands upon thousands of years of uneasy wandering." His poems, consequently, are "gentle, pallid, and a little anxious, like certain springlike autumn days"; only the military verses are conceded to show a bit of backbone, and this is because the past has been made to shape up by means of forced marches and barracks society. Gleefully, Slataper expresses his own reaction to a first reading of *Poesie di Umberto Saba:*

> First of all, with something of that indulgent pride and kindliness that any more robust animal might have when he hesitates in order not to squash the tiny insect groping confusedly in the maddening light of a pavement pounding with perennial din; and after, with a sympathetic sadness, with a wish to lend a hand to support a weary head.

His notice was, in fact, what Italians call a *stroncatura,* a slating, a jeering onslaught on the poet's character—or lack of it. (Slataper's own standard for the poet is sheer Zarathustra: "[he] is always a strong man, someone who makes himself master of everything: *tutto!*")

Ten months later, Slataper completed the hatchet job with a facetious *Voce* essay that repeated the timid insect image and lumped Saba together with a little school of five other so-called "crepuscular" poets from Italy, followers of Pascoli whose aim, according to Slataper, was to articulate a "timid but human response—sweetly, femininely human—to the false and gorgeous magniloquence of Carducci and D'Annunzio." He went so far as to imagine Saba's reaction to the charge of *crepuscolarismo:* "surely some little brother is going to raise up his peeled head, stare at me with his little eyes full of a horrified fear, and say to me in falsetto: 'Saba and Gozzano? With Palazzeschi and Corazzini? But how could they live together?'" But, insisted Slataper, they were all interchangeably alike, "shaped by literary convention, not animated by life" (as he had put it in the *Lettere triestine*). He found their wan debilities and little perplexities "morally repugnant." Yet the malicious ad hominem thrust, the anti-Semitism and "virile" contempt for the effeminate aesthete, are reserved for Umberto Saba, townsman and *fratellino.*

A friend remembers Saba's reaction. " 'Peeled head?' he exclaimed, pretending to be angry. 'But mine is a venerable baldness!' " Beneath the pretend anger there was real anger, however: Slataper's piece had been disproportionate, ungenerous, and unfair. That *Poesie* was imperfect Saba knew very well. Its language was sometimes awkward; he had gone to Florence in the first place to "correct"—his own word for it—his dialect-prone Italian. Some of its poems *were* derivative—but of Leopardi, as Benco had noted and he himself would later point out with pride, rather than of Pascoli or the crepusculars. In the gift copy he sent to Papini in 1910, he begged him, with an ironic modesty of course, to read only the poems on pages 65, 100, and "perhaps" 114. Yet Saba's response to Slataper himself can only be called diplomatic.

Egregio Slataper! he wrote from Trieste after the first *Voce* piece: "Distinguished Slataper! I have read your review. I thank you for it and we will talk about it, if we ever do, when we meet." (For what it is worth, the "you" here is formal, *Lei* rather than *tu*.) The notoriously thin-skinned and "difficult" Saba left it at that, I think, not only because Slataper was on the editorial board of a periodical that had undertaken—as part of its interest in Triestine matters and chiefly at the behest of Papini—to bring out Saba's next book in the Libreria della Voce, but because his real response to Slataper was contained in an enclosed essay he hoped *La Voce* ("the only review possible") would publish.

"Quella che resta da fare ai poeti" [What remains for poets to do] is introduced in the same note to Slataper as "an exposition of a method of work and a program for living" written, according to its author, "like a first love letter." In it, one can see in retrospect, Saba set his own lifetime standards as a poet.

"What remains for poets to do" is to make poetry *honest*. Theoretically at least, the point is very simple.

Whoever does not write verse out of a sincere need to support the expression of his passion with rhythm, whoever has commercial or otherwise ambitious intentions—he for whom the publication of a book is like winning a medal or opening a shop—such a one cannot begin to imagine what stubborn force of intellect, what disinterested grandeur of soul, is needed to resist all seduction and to keep oneself pure and honest in front of oneself—this even when the dishonest line of verse, taken by itself alone, may seem best.

The sole criterion for good poetry—the ethical sense of the adjective conditions the aesthetic—is its truthful correspondence to its poet's experience. Saba perhaps naively assumes that the habitual reader of poetry ("he who is able to go ever so slightly below the surface") will recognize transgressions of this moral imperative, but whether or not the delinquent is publicly caught is irrelevant—"Quella che resta" is written as a declaration of faith by a poet for poets. And it says that the poet's crucial responsibility lies in the sphere of moral awakeness, *coscienza,* in order that expression may be as faithful as possible to the engendering perception or passion.

[A] long discipline is needed in order to prepare oneself for receiving a moment's grace with one's authentic being; making a daily examination of one's conscience, rereading what one has written in those periods of quiet when analysis is possible, seeking always to recall the state of mind that first generated these lines, noting with heroic meticulousness the discrepancies between what was thought and what was written.

The position articulated here is, of course, not unsimilar to Slataper's *moral* contempt for literary schools and conventions, for mellifluous golden nightingales as opposed to plainspoken and honest crows. Saba's title for his second book—"With My Own Eyes"—makes the same point in a different way. But "Quella che resta da fare ai poeti," intended to provide a poetics for that book, was rejected by Slataper as being, once again, derivative ("E così ha fatto il Pascoli" he noted in the margin: warmed-over Pascoli), and was returned to its author. The next time it was read by anyone other than Saba himself (who never mentioned it again) was a short time after his death in 1957 when it was found among his papers and read aloud by Carlo Levi to Saba's daughter Linuccia, Giani Stuparich, Anita Pittoni,* and a few others of the old poet's intimate circle.

As for *Coi miei occhi,* published like *Poesie di Umberto Saba* at the poet's own expense but this time under the auspices of *La Voce,* it had, in Saba's words, "no fortune." (I think we know why.) Only later, after the war, revised into *Trieste e una donna* (Trieste and a lady) as a part of the *Canzoniere,* was it gradually recognized as perhaps Saba's greatest sequence, the quintessential chapter on "his" city ("Mine/because I was born there, more than others' mine who discovered it as a boy, and as a man/married it to Italy forever with my song") and his "moody, secret life" within it. (See appendix entitled Translations for translations of select Trieste poems by Umberto Saba.)

In any case, his undeclared and intramural struggle with Slataper for primacy was ended in all but Saba's very tenacious memory at the close of 1915, when Slataper, aged twenty-seven and fighting as a volunteer for Italy, was shot dead on the Carso. In his life as in his writing, as his friend and editor Giani Stuparich noted, Slataper's youthful arrogance, reckless energies, and precocious gifts made his prickly presence in literary Trieste its single, stunning moment of *Sturm und Drang.*

Circa 1907–8: "Mr James Joyce described [in English] by his faithful pupil Ettore Schmitz":

When I see him walking on the street I always think that he is enjoying a leisure, a full leisure. Nobody is awaiting him and he does not want to reach an aim or to meet anybody. No! He walks in order to be left to himself. He also does not walk for health. He walks because he is not stopped by anything. I imagine that if he would find his way barred by a high and big wall he would not be shocked in the least. He would change direction and if the new direction would also prove not to be clear he would change it again and walk on his hands shaken only by the natural movement of the whole body, his legs working without any effort to lengthen or to fasten [*quicken*] his steps. No! His step is really his and of nobody else and cannot be lengthened or made faster. His whole body in quiet is that of a sportsman. If moved [*that is in movement*] that of a child weakened by the great love of his parents. I know that life has not been a parent of that kind for him. It could have been worst and all the same Mr James Joyce would have kept his appearance of a man who considers things as points breaking the light for his amusement. He wears glasses and really he uses them without interruption from the early (?) morning until late in the night when he wakes up. Perhaps he may see less than it is to suppose from his appearance but he looks like a being who moves in order to see. Surely he cannot fight and does not want to. He is going through life hoping not to meet bad men. I wish him heartily not to meet them.

It is a pleasure to think that the several corrections (in brackets) made in the lightly cracked English of this assigned portrait of the teacher as a young man may have been made by Joyce himself, no doubt a lenient master. But there are felicities in this exercise ("a man who considers things as points breaking the light for his amusement," "a being who moves in order to see") that could not have been better done by a full-time artist composing in his own tongue. Even if Joyce recollected himself as nothing more than a "paid teacher" in the Schmitzes' eyes, the job relationship was clearly a genial one.

He had begun giving English lessons at the house adjoining the marine paint factory at Servola at the southern edge of Trieste in 1907. Was his reading them from the newly completed manuscript of "The Dead" an assignment in oral comprehension? It is an old story at any rate, and one best told by Stanislaus Joyce, that the occult peripeteia of the *caso Svevo* occurred here one morning, some eighteen years before its climax.

When he read them "The Dead," la Signora Schmitz was so impressed by it that she went out into the garden of the villa that adjoined the factory and gathered a bunch of flowers to present to the budding author. It was the first genuine appreciation of my brother's literary work by the common reader that I can recall, and in part sets off my brother's discovery of her husband.

It may have been at the next lesson, perhaps, that Schmitz began to say to my brother that he, too, had once had ambitions to be a writer and had, in fact, published two novels many years before. He went up to his study, and, after searching for a while, fetched down two small, badly printed, badly bound volumes that had been published at the author's expense ten years before by Ettore Vram, a bookseller in Trieste, who was also a publisher in a very modest way. He almost apologized for giving them to my brother to read. I remember quite distinctly the day my brother brought them home. Laying them on the table he said:

—Schmitz has given me these two novels of his to read. Who knows what kind of stuff it is?

After he had read them, the teacher judged his pupil to be a "neglected writer" and told him so on his next visit to Villa Veneziani. "There are passages in *Senilità* that even Anatole France could not have improved"; Joyce already knew several of them by heart. Schmitz was moved "almost to tears" and, forgetting about his lunch, walked his teacher halfway home (up the Servola road today called Via Italo Svevo) "talking to him without further reserve of his disappointed literary ambitions."

By early 1909 Svevo had read the first three chapters of *A Portrait of the Artist as a Young Man* in manuscript and wrote acutely of them to Joyce in English. He praised his "method of observation and description [that] does not allow you to enrich a fact that is not rich of itself . . . [using no] artificial colours to lend to the things the life they wanted in themselves." This in fact was very much the method ("grey, very grey") that had helped contribute to the failure of Svevo himself ten years earlier. As Stanislaus remarks, "What my brother found in Italo Svevo was a mentality akin to his own, an analytic method which was congenial."

But when Joyce communicated his high opinion to another of his pupils who happened to be president of the Gabinetto Minerva, the literary society of Trieste, president Niccolò Vidacovich "pursed his lips, half-closed his eyes, and shook his head slowly and sadly." How was an

Irishman to judge poor Schmitz's execrable Italian? How could a literary Triestine, a lover of the Italian classics and translator (with Signor Joyce) of Synge's *Riders to the Sea* and Yeats's *The Countess Cathleen* into the language of Dante and Boccaccio, countenance such shoddy workmanship? Despite the sarcasms lately directed toward Triestine culture by the renegade Slataper—who in any case did not see fit to mention Svevo—despite the qualified praise of Svevo over a decade ago by someone like Silvio Benco who represented an important component of current Triestine culture, the president of the Gabinetto Minerva could only, regretfully, make his face. The *caso Svevo* was an intramural affair that was embarrassing and best forgotten.

Could indeed a foreigner, even a gifted and quadrilingual one like James Joyce, accurately judge prose like Svevo's on its merits? "Almost always," wrote Slataper, "our style is heavy handed . . . shaped by literary convention, not animated by life." But if Slataper's own "Alpine locomotive" style is modeled on Nietzsche, or Benco's on D'Annunzio, or Saba's on Leopardi, Svevo's awkward prose is certainly not the way it is because of an overdose of Italian or even German literature. And clearly it constituted a problem for those few Italian-speaking readers, entirely citizens of Trieste, who were aware of it.

(A colleague of Benco's once tried to explain why Svevo wrote "*so badly*": "That blessed father of his had a prejudice for German education. He sent the boy to Germany and shackled him for life with this slow, improper, and convoluted way of expressing himself." Still, Svevo's daughter bears witness that Svevo's German was fluent but flawed; Saba is only half correct when he says that "Svevo could write *well* in German; he preferred to write *badly* in Italian." The cause of his ponderous and often incorrect Italian seems to be, as Giorgio Voghera has pointed out, that he generally "thought" in *triestino,* the Venetic dialect of the wharves and warehouses, and used German locutions to structure his more complex or abstract passages; he then "translated" this amalgam into a tongue of which he was by no means perfect master. But others, genuine admirers like Bazlen and Quarantotti Gambini, felt Svevo's language was ultimately a manifestation of his laziness. For example his "corrections" for the second (1927) edition of *Senilità* seem dutiful, partial, and frequently arbitrary, as though his heart were not in it.)

So who knew better, Niccolò Vidacovich or James Joyce? According to a fellow Berlitz teacher, Joyce's own Italian when he first arrived in Trieste, if bookish and medieval enough to be virtually a dead language, was grammatically faultless. A few years later, Silvio Benco, asked by Joyce to vet the Italian of the pieces on Ireland he had written for the *Piccolo,* found it lacked neither precision nor contemporary expressiveness: "The manuscripts had no need of my corrections." Joyce was surely not unaware of the linguistic failings of *Una vita* and *Senilità.* But as a reader for whom Italian was a second language—like the French *italianistes* Larbaud and Crémieux to whom he would later recommend Svevo—he was less likely than the typical Italian *letterato,* or than the president of the Gabinetto Minerva of Trieste, to be in utter thrall to standard norms of correctness and decorum in matters of diction, and therefore more free to perceive values of a different, compensatory order where they might exist. He might see, for instance, that Svevo's grey and graceless crow's talk, odd semidemotic variant of the "style of scrupulous meanness" the artist as a young man had devised for his *Dubliners,* might be *right* for the world and worldview it was meant to purvey, might be—in Montale's phrase of 1925—"anti-literary, but fervid, essential." †

---

†Even so, it is interesting to note that Joyce, also very fond of an aureate style (Newman, D'Annunzio), knew by heart and selected for particular praise the uncharacteristically "high" close to *Senilità:*

> Sí! Angiolina pensa e piange! Pense come se le fosse stato spiegato il segreto dell'universo e della propria esistenza; piange come se nel vasto mondo non avvesse piú trovato neppure un *Deo gratias* qualunque.
> [Yes! Angiolina thinks and weeps! Thinks as though the secret of the universe and of

Yet Joyce's discovery in 1907 that his employer and pupil was unjustly neglected as an author made no change at all in the writing life of Italo Svevo at that time; his iron resolution still held. (And who, after all, was *James Joyce* in 1907? An itinerant "merchant of gerunds"—Svevo's phrase—with one slender and conventional volume of verses and a couple of short stories to his published name: "promising" to the Schmitzes and Nora and Stanislaus and himself alone.) But for *La coscienza di Zeno* to be conceived and written, a cessation of usual routine—local supervision and business travel—was required, and this came only through the war.

By 1916 factory production had been curtailed considerably owing to a scarcity of raw materials and personnel. The chief customer for Veneziani marine paint was Great Britain, and Great Britain was an enemy. Trieste was within earshot of the fighting on the Carso, and travel was absolutely forbidden. In his newfound, relative freedom (reflected in the closing chapter of *Zeno*), Ettore Schmitz was able to become what he chose to call a "dilettante" again. He practiced his violin, though war had broken up the local string quartet. He read deeply in Freud, "preoccupied," as he put it much later, "with understanding the nature of a perfect moral health." With a nephew he worked on an Italian translation of *The Interpretation of Dreams,* and in complete solitude ("that is, in perfect contradiction to the theory and practice of Freud") undertook to conduct a psychoanalysis upon himself. This comic and inconclusive experiment, along with the related memoirs that Svevo took notes for during this period, would later provide the narrative structure for the so-called confessions of Zeno Cosini. During the long "repose" induced by wartime, he

---

her own existence had been explained to her; weeps as though in the vast world she had no longer found even one *Deo gratias* whatsoever.]

Of course the whole haunting passage is fraught with harshest irony: this image of *la figlia che piange* is the last and lasting illusion of the "senile" protagonist Emilio.

Nov. 1985–June 1986), 24–5, 140, 179

Trst, 23, 48, 91, 110, 175–7, 179

Tuoni, Dario di, 10

Ungaretti, Giuseppe, 238

Università popolare, 98, 231, 245

University of Trieste (or lack of), 28, 32, 74, 128, 140, 141, 231, 232–3, 237, 245

usurpazione (1382). *See dedizione* (1382)

Venice, 11, 39, 44–7, 65, 73, 80, 82, 85, 95, 106, 111, 141, 144, 176, 177–8, 236, 238

Verdi, Giuseppe, 121–2

Verga, Giovanni, 127

Verlaine, Paul, 10

Veruda, Umberto, 120, 164, 167, 168, 169

Vidacovich, Niccolò, 151–2, 153, 231, 232

Vienna, 12, 16, 19, 21, 27, 42, 53, 67, 69, 74, 97, 105–6, 111, 142, 155, 228, 232, 234, 237, 245

Villa Veneziani, 5, 7, 8, 35, 150–1, 158

Virgil, 45–7, 59, 128, 168, 244

La Voce, 130, 139–40, 142–9, 158, 233, 244

Voghera, Giorgio, 152–3

Voghera, Guido ("anonimo triestino"), 160, 250

Vram, Ettore, 124, 125, 126, 130, 151

Weaver, William, 26–7, 33

Weiss, Edoardo, 224, 228

Winckelmann, Johann, 21, 35, 61, 66–71, 82, 97, 237

wind rose, 1, 53, 56, 206–7

Yugoslavia (Kingdom of, then People's Republic of Serbs, Croats and Slovenes, 1918–91), 11, 12, 15, 23, 34, 35, 46–8, 88, 91, 135, 169, 175–7, 236

Lo Zibaldone, 235

Ziliotti, Baccio, 128–31, 133, 156, 168

Zola, Émile, 116, 241

Personal Acknowledgments

to the memory of my sister Dino Read, who gave this adventure her blessing;

to Donatella Pirona and James Davey of Trieste, and to Anna and Dorian, for their generous hospitality;

to the Research Foundation of the University of Connecticut for its contribution toward travel expenses;

to Scott Kennedy and Mohini Mundkur and Lynn Sweet and Robert Vrecenak of the Homer Babbidge Library of the University of Connecticut for their consideration and help;

to Ellen Feldman, Jo Ann Kiser, Randolph Petilos, and Joan Sommers of the University of Chicago Press for their invaluable professional skills;

to the following individuals for services graciously rendered: the late William Arrowsmith (who gave this book its rightful name), Jane Blanshard, Maria Romagnoli Brackett and John Brackett, Nathaniel Brackenridge Cary, Jack Davis, Dario Del Puppo, Robert Dombroski, Louise Guiney, Margaret Hemphill, W. E. Kennick, Alicé Andreina Montera, Anne Renfro Read, Paul Ryan, Stephanie Terenzio, and Eve Webster;

to my godson Nick Read for his gifts as an artist as well as for his companionship during the third week;

and, once again most of all, to my dear wife, Edith Howes Cary, who saw me off and welcomed me home.

J.C.

Trieste, Italy
Mansfield Center, Connecticut
1985–1993

recalled, "I was again taken over by my ancient phantasms but, distrustful, I did not set them down. I had to hold myself in readiness to resume my normal life whenever that became possible."

With war's end and Trieste's redemption by Italy, a greater urgency to write with a public in mind presented itself. The irredentist *Piccolo* had earlier been closed down and its plant destroyed on orders from Vienna; now, in 1919, an old friend planned a new paper, the significantly named *Nazione,* and Svevo was invited to write for it. And so he did, most notably an amusing set of pieces on the system of public transportation, "the slowest tramway in the world," operating between central Trieste and his Servola suburb. But he himself felt that the crucial factor in his return to writing was having become, at long last, an Italian citizen. "It's certain," he wrote in 1923,

> that if Italy had not come to me, I would not even have thought of being able to write. This is a curious thing that not even I, to whom it happened, know how to explain. Our milieu has not changed all that much! And yet I set out to write my novel four months after the arrival of our troops. As if it were quite natural! At 58 years of age! I believe that with the peevishness of anyone just freed I thought that right of citizenship had been granted to me and to my sublanguage [*linguetta*].

Triestine writers—Svevo in the 1890s, Slataper and Saba a few years before the war—had always known it: recognition, to be worth having, would have to come from outside, from abroad. That Svevo put his money down to have his first two novels published in Trieste only shows the young bank clerk's impecuniousness (printing costs were cheaper there) and lack of strategic sense; even so, the sole review that mattered to him came from Milan. Most sought and if necessary paid to have their books published and distributed on the peninsula—Benco qua novelist in Milan, Slataper and Saba and Giotti in Florence, Stuparich in Naples and Rome. When Saba returned to Trieste after the war and bought an antiquarian bookshop, and brought out his reshaped and collected poems as

the *Canzoniere* in an edition of five hundred copies under its aegis, this was a sign of defeat and proud resignation. No one else would take the risk of publishing him.

La coscienza di Zeno was written between 1919 and 1922 and published in Bologna in 1923, again at the author's expense. Its few reviewers noted its length and casual structure, its apparent shapelessness, above all its slovenly Italian. Even Benco was lukewarm, finding the book original but also prolix and uneven, written in a language he found "pathetically harsh and eccentric." History was repeating itself and Svevo inscribed his despair on the flyleaf of the copy he sent Joyce in Paris.

"And into the consecrated tomb they descended, comforted by the vision of a radiant future." In January 1924, while Professor Ziliotto was composing the final, oddly prophetic sentence of his literary history of Trieste and evoking the shades of Trieste's young writers cut off in their prime, Joyce wrote Svevo acknowledging his gift of *La coscienza di Zeno* and comforting him for its lack of serious notice in Italy. ("Why despair? You must know that it is by far your best book. . . . I see that the last paragraph of *Senilità*—'Yes Angiolina thinks and weeps etc.'—has blossomed magnificently in secret." Most important of all, he was inspired to advise his former pupil to look for help outside of Italy and able to provide specific names and addresses. Copies of the novel were duly sent to Valery Larbaud, Benjamin Crémieux, and Ford Madox Ford in Paris, T. S. Eliot in London, and Gilbert Seldes in New York. The *caso Svevo* was about to become *commedia sveviana*.

The "public" discovery of Italo Svevo occurred on both sides of the Italian border roughly two years later. Within Italy it took place in the November–December 1925 issue of the Milanese journal *L'Esame* when a twenty-nine year-old poet from Genoa published his initial and still valuable essay on the work of a "contemporary narrator who is beginning to arouse interest and admiration in more than one *letterato* and Italophile on the far side of the Alps, and who is up to now in fact unknown in his own country." Montale felt obliged to reassure his readers that his piece was not an "imaginary portrait" in the manner of Walter Pater—"such is the shadow that obscures the work and even the name of the novelist who calls himself Italo Svevo." (Behind Montale stood another shadowy figure, the young Roberto Bazlen of Trieste, who had read and sought out Svevo earlier that year—*Stile tremendo!* he wrote without irony of *Senilità*, "Italy's single modern novel (published in 1898!)"; who had procured from the author copies of all three novels to send to Montale in Genoa; who had timed what he called *la bomba Svevo,* the firework shock of recognition executed by Montale, so that it was the first to burst in Europe.) Montale's "Omaggio a Italo Svevo" appeared just two months before the Svevo number of Adrienne Monnier's *Le Navire d'Argent* of February 1926, in which Crémieux wrote his famous essay on the man whom Larbaud had already privately designated *maestro,* appraising the nature of Svevo's isolated genius and offering forty pages of translation from his work. "Reading him translated . . . by Crémieux and Larbaud, Svevo seems another man," wrote one disgruntled Italian reviewer. "If this unknown Italian is destined to be rewarded by a European recognizance, it will be providential if this be begun [not only] in another language but *in a language.*"

The sensational discovery-recovery of Italo Svevo stimulated the subsequent mapping of a literary Trieste by younger members of the Italian avant-garde. In the spring of 1926, for example, Montale visited Trieste at Svevo's invitation and stayed as a guest at the Villa Veneziani; Bazlen at this time introduced the young poet to Saba, Benco, Giotti, Stuparich, and the painter Vittorio Bolaffio. Triestine figures began to turn up in Montale's own poetry: Saba's daughter Linuccia; Austrian friends of Bazlen's like Gerti Tolazzi, Liuba Blumenthal, and Dora Markus (whom Montale, in fact, never met but whose "marvelous legs," photographed by Bazlen, occasioned one of his most disquieting lyric portraits); Bazlen himself. Montale essays followed on Saba and Giotti. In 1928 the important Florentine magazine *Solaria,* heir to the deceased *La Voce,* published editions of Giotti's poems in Triestine dialect (with a glossary) and Saba's latest lyric sequence; in the same year it brought out a single issue devoted entirely to the work of Saba. In 1929 an "obituary" issue was devoted to the fiction of the late Svevo.

Montale ended his first essay on Saba by evoking the figures of Saba, Svevo, and the painter Arturo Fittke—"the three great, very different, Triestine artists"—against a backdrop of the city, lately on the other side of the frontier, that these figures had revealed to all Italians "seriously concerned with contemporary thought and art." Thirty-seven years later, in his great discourse to the Circle of Culture and Arts in Trieste on the centenary celebration of Svevo's birth, Montale addressed himself to the matter of a literary Trieste, that is, the "sole Italian city that derives its glory from its writers":

The fact is undeniable and the reasons for it obvious. More than any other Italian city Trieste has felt the need of affirming the link uniting it to Italian culture—uniting it and at the same time differentiating it. And perhaps it is because of this that the term 'Triestine writer' may be said to have acquired a very special meaning: that of a writer closely bound to the life, customs, and difficult destiny of his city. Not to its folklore, needless to say, or to its local color, but to the image of a city unlike any other in Italy.

This splendid peroration to Slataper's "Trieste is Italian in a different way than other Italian cities are" amounts, in fact, to an epitaph.

A "Triestine writer," one may safely say, is a writer from the area of Trieste; it is certainly this topographical feature that links the writers listed in the appendix entitled Literary Trieste: Evidence of Its Existence. And since the gestalt of Trieste III is presumably different from the gestalt of Trieste II, one might add the temporal-historical notation that a "Triestine writer" of the sort envisaged by Montale had to *know both:* had to be born no earlier than 1861 and die no earlier than 1928 (using Svevo's dates as *termini ad quem*). But beyond this there is neither a common style nor a common matter. One only has to think of specimen writers from Trieste like Svevo, Benco, Saba, and Slataper to be made more aware of differences, sometimes bitter, than of similarities.

Slataper notwithstanding, there is no "stylistic *triestinità*": there are crows and nightingales and a range of voices in between. (Even the dialects of lyricists like Marin and Giotti are idiosyncratic.) And Montale notwithstanding, the "image of the city" binding every Triestine writer varies enormously: a normal contingency in Svevo, more or less irrelevant in Benco, an ontological issue in Slataper, a mirror for the moods in Saba (who late in life declared the city *his* not only because he was born and bred there but because he alone had *redeemed* it, made it truly Italian, by an act of poetic language: "married it to Italy forever with my song").

In the late 1920s the critic Pietro Pancrazi attempted a thematic synthesis.

> Today it is possible to affirm that a Triestine literature exists. . . . Common to all these writers [Slataper, Saba, Giotti, Svevo, Stuparich], more than is usual in the Italian tradition, is the moral obsession. . . . These writers, mixed in language, culture, and often blood, are usually intent on self-discovery, self-definition, seeking what is their reality—but almost with the presupposition that they will not find it, as one who sees his search as an end in itself, rather than a means.

This sounds, in fact, like one definition of a worldwide feature of "modern" literature, in which "literature" itself is a suspect word (like "rhetoric"), in which *coscienza*—consciousness = conscience—is crucial, in which "seeing through" is everything. Conceivably the hypochondriac edge to so much Triestine writing from Svevo and Saba and Slataper to Bazlen and Guido Voghera (the self-styled *anonimo triestino*) is an impassioned variation on this theme,† even Trieste's own contribution to the modernity of modern Italian literature.

Montale's noble words amount to an epitaph because the conditions that made Trieste what it was (and its writers, therefore, what they were), the conditions that once upon a time were distillable into such locutions as "the unredeemed," "the marches of Italy," "frontier identity," and "double soul," have either disappeared or altered. Trieste is different from other Italian cities still, but what Italian city isn't? Its difference is different than it used to be. To a degree it has been assimilated.

Economics and Slav irredentism apart, Trieste III is a stylish, testy city with much folklore, a cherished palette of local colors, and unusual

---

†Similar to Svevo's preoccupation "with understanding the nature of a perfect moral health." See appendix entitled Translations for a love letter on this theme, written while Svevo was finishing *Senilità* in 1897 but anticipating the humor and vision of *Zeno* composed over a quarter of a century later.

memories. One of its main memories, as Montale didn't quite say, is "literary Trieste," and in testament to this notable, poignant, famous, and relatively recent phase of its long past, Trieste III has devised a series of civic pieties: centennial dinners and conferences, marble plaques affixed to certain facades, altered street names (Via Svevo, Corso Saba, Scala Joyce, Piazza Giotti, and so on), and busts set up in the Public Garden.

Literary Trieste exists, of course, but in a ghostly way entirely. It is a city made of books that were written by writers born about a century ago.

And now dead. And in another world.

MIRAMAR &
DIUNNO

⑧

⑫

⑩

PIAZZA
UNITÀ
D'ITALIA

① ② ③

CORSO ITALIA

⑮

⑭

PIAZZA
BENCO

V. M

⑪

⑦

⑥

V. LAZZARETTO VECCHIO

⑨

TRIESTE

LITERARY TRIESTE

SERVOLA & ISTRIA

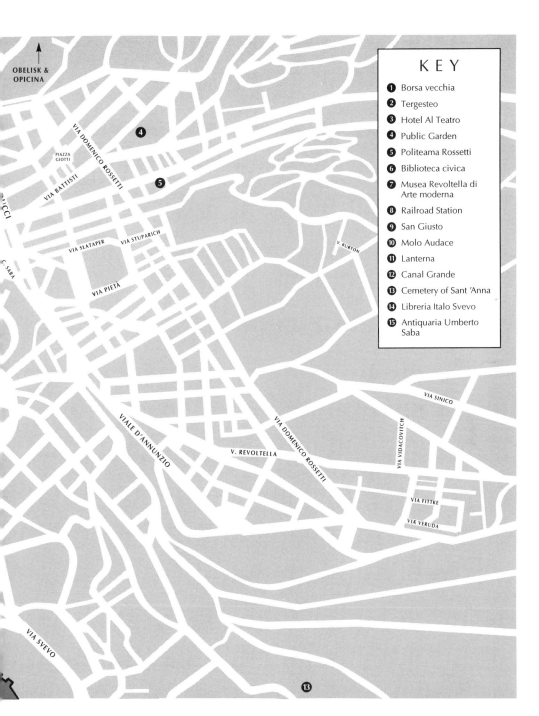

OBELISK &
OPICINA

PIAZZA
GIOTTI

VIA DOMENICO ROSSETTI

VIA BATTISTI

❹

❺

C. SABA

VIA SLATAPER   VIA STUPARICH

VIA PIETÀ

V. BURTON

VIALE D'ANNUNZIO

V. REVOLTELLA

VIA DOMENICO ROSSETTI

VIA SINICO

VIA VIDACOVITCH

VIA FITTKE

VIA VERUDA

VIA SVEVO

❸

KEY

❶ Borsa vecchia

❷ Tergesteo

❸ Hotel Al Teatro

❹ Public Garden

❺ Politeama Rossetti

❻ Biblioteca civica

❼ Musea Revoltella di
Arte moderna

❽ Railroad Station

❾ San Giusto

❿ Molo Audace

⓫ Lanterna

⓬ Canal Grande

⓭ Cemetery of Sant 'Anna

⓮ Libreria Italo Svevo

⓯ Antiquaria Umberto
Saba

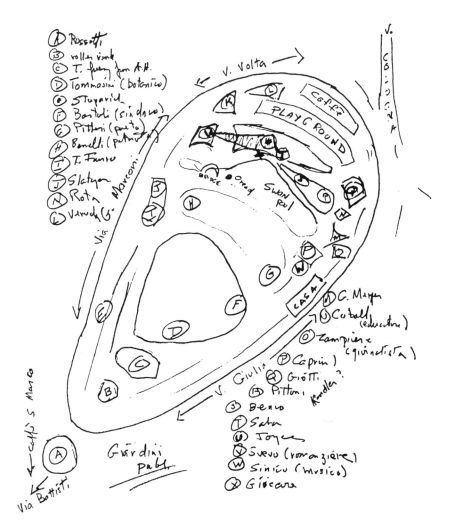

Public Garden in Trieste

The Masters in the Public Garden

he leaves are fallen.

(Raked into fat copper and manila heaps beneath the poplars, waiting for wind or pickup. Pinned trembling on the points of stubby boxwood edging the grass across the way. Lightly rocked and swamping slowly in the swan pool, unnoted by the stone oread with pigtails clutching the stone swan to her belly upon her rock isle as by the living, preening swans. Or—dropped upon my clipboard—this one, tan and desiccated, that shatters when I press it with my hand.)

Green persists in the hedged borders of the grassy islands among the walks and alleys, in the brakes of massed laurel, in holm oak and pine. The four o'clock winter sun glints from brass tags affixed to the exotics (Spanish and Himalayan fir, cork, cedar of Lebanon, great sequoia . . .). Off towards the park railings and the streets beyond are dark clumps and coverts and thickets of thorned and berried bush where stray cats prowl and peahens rummage and candy wrappers decompose. Above, filtered through a tangle of bare branch and evergreen, a dream pueblo of beige and brick: the apartment dwellings of the fortunate.

A bus exhales on Via Battisti. Shouts of children in the playground, murmur of mothers on the cold benches. (Warm life, *calda vita,* despite the chilly air.) The scratch of my pencil on the pad. Snarl of skateboards on the asphalt terrace of the cafeteria, closed for the season. (Several Peking

ducks interrogate a gentleman in a maroon overcoat, who fumbles in his pockets.) Squeak of my eraser when I have to correct. The homely rise and fall of the city air in my nostrils.

X marks the spot where I sit in the midst of it all, back to the swan pool, twenty blue-gray pigeons poking sullenly at the gravel by my shoes for the crumbs I have not tossed them. I am making my map of the Public Garden.

It is shaped like a plectrum, like an inverted tear, like a savage arrowhead aimed straight down Via Battisti at the Lloyd Adriatico billboard, like a stubby exclamation point (if you take as its dot—marked *A* on the map—the small circle at the entrance where Domenico Rossetti is poised upon his lofty pedestal facing today's traffic and utterly ignoring three garland-proffering nymphs, a dignified city father in a Spanish cape with one hand on his heart and an untitled book in the other. Behind his worthy back, past the gates forbidding dogs and bicycles, is *B,* the small oval roller rink that never seems to be used, and past that, easy to miss in the encroaching yew and ilex, Trieste strenuously liberating herself from the Austro-Hungarian eagle, *C.* Then things get complicated, labyrinthine. I have not done well by the walks and actual shapes of the islands. But the approximate location of the busts is clear enough.)

There are twenty-one of these, and it requires more than death to get to be one. "Alas, we are so fashioned," wrote Biagio Marin thirty years ago, "that the presence of these likenesses and of the solemn epitaphs accompanying them are not enough to revive in our *coscienza* the life and worth of these men who lived and worked for us, neglecting, in their love of city, their own private concerns." Gratefully commissioned over the years by the selfsame city, the busts sit upon their columns in the Public Garden and wait to be inspiring. These pigeon-fouled heads and shoulders with their weathered names and dates and callings (*botanico, educatore, giornalista, musico, patriota . . .*) are meant not only to be remembered but to remind the passing Triestine that he or she is citizen of a city with an arduous history not yet done.

> No, quella voce non fu bugiarda
> che agli avi nostri parlò nel cor . . .

as one of them, Giuseppe Sinico (*musico,* for a short time voice teacher of James Joyce) wrote in the now-forgotten San Giusto hymn from his opera *Marinella* (1854). "No, that voice was not deceiving that spoke in the hearts of our forefathers." These busts are meant to stir.

(But the passersby pass by. The skater's knee is bleeding badly. The lovers trail off toward the railings in search of privacy. The sere leaf falls, and the ducks demand their tip for being ducks in a public place. The lady on the bench taps her foot and glances once more at her wristwatch. And the elegant gold cockerel with scarlet comb and wattle shadows its snow white mate into the laurel behind the plinth of Umberto Veruda. The warm life passes, too full of itself to be inspired or stirred. Unmappable.)

Task in hand and happy at last, I watch it pass and the cold busts waiting, and make a map to help me remember where they wait, poor bronze and marble pieties, along the garden paths. *Sinico, musico, 1836–1907:* far end of swan pool by the playground. And also, if possible, what they stand for, since—three weeks in Trieste notwithstanding—I am a stranger still, with time and inclination to read and to ponder inscriptions. The busts in the Public Garden depend upon people like me.

Giuseppe Sinico, for instance, believed that Joyce's light tenor had a beautiful timbre and posthumously left his name to an alcoholic lady run over by a locomotive in "A Painful Case," of the *Dubliners* stories. Riccardo Pitteri, *poeta,* died of natural causes in 1915 and never knew that posterity—Professor Ziliotto at least, and myself—would think of him as "a Carduccian with Virgilian soul." Poor Umberto Veruda, *pittore* with his butterfly collar and lock of hair over one eye, Svevo's closest friend and model for the exuberant sculptor Balli in *Senilità,* frightened his beloved mother into cardiac arrest by pretending to be furious with her for not obeying her doctor's orders; she died in his arms and he spent the year of life remaining him wandering from city to city correctly convinced he was a dead man, pockets stuffed with notes and identification papers so that he would be known to whoever found his body in the street or hotel bed . . .

The sensitive stranger registers that there are none of Franz Josef's *fedelissimi triestini* here and no Slavs either, unless you want to count Scipio Slataper. Ten of them lived and died in Trieste II, perforce content with the view from Mount Pisgah; all of the others but one entered the Promised Land and became certified Italians at war's end. The garden, recall, is a public one, and features concerns that are civic and Italian in focus. Slataper is present not as the author of "the most beautiful book produced by a writer from our city" (Benco's phrase) but, according to his epitaph, as a "Giulian volunteer" who "fell" on a hill near Gorizia on March 12, 1915. Giani Stuparich, *scrittore,* almost the latest dead of all in 1961, is chiefly remembered here for his *medaglia d'oro al V.M.,* the medal for military valor that Montale, himself a veteran, used to tease him about, calling him *warrior* and *lion.* Giuseppe Sinico composed the San Giusto hymn, an irredentist favorite. Besides writing Carduccian verse, Riccardo Pitteri was president of the National League and campaigned vigorously for Italian schooling for the children of irredentist families. Gianni Bartoli, *sindaco,* was mayor of the city during the tormented period of Yugoslav presence and military partition in the years following World War II.

Animae patriae . . .

Over the years of Trieste III, however, the busts in the Public Garden have slowly spread east towards the children's playground and the cafeteria, away from Domenico Rossetti upon his pedestal rising above the stink and racket of Via Battisti. At *X,* the eastern end just past the swan pool where I sit witness upon a bench with my clipboard, Biagio Marin's grave pronouncement upon the busts and their originals ("these men who lived and worked for us, neglecting, in their love of city, their own private concerns") seems less apropos. For here I am surrounded by the likenesses of men who took and worked their own private concerns and made something public out of them that in the long run, to the city's surprise, brought the city fame. These, I believe, are the masters.

Not all of them of course, but some. Among the painters, neither Arturo Fittke nor Vittorio Bolaffio, but at any rate Veruda. Not Montale, self-styled *triestino d'elezione,* who remembered Trieste as his chosen *patria,* fatherland. Writers despite their war honors, Stuparich and Slataper are a few steps down the path to the west. Over my shoulder is Silvio Benco, severe and spade-bearded, looking a bit like Jan Smuts. A small-scale and oddly elongated Giotti stands, in the Public Garden as in life, a little at the edge of things. Biagio Marin died in 1985, the last of all to go, and is not here as yet.

Literary Trieste. Within geometrical range of me where I sit happy athwart the hypotenuse, together at last and gathered into a triangle which although obtuse rather than equilateral is beautiful all the same, are the ghostly simulacra of the three who drew me here with their words in the very first place. The industrialist looks manic, pop-eyed, richly dark as the prewar bronze of which he is made. The merchant of gerunds is cast in the image of an early passport photo, a framing frame of beaten bronze helping to make the point. The antiquarian bookdealer who married Trieste to Italy forever with his song looks overly plump and, with his starched sportshirt and turned-up overcoat collar, too dapper for the proletarian persona he favored in his maturity.

·

ITALO SVEVO
NOVELIST 1861–1928

·

TO JAMES JOYCE
IN THE CENTENNIAL YEAR OF HIS BIRTH 1882–1982

·

TO UMBERTO SABA
IN THE CENTENNIAL YEAR OF HIS BIRTH 1883–1983

·

Civic pieties, of course, but not good likenesses. And as it turned out, they were not to be my particular business here after all.

But I mark them down on the map with a special pleasure.

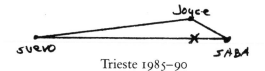

Trieste 1985–90

One morning there appeared to me something I had long desired to see, although it is not frequent in these parts: a fata morgana [mirage] upon the sea. After breakfast we had walked out to the little hill from which the sea can be viewed in all its vastness, and here I seemed to see rise up above the level of the horizon a mass of water across the lower portions of which ran sailing ships, upside down; coasts never before seen appeared before my eyes. It was the enchanting vision of a double sea of the most extraordinary aspect. A splendid sun illuminated this spectacle which lasted long enough to allow one to inspect it with tranquility. At length it disappeared like a lovely dream in the azure water-vapors.

ARCHDUKE MAXIMILIAN
Journal

Everything in Trieste is double or triple . . .

SCIPIO SLATAPER
"Irredentismo"

Three Farewells

Sua mare grega

On the flight home I read one of the many books I had bought at the Libreria Italo Svevo, Signora Livia Veneziani Svevo's charming life of her husband. She quoted in its entirety a letter from Joyce to Svevo written in 1921 in which the latter was asked to bring with him, possibly on his next business trip to Paris, a bundle of notes for the final two chapters of *Ulysses,* which had been left with brother Stanislaus at the time of Joyce's definitive departure from Trieste in the summer of 1920. They would be easy enough to spot since they were "bound with a rubber band the color of a Sister of Charity's belly."

The letter was interesting for a number of other reasons. For one thing, as Signora Svevo pointed out, it illustrated the *cordialità* existing between the old man of sixty who had failed to find recognition as a novelist and the Irish exile of nearly forty already acknowledged as a master. And then it was written, like so much of Joyce, in a brilliant array of styles. There was, to begin and end with, a plain, conversational, functional Italian. There was a parodically pedantic and elaborately formal caricature Italian composed as if by a demented *cinquecento* humanist obsessed with exactitude (the desired packet of notes had an "approximate" size of 95 × 70 centimeters and "a gross weight without tare of 4.78 kilograms"), rather in the mode of the Ithaca chapter Joyce was currently working on. Finally, there was a gossipy paragraph in the Triestine dialect.

Some of this was not so easy to read. The notes were wrapped, for example, in *una mappa di tela cerata,* which could be understood to be an oilcloth *map.* Very odd! (Later, at home, I learned that *mappa* might also signify not a "briefcase," as it is translated in the Joyce *Letters,* but a cloth that could be used for liturgical purposes, as in covering an altar or the implements thereon; a mot juste, therefore, with a properly Joycean swirl to it.) The dialect had mainly to be pronounced aloud in the head and guessed at in an educated way.

One phrase in particular fired my imagination and ended by elating me. Joyce wrote of his urgent need of the notes in order to bring to an end his *lavoro letterario intitolato «Ulisse» ossia «Sua mare grega».* Which was to say: his literary labor entitled *Ulysses, or.* . . . Or what?

It was *triestino. Mare* was simple enough: sea. But what was strange was that it seemed here to be feminine. *Il mare* would be good Italian. But wasn't it written in the very first chapter of *Ulysses* itself that the sea was our mighty mother? Perhaps to a seafaring folk like the Triestines the sea would be grammatically feminine. *La mare:* the sea in *triestino.*

The rest was a matter of educated guess and sudden insight. I balanced between a dialect version of "herded" (as in gregarious) and "grey" for the adjective *grega;* then, remembering my week in Trieste, I knew the latter was correct. *Sua* was an elision of a preposition plus the feminine article. On a grey sea. *Ulysses, or Upon a Grey Sea.*

Soaring over the broad Atlantic on my way home, I put the book down and felt pleasure. For I too had been, this week past, a stranger in a strange place. I recalled the first morning up at the Obelisk, the scene on the tram, the dog Rex, the blurred view looking down from Opicina on the self-sufficient town; how grey it had all seemed both outside and inside me! *Upon a Grey Sea.* It carried a precious connection—necessary to explain it all lightly and without self-pity!—between the books and the writers I cared for and the town they lived in in their time, and the town I in my time had come to and myself in the town.

It could even be my title—not *Literary Trieste* but *Upon a Grey Sea*. (Naming things conferred a certain reality.)

There might even, as in the letter, be a subtitle: *Upon a Grey Sea, or* . . .

Or what? I wondered.

Do vidjenja Trst

The #30 bus for Piazza Libertà and the train station. Down the sun-drenched *riva* past the Molo Audace. Past the Greek Orthodox Church with the glittering iconostasis, where in the gloom the gold had gathered light against it. Past imposing, neoclassical Palazzo Carciotti (now an office building) with its grandiose statues of Minerva, Fame, Justice, Mercury, Abundance and, for good measure, a "sylph" (picked out and identified one lackluster morning with the help of Dottoressa Ruaro Loseri) ensconced on the balustrade above the columns of the upper facade; above *them* a green copper dome upon which was perched an aggressive, bronze Napoleonic eagle. Past the currently not very grand Canal Grande. Past, after the bus turned up from the harbor, the little restaurant that to my dismay had served up exclusively *wurst* and *krauti* for my first supper that second week in Trieste. I had lacked the moral courage to get up and leave.

The stalls were shut on Piazza Libertà; at this hour on Sunday no day-trippers from Yugoslavia were buying blue jeans and transistors cheap. The almost empty train was waiting on its track. It was clear from the disheveled state of the compartments—ashtrays overflowing and crumbs in the velour pillows mashed into the sidewalls beneath the sills or fallen on the filthy floor—that it had come through the night and originated elsewhere. I picked what seemed to be the cleanest compartment and arranged my bags on either seat to discourage company.

There was time enough to return to the station and buy a last *Piccolo* at the newsstand, a sandwich and a beer at the cart by the platform gate. Time also to observe a blue-smocked janitor with broom and bucket falter at my door before proceeding further up the line. Time to face down three or four candidates for company by the resolute spread of my presence within my chosen space. I also had time to study the faded color photographs set behind celluloid in metal frames above the headrests.

No Forum, no Rialto Bridge, no leaning Tower of Pisa. No view of Castle Miramar. Nothing Italian at all. Instead, a huge pockmarked limestone boulder with a crude face carved into it set upon the bank of some river or lake at Lepenski Vir; a hydroelectric plant at Novi Sad; someone's gloomy castle keep or tomb on the top of Mount Lovcén; the underground caffè in the floodlit grottoes of Postojna; a high-rise Hotel Crna Gora in Titograd. Strange Balkan sights from over the Carso lip, captioned in a strange tongue translated below into German, French, English, and Greek. A world I knew nothing about, not very far from here. Even—in a way—here.

With a sudden start, the train began to move west towards Venice. I slid open the compartment door into the corridor to take a last look at the receding station, the slowly rotating port. Farewell to Trieste. On the corridor wall, screwed under celluloid, a large blue and green and orange map caught my attention and held it just to the left of the flowing window.

In green, set against a blue sea called Jadransko More, with a shape that suggested absolutely nothing (no dreadnought, no hip boot) to my imagination, was Jugoslavja, an eastern region of *Mitteleuropa,* the western limit of the Balkan Peninsula where I had never been. Black stars marked Zagreb, Sarajevo, Beograd, Skopje; black dots for smaller towns. Surrounding this with orange were the contiguous nations: Albanija, Grčka, Bugarska, Rumunija, Madarska, Austrija, and, at the far left, in the far west, commencing in a slender curl of shore at the very top of the blue Jadransko, Italija. And Trst.

I was moving at a rising speed past things seen—Miramar, Duino, the striped smokestacks and giant cranes of Monfalcone—back toward a world I considered myself to some extent familiar with: Venice, Milan, and home. But the map before my eyes declared a different perspective. From its point of view I had been in Trst. *Slovensky Trst.* Farewell to Trst.

I could touch my finger to the very spot I was on the point of leaving. Trst: westmost city of an unknown world. North up the coast from Pula where, when it was Pola, Joyce had first taught at the Berlitz School (which he called Cul). Across the neck of Istria from Rijeka, *river,* the Fiume that D'Annunzio and his legionnaires held hostage over sixty years ago. An easy trip from Ljubljana, the Laibach that was when young Franz Josef with his cavalcade of horse-drawn carriages passed through en route to laying the foundation stone for the new Südbahn station in Trieste. Not Trieste now but Trst. Or Trieste but also Trst.

Do vidjenja Trst. Farewell to Trst. The end of one thing and beginning of another. I hadn't thought to recognize it during my time there.

Seagulls

Cork tips. A bobbing archipelago of gutted lemon and orange halves. A few artichoke leaves. A crumpled carton of pear nectar. A pretty blue-tinted Fanta bottle, empty, 1.5 litre size.

There were no seagulls in Venice. Lots of other stuff sliding by on the face of the filthy Canale, however: a plain transparent plastic bag that looked like a jellyfish, slicks of viscera or oil, a police launch, a *vaporetto.* But no sobbing gulls afloat, nor flying through the air to swoop or pluck. And pigeons everywhere, fidgeting about the chairs and tables looking for crumbs. Was it possible that the pigeons kept them off?

Had there been seagulls in Trieste?

I had quietly raised my eyes from yesterday's edition of the *Piccolo* and, looking out from where I sat across those foul grey waters, suddenly saw what wasn't there. I saw, that is, no seagulls. Or invisible seagulls. I confirmed them again and again. There were no seagulls visible at this hour in Venice. I hadn't thought to look or listen for them in Trieste. Three weeks there, and I had no memory of them. I hadn't even taken them for granted.

Perhaps pigeons kept them off but I doubted it.

Late one night towards the end of my third week there I had lain in the dark and been assaulted by an unclassifiable clattering: sticks drawn fast across iron palings, the flourish of drums at a hanging, a cloudburst of hailstones smashing on the nearby gutters. The racket had broken off as suddenly as it had begun.

Then dawn. A wash of pale grey touched the corners of my room while the streetlamp burned on beneath the louvred window throwing thin orange stripes across the ceiling. It began again. Downfalls of boreal showers, I decided, driven south off the limestone mesa by winter gusts out of Pannonia and Scythia. I curled up and dreamed myself in a seaport refreshed and gleaming with rain.

But rising later I saw from the bathroom window the *città vecchia* below still unwashed, dry in its untroubled dust. Gradually I heard the soft persistent squabble-squabble of the earliest risers, those pigeons of terra firma in their thousands in the eaves above my head.

Later still, an hour before the breakfast knock, the clattering renewed. It was the pigeons' risings that I heard, their fluster and great inexplicable shrugs and resettlings on the tin gutters and flashings of the hotel. After that came the human bells, the crash of the *saracinesche* drawn up in the shop below (cherished word: metal blinds against break-in), the clack of wooden clogs in the narrow street, the first exchanges of the day in the dialect I never mastered.

In Trieste, immersed in my ghostly business, I never dreamed of listening or looking for the seagulls. In Venice a few days later, prompted by their strange, temporary absence from the passing scene, I remembered my time in Trieste. I could not recall actually *not* seeing gulls there. Nor, more disturbing to me, could I recall seeing them. A hundred miles away on the shores of the same grey sea, the matter of seagulls had simply never come up.

And, since I had gone to Trieste in the first place to find my business—which required me to be especially sensitive, to be one on whom nothing is lost, to see and to hear everything—I felt both chagrined and annoyed. As if I had been rebuked, perhaps unfairly.

"Pour 'Trouver Trieste,' s'il vous plait?" It is hard to know what to answer. A friend of mine remembers Trieste mainly because he had a nosebleed there, in the lobby of the Hotel Jolly of all places. The child of another cut its hand on the point of the nail scissors in her purse while they waited in the station for the Zagreb train. Unlucky.

Farewell to Trieste—triste Trst, or *Triest* as the Austrians say, far-off Tergeste on her coast of curving salt—farewell to Trieste with mixed feelings. I leave it, three weeks plus sixty months later, much as I found it. An inconclusive encounter.

At home, reading again, I discovered in Svevo that there are indeed seagulls in Trieste, or were anyway in 1892. They uttered little cries from tiny heads and looked lonely. Their great white wings outstretched, they wheeled above the crowded port intent on fish alone. No need of many brains with such big wings, such appetites. Instinctual life mocks bookishness wrote Svevo in his first book.

At home I read that *sua mare grega* is indeed *triestino:* "his Greek mother" literally, but more precisely "his whore of a mother" in the dialect. *Ulysses, or* . . . Joyce had had his Penelope in mind, Molly Bloom, both slut and mothering consort. (Nevertheless, for much of my time there, the sea had been grey indeed.)

And at home I learned at last the nature of my business there. Not *Literary Trieste,* although there are good grounds for the belief in it. Not, certainly, *Upon a Grey Sea,* for this is a partial picture that leaves out the fata morgana and visions of azure, the radiant walk from the station. Better because truer: *My Three Weeks in Trieste.*

But a ghost story with, if you finish it, a happy ending. Or a ghost's story with, at the end, a happy turn of phrase . . .

A Ghost in Trieste.

Appendixes

Translations

1. Nine Trieste poems from the *Canzoniere* of Umberto Saba
2. Two passages from Scipio Slataper, *Il mio Carso*
3. Ettore Schmitz, "Cronaca della famiglia"(Family chronicle)
4. Two Trieste poems by James Joyce, with Italian translations by Eugenio Montale

Nine Trieste Poems from the *Canzoniere* of Umberto Saba

Città Vecchia

Spesso, per ritornare alla mia casa
prendo un'oscura via di città vecchia.
Giallo in qualche pozzanghera si specchia
qualche fanale, e affollata è la strada.

Qui tra la gente che viene che va
dall'osteria alla casa o al lupanare,
dove son merci ed uomini il detrito
di un gran porto di mare,
io ritrovo, passando, l'infinito
nell'umiltà.
Qui prostituta e marinaio, il vecchio
che bestemmia, la femmina che bega,
il dragone che siede alla bottega
del friggitore,
la tumultuante giovane impazzita
d'amore,
sono tutte creature della vita
e del dolore;
s'agita in esse, come in me, il Signore.

Qui degli umili sento in compagnia
il mio pensiero farsi
più puro dove più turpe è la via.

(1911)

Old Town

Often, homeward bound, I choose
a dark way through the Old Town.
Puddles mirror yellow lamps
and the streets are packed.

Here amidst those who come and go
from bar to home or brothel,
where wares and men are flotsam
of a great seaport,
I pass, and find again the infinite
in lowliness.
Here whore and sailor, the old man
cursing, the railing female,
the trooper seated at the fish-fry
counter,
the reckless girl made mad
by love,
all, all are creatures of life
and of sorrow;
there stirs in them all, as in me, the Lord.

Here in lowly company
I feel my thought grow purer where
more foul is the way.

(1911)

Tre Vie

C'è a Trieste una via dove mi specchio
nei lunghi giorni di chiusa tristezza:
si chiama Via del Lazzaretto Vecchio.
Tra case come ospizi antiche uguali,
ha una nota, una sola, d'allegrezza:
il mare in fondo alle sue laterali.
Odorata di droghe e di catrame
dai magazzini desolati a fronte,
fa commercio di reti, di cordame
per le navi: un negozio ha per insegna
una bandiera; nell'interno, volte
contro il passante, che raro le degna
d'uno sguardo, coi volti esangui e proni
sui colori di tutte le nazioni,
le lavoranti scontano la pena
della vita: innocenti prigioniere
cuciono tetre le allegre bandiere.

A Trieste ove son tristezze molte,
e bellezze di cielo e di contrada,
c'è un'erta che si chiama Via del Monte.
Incomincia con una sinagoga,
e termina ad un chiostro; a mezza strada
ha una cappella; indi la nera foga
della vita scoprire puoi da un prato,
e il mare con le navi e il promontorio,
e la folla e le tende del mercato.
Pure, a fianco dell'erta, è un camposanto
abbandonato, ove nessun mortorio

Three Streets

In Trieste there is a street that mirrors me
in my long days of sealed sorrow:
it is the street called Lazaretto Vecchio.
Its buildings all alike as ancient almshouses,
it has one note—one only—of gaiety:
the sea you see beyond its narrow alleys.
Smelling of spices and tar
from the dreary storerooms nearby
it does a trade in fishnets, in ships'
tackle. One shop has for its sign
a flag; inside, facing towards
the passerby who rarely deigns
a glance, their faces worn and sunken
above the colors of every country,
workers work out the pain
of living: innocent prisoners
sewing in gloom gay flags.

In Trieste where there are many sorrows
and much loveliness of street and sky,
there is a hillside street called Via del Monte.
It begins with a synagogue
and ends with a cloister; halfway up
there is a chapel with a field
where you can view life's dark passion,
and the sea with its ships, and the promontory,
and the crowds, and the marketplace awnings.
On one flank of the hill there is also
an abandoned graveyard where no funeral comes,

entra, non si sotterra più, per quanto
io mi ricordi: il vecchio cimitero
degli ebrei, così caro al mio pensiero,
se vi penso i miei vecchi, dopo tanto
penare e mercatare, là sepolti,
simili tutti d'animo e di volti.

Via del Monte è la via dei santi affetti,
ma la via della gioa e dell'amore
è sempre Via Domenico Rossetti.
Questa verde contrada suburbana,
che perde dì per dì del suo colore,
che è sempre più città, meno campagna,
serba il fascino ancora dei suoi belli
anni, delle sue prime ville sperse,
dei suoi radi filari d'alberelli.
Chi la passeggia in queste ultime sere
d'estate, quando tutte sono aperte
le finestre, e ciascuna è un belvedere,
dove agucchiando o leggendo si aspetta,
pensa che forse qui la sua diletta
rifiorirebbe all'antico piacere
di vivere, di amare lui, lui solo;
e a più rosea salute il suo figliolo.

(1911)

where, within my memory, no one
has been buried: the old cemetery
of the Jews, dear to my thought
when I think of my old ones, after such
suffering and bargaining, so alike
in face and soul, there buried.

Via del Monte is the street of holy affections,
but the street of joy and love
is forever Via Domenico Rossetti.
This green suburban street
which loses day by day its color
—always more city, less of country—
still keeps the charm of its loveliest
years, of its first scattered villas,
of its slender rows of trees.
Who walks upon it in these last summer
evenings, when the windows all are open
and each house seems a belvedere
where, sewing or reading, someone waits,
must think that here perhaps his heart's delight
might once more flower in her ancient love
of life, her love for him and him alone;
and in her child revive a rosier health.

(1911)

Via della Pietà

Accennava all'aspetto una sventura,
sì lunga e stretta come una barella.
Hanno abbattute le sue vecchie mura,
e di qualche ippocàstano si abbella.

Ma ancor di sé l'attrista l'ospedale,
che qui le sue finestre apre e la porta,
dove per visitar le gente morta
preme il volgo perverso; e come fuori
dei teatri carrozze in riga nera,
sempre fermo ci vedo un funerale.
Cerei sinistri odori
escon dalla cappella; e se non posso
rattristarmi, pensare il giorno estremo,
l'eterno addio alle cose di cui temo
perdere sola un'ora, è perché il rosso
d'una cresta si muove fra un po' d'erba,
cresciuta lungo gli arboscelli in breve
zolla: quel rosso in me speranza e fede
ravviva, come in campo una bandiera.

La gallinella che ancora qui si duole,
e raspa presso alla porta funesta,
mi fa vedere dietro la sua cresta
tutta una fattoria piena di sole.

(1911)

Via della Pietà

As long and narrow as a stretcher
it has always suggested hard luck.
Now they've broken down its old walls
and planted chestnut trees to make it pretty.

Yet still the hospital saddens it
whose doors and windows open on this street,
where still a stubborn crowd pays call
upon the dead, and, like a black line
of carriages queued outside some theater,
a funeral seems forever fixed.
Waxy, sickish odors
escape from the chapel; and if I cannot
sink back into my sorrow, or think again
of my last hour or my eternal farewell
to those things I fear to lose
if only for an hour, it is because
that red comb is moving in a tuft of grass
which grows upon a mound beneath a chestnut tree:
that small red crest which quickens in me hope
and faith, like a banner on a battlefield.

That little hen that suffers there,
that by the grim door scratches on the earth,
empowers my eye beyond its tiny comb:
I see a farmyard, fair, and bathed with sun.

(1911)

Il Molo

Per me al mondo non v'ha un più caro e fido
luogo di questo. Dove mai più solo
mi sento e in buona compagnia che al molo
San Carlo, e più mi piace l'onda e il lido?

Vedo navi il cui nome è già un ricordo
d'infanzia. Come allor torbidi e fiacchi
—forse aspettando dell'imbarco l'ora—
i garzoni s'aggirano; quei sacchi
su quella tolda, quelle casse a bordo
di quel veliero, eran principio un giorno
di gran ricchezze, onde stupita avrei
l'accolta folla a un lieto mio ritorno,
di bei doni donati i fidi miei.
Non per tale un ritorno or lascerei
molo San Carlo, quest'estrema sponda
d'Italia, ove la vita è ancora guerra;
non so, fuori di lei, pensar gioconda
l'opera, i giorni miei quasi felici,
così ben profondate ho le radici
nella mia terra.

Né a te dispiaccia, amica mia, se amore
reco pur tanto al luogo ove son nato.
Sai che un più vario, un più movimentato
porto di questo è solo il nostro cuore.

(1912)

Molo San Carlo

No place on earth is dearer and more my very own
than this. Where should I be more alone,
where in better company, than Molo San Carlo?
Where, for me, a sea and shore more lovable?

Here I see ships whose very names recall
my childhood. Then as now,—sweaty, tired
perhaps awaiting the hour to weigh anchor—
those sailors loitered. Those sacks upon that deck,
those crates aboard that great three-master,
these once upon a time were treasure trove
with which I might amaze my faithful ones
gathered in joy the day of my return.
Not now for any such return shall I depart
Molo San Carlo, this final shore of Italy,
where life is conflict still.
Where else could I take joy in my life's work,
or dream my daily life was almost happy?
So deep-struck are my roots
in my place.

(Lina, beloved, do not be hurt
if so much love I bear where I was born.
We know there hammers in the heart
a stranger and more agitated port.)

(1912)

L'Osteria "All'isoletta"

La notte, per placare un'aspra rissa,
e più feroce quanto è solo interna,
penso lotte più estranee: penso Lissa,

i Bàlcani, Trieste, il vecchio ghetto;
infine mi rifugio a una taverna;
dal suo solo ricordo il sonno aspetto.

Deserta com'è lungo il caldo giorno,
sulle pareti un'isoletta è pinta,
verde smeraldo, e il mar con pesci ha intorno.

Ma di fumi e di canti a notte è piena;
un dalmata ha con sé la più discinta;
ritrova il marinaio la sirena.

Io ascolto, e godo della compagnia,
godo di non pensare a un paradiso,
diverso troppo da quest'allegria,

che arrochisce nei cori e infiamma il viso.

(Bologna, 1913)

The Tavern of the Desert Isle

Nighttimes, to assuage a bitter quarrel
—inner, and thereby all the more ferocious—
I think of other, outer battles: I think of Lissa,

of the Balkans, of Trieste and its old ghetto;
finally my mind takes refuge in a tavern
from whose memory alone sweet sleep should come.

Vacant all the long hot afternoons,
someone has painted on its walls a desert isle
green as an emerald, adrift in a fishy sea.

At nights the place is full of smoke and song:
a Dalmatian hugs his all but naked girl,
a sailor here can claim his promised siren.

I listen, and take my joy in such rough trade,
mercifully unable to conjure any paradise
much different from this sort of happiness

where choruses grow hoarse and faces redden.

(Bologna, 1913)

Caffè Tergeste

Caffè Tergeste, ai tuoi tavoli bianchi
ripete l'ubbriaco il suo delirio;
ed io ci scrivo i miei più allegri canti.

Caffè di ladri, di baldracche covo,
io soffersi ai tuoi tavoli il martirio,
lo soffersi a formarmi un cuore nuovo.

Pensavo: Quando bene avrò goduto
la morte, il nulla che in lei mi predico,
che mi ripagherà d'esser vissuto?

Di vantarmi magnanimo non oso;
ma, se il nascere è un fallo, io al mio nemico
sarei, per maggior colpa, più pietoso.

Caffè di plebe, dove un dì celavo
la mia faccia, con goia oggi ti guardo.
E tu concili l'italo e lo slavo,

a tarda notte, lungo il tuo bigliardo.

(Bologna, 1914)

Caffè Tergeste

Caffè Tergeste, at your white-clothed tables
the drunk insists on his delirium,
and here I write my gayest songs.

Caffè of thieves and harlots' nest,
at your tables I have suffered martyrdom,
suffered it to make my heart anew.

I have thought: when at last I shall have tasted
death—or that nothingness I anticipate is death—
what will repay me for having lived?

I do not dare to call myself great-hearted
but if to be born at all is a transgression
I shall act, for all my sins, great-heartedly.

Caffè of my people, where once I hid my face
in cupped hands, today with joy I see you.
In the dark hours, above your billiard tables,

you reconcile Italian and Slav.

(Bologna, 1914)

Mezzogiorno d'Inverno

In quel momento ch'ero già felice
(Dio mi perdoni la parola grande
e tremenda) chi quasi al pianto spinse
mia breve gioa? Voi direte: «Certa
bella creatura che di là passava,
e ti sorrise». Un palloncino invece,
un turchino vagante palloncino
nell'azzurro dell'aria, ed il nativo
cielo non mai come nel chiaro e freddo
mezzogiorno d'inverno risplendente.
Cielo con qualche nuvoletta bianca,
e i vetri delle case al sol fiammanti,
e il fumo tenue d'uno due camini,
e su tutte le cose, le divine
cose, quel globo dalla mano incauta
d'un fanciullo sfuggito (egli piangeva
certo in mezzo alla folla il suo dolore,
il suo grande dolore) tra il Palazzo
della Borsa e il Caffè dove seduto
oltre i vetri ammiravo io con lucenti
occhi or salire or scendere il suo bene.

(1919)

Winter Noon

Once upon a time when I was happy
(may God forgive that great and fearsome word!)
what was it turned nearly to tears
my fragile joy? "Some lovely thing who smiled,"
you'd say, "as she was passing by . . ."
and you'd be wrong. It was a toy balloon,
a bright and bluish-green balloon adrift
in the azure air, the sky of home
never so brilliant as in that clear, cold
winter noon. It was the sky
with a small white cloud or two, the sun
setting the windowpanes on fire, the thread
of smoke from several chimneys and, over all,
over every blessed thing, it was that globe
fled upward from some child's careless hand
(surely sobbing out his grief, his matchless grief)
somewhere in the crowd between Palazzo Borsa
and my caffè while I sat staring,
tracking out the window with my shining eyes
the soar and dip of all his heart's desire.

(1919)

Avevo

Da una burrasca ignobile approdato
a questa casa ospitale, m'affaccio
—liberamente alfine—alla finestra.
Guardo nel cielo nuvole passare,
biancheggiare lo spicchio della luna,

Palazzo Pitti di fronte. E mi volgo
vane antiche domande: Perché, madre,
m'hai messo al mondo? Che ci faccio adesso
che sono vecchio, e tutto s'innova,
che il passato è macerie, che alla prova
impari mi trovai di spaventose
vicende? Viene meno anche la fede
nella morte, che tutto essa risolva.

Avevo il mondo per me; avevo luoghi
del mondo dove mi salvavo. Tanta
luce in quelli ho veduto che, a momenti,
ero una luce io stesso. Ricordi,
tu dei miei giovani amici il più caro,
tu quasi un figlio per me, che non pure
so dove sei, né se più sei, che a volte
prigioniero ti penso nella terra
squallida, in mano al nemico? Vergogna
mi prende allora di quel poco cibo,
dell'ospitale provvisorio tetto.
Tutto mi portò via il fascista abbietto
ed il tedesco lurco.

I Had

Cast up by a brutal storm
into this friendly house, freely at last
I can show myself at the window.
I watch the clouds that pass in the sky,
the whitening crescent moon,

Palazzo Pitti opposite. And I ask myself
the old, impossible questions. Why, mother,
did you give me birth? What shall I do
now I am old, now everything is strange,
now the past is a shambles and I have shown
myself unequal to the test of terrible events?
Even my faith in death, that it solves
everything, has faltered.

I had a world, and in that world I had
my sacred places. And there I found such light
that, for moments, I was a light myself.
Do you remember? you, the dearest
of all my young friends, almost my son,
whose whereabouts I do not know, dead
or a prisoner in that squalid land, in the hands
of the enemy? And now shame fills me
for this crust of bread, this hospitable
and temporary shelter.
All that I had they have taken,
the vile fascist and the swilling german.

Avevo una famiglia, una compagna;
la buona, la meravigliosa Lina.
È viva ancora, ma al riposo inclina
più che i suoi anni impongano. Ed un'ansia
pietà mi prende di vederla ancora,
i non sue case affaccendata, il fuoco
alimentare a scarse legna. D'altri
tempi al ricordo doloroso il cuore
si stringe, come ad un rimorso, in petto.
Tutto mi portò via il fascista abbietto
ed il tedesco lurco.

Avevo una bambina, oggi una donna.
Di me vedevo in lei la miglior parte.
Tempo funesto anche trovava l'arte
di staccarla da me, che la radice
vede in me dei suoi mali, né più l'occhio
mi volge, azzurro, con l'usato affetto.
Tutto mi portò via il fascista abbietto
ed il tedesco lurco.

Avevo una città bella tra i monti
rocciosi e il mare luminoso. Mia
perché vi nacqui, più che d'altri mia
che la scoprivo fanciullo, ed adulto
per sempre a Italia la sposai col canto.
Vivere si doveva. Ed io per tanto
scelsi fra i mali il più degno: fu il piccolo
d'antichi libri raro negozietto.
Tutto mi portò via il fascista inetto
ed il tedesco lurco.

I had a family, a companion:
the good, the marvelous Lina.
She is alive still, but weary
beyond her years. And a troubled
pity fills me now to see her
busy by hearths that are not her own,
feeding a little fire with hard-won wood.
The heart twists in the chest like remorse
at the dolorous memory of other times.
All that I had they have taken,
the vile fascist and the swilling german.

I had a baby girl, today a woman.
Once in her I saw the best part of me.
The dark times have found the way
to take her from me, who must see in me
the root of all her troubles, who cannot turn
her bluest eye on me with her accustomed love.
All that I had they have taken,
the vile fascist and the swilling german.

I had a city, lovely between the rocky
highlands and the shining sea. Mine
because I was born there, more than others'
mine who discovered it as a boy, and as a man
married it to Italy forever with my song.
One cannot live by singing so I chose,
of all burdens, the worthiest: the little shop
of rare and antique books.
All that I had they have taken,
the vile fascist and the swilling german.

Avevo un cimitero ove mia madre
riposa, e i vecchi di mia madre. Bello
come un giardino; e quante volte in quello
mi rifugiavo col pensiero! Oscuri
esigli e lunghi, atre vicende, dubbio
quel giardino mi mostrano e quel letto.
Tutto mi portò via il fascista abbietto
—anche la tomba—ed il tedesco lurco.

(Firenze, 1944)

Tre Poesie a Linuccia

I

Era un piccolo mondo e si teneva
per mano.

Era un mondo difficile, lontano
oggi da noi, che lo lambisce appena,
come un'onda, l'angoscia. Tra la veglia
e il sonno lento a venire, se a tratti,
col suo esatto disegno e i suoi esatti
contorni, un quadro se ne stacca e illumina
la tua memoria, dolce in sé, ti cerca,
come il pugnale d'un nemico, il cuore.

Era un piccolo mondo e il suo furore
ti teneva per mano.

I had a cemetery where my mother rests
and my mother's parents. It was lovely
as a garden, how many times in my thought
I've taken refuge there! But abrupt
exiles and the skein of dark events have shown
how spectral are that garden and that resting place.
All that I had—even the tomb—they have taken,
the vile fascist and the swilling german.

(Florence, 1944)

Three Poems for Linuccia

I

It was a small world and you could clasp it
in your hand.

It was a hard world, very far from us
today, whose loss and longing lap it softly
like a wave. Between the night's long watch
and sleep so slow to come, there comes
in flashes—precise pattern, precise contour—
its image breaking clear and flooding memory
with its sweet light, sweet although it seeks,
like an enemy's blow, your heart.

It was a small world and its fury
could clasp you by the hand.

2

In fondo all'Adriatico selvaggio
si apriva un porto alla tua infanzia. Navi
verso lontano partivano. Bianco,
in cima al verde sovrastante colle,
dagli spalti d'antico forte, un fumo
usciva dopo un lampo e un rombo. Immenso
l'accoglieva l'azzurro, lo sperdeva
nella volta celeste. Rispondeva
guerriera nave al saluto, ancorata
al largo della tua casa che aveva
in capo al molo una rosa, la rosa
dei venti.

Era un piccolo porto, era una porta
aperta ai sogni.

3

Da quei sogni e da quel furore tutto
quello ch'ài guadagnato, ch'ài perduto,
il tuo male e il tuo bene, t'è venuto.

(Milano, 1946)

2

At the top of the wild Adriatic
a port flowered to your innocence. Ships
steamed for the distances. White
at the tip of green San Giusto hill,
from the parapet of the old fort, a puff
of smoke would follow the flash and bang
to be gathered into the blue immense,
dissolving into arching heaven. From the gulf
below the window where you watched,
the anchored warship would salute
back, back to where the pier proffered
its bouquet, a wind rose.

It was a small port, a door open
to your dreams.

3

From those dreams and from that fury, all
you've won and lost, all that's bad, all that's good,
everything has come to you.

(Milan, 1946)

Two Passages from Scipio Slataper, *Il mio Carso*

1. Overture

I would like to tell you I was born on carso, in a hovel with a thatched roof black-
ened by rain and smoke. There was a mangy cur barking hoarsely, beneath its
belly two muddy geese, a hoe, a spade, and from the nearly fodderless dungheap
oozed, after rainfall, rivulets of brownish juice.

I would like to tell you I was born in Croatia, in the great oak forest. In
winter everything was white with snow, the door could be opened only a crack
and I heard the wolves howl at nighttime. Mama wrapped my swollen reddened
hands with rags and I flung myself down by fireside whimpering with cold.

I would like to tell you I was born on the Moravian plain and I ran like a
hare up the long furrows, scaring off the cawing crows. I threw myself belly first
on the ground, I tore up a beetroot and gnawed on its earthiness. Then I came
here, I have tried to domesticate myself, I have learned Italian, I have chosen my
friends from among the best educated of the young—but soon I must return to
my country because I am very unwell here.

I would like to fool you, but you would not believe me. You are cunning
and wise. You would quickly understand that I am a poor Italian trying to make
his solitary preoccupations seem primitive. It is best if I confess that I am your
brother, even if sometimes I watch you, daydreaming and far away from you,
and I feel myself timid before your culture and your reasoning. Perhaps I am
afraid of you. Your objections little by little shut me up in a cage while I listen to
you impartial and content and do not notice how you are enjoying your intellectual bravura. And then I get red and tongue-tied at my end of the table, and I
think of the consolation of the great trees that are open to the wind. I avidly think
of the sun upon the hills, of the rich freedom of life up there, of my true friends

who love me and recognized me with a clasp of the hand, calm laughter welling up. They are strong and good.

I think of my faraway and unknown origins, of my ancestors plowing the endless field with the harrow drawn by four spotted nags, or stooping in their leather aprons above the boilers of molten glass; of my enterprising forebear who came down into Trieste in the epoch of the *portofranco;* of the great green-stained house there where I was born, where our grandmother, hardened by sorrow, lives still . . .

2. Descent from the Carso into Trieste's Old Town†

I swing around abruptly. Mount Kâl [Monte Calvo, "Bald Mountain," due east of Trieste] is up *there*. Why have you come down here?

Very well, now you are here. And here you must live. I thump my chest with my hands to feel if my body is here; and it is, it resists. I mean to enter the lowest tavern in the Old Town.

Smoke and stink . . . I'm suffocating. But I light my pipe, I smoke in the smoke, I spit.—Waiter! a half quart of *petess.*—I can drink grappa too if the others drink it, and this glass must be clean if the others can touch their lips there and swill. (On the rim of this glass may be, quite invisible, my lifelong agony.) But I drink. And I raise my eyes to my companions.

A coal heaver, head growing out of his left shoulder like an enormous tu-

---

†(see Saba, "Old Town," "The Tavern of the Desert Isle," "Caffè Tergeste")

mor, spits up black gobs. A woman with thick hairs sprouting above her lip, spotted with powder, cleans her mouth with her fat fingers. Under the table the cold-eyed man in shirtsleeves opposite shoves his knee between her legs. In the padrona's black and greasy hair a wen glints rosy in the gaslight. I watch it through the wet bottom of my glass.

—Waiter! another half quart!—And I beat with my fist upon the shaky table. They look at me and go on with their talk.

Beside me two figures, coats flung over their blue-shirted shoulders, discuss the theft of a tin jug. The others carouse and sing. Good. Nothing is strange here, every thing as hard and defined as the carso's edges. If I slam my fist into the face of that porter he'll give me two fists back. If I deliver a little lecture on morals to that whore there, she'll pat her little ass in answer. I am among thieves and assassins. But if I leap up on this table and if Christ fill me with the word I destroy the world and them and then rebuild it.

This is my city. I am well here.

The occasion for this tender scrutiny (and portrait of Livia as embodiment of "perfect moral health") is the photograph above, taken on the Schmitzes' first wedding anniversary. The young author of *Senilità* wrote it to accompany the picture, and sent it to his wife two weeks later, calling it "Family Chronicle."

Ettore Schmitz, from "Cronaca della famiglia"
(Family Chronicle)

Even though it doesn't show in this photograph, there is a baby in it. The balustrade is there for its comfort: that was the photographer's grand idea. Naturally, if the balustrade were removed the baby would still be quietly there all the same and the photographer would have had no trouble at all in photographing it. Although in that case the lady carrying the baby would have appeared as she really is and not so youthfully symmetrical as her face leads one to suppose.

So the baby has been photographed while still deprived of a name. We call it Letizia or Francesco [Letizia = Joy, in honor of the writer's mother Allegra. His father was Francesco. The baby, an only child, turned out to be Letizia.] and we still don't know which we prefer because we are resolved to prefer whichever name comes. I should have liked to look at it by means of that Roentgen ray, which has just been invented, but its mother refused to lend herself to that sort of photograph and I have had to content myself with this very imperfect one . . .

The distinctly blond lady who has the honor of being photographed at my side is named Livia Fausta Veneziani and she has been my wife for precisely one year. I must confess that she amazes me. She takes everything seriously: her cook Maria, her husband, life itself. Her cook Maria . . . is not in the photograph, not even behind the balustrade. But even after a year my wife takes everything seriously, her husband—the father of her children after all!—in particular. In fact she takes every degree of relationship seriously. The mother is she to whom we owe our lives, the father *idem* and beyond that is the lord and master of the mama and of all he surveys. She has no doubts whatever on this score though I believe that in this matter she has not yet heard of the French Revolution and that if a *lettre de cachet* [i.e., an order for incarceration under the King's private seal] came for her from the patriarchal authorities and countersigned by the King himself, she

would not be so very indignant. It was the King, after all! What an honor to be
shut up in prison by order of the King! She is always the first to bow to the head
of the commune or the bishop of the diocese and if these do not bow back it
makes no difference because one bows to authority and those who represent authority have no further duty to us than to represent it. Thus the world is a beautiful ideological construct in which everyone has his or her place to occupy and
owes respect to every other place. As a sociologist my wife is not an evolutionist
because for her it is in the nature of things that people change but the places remain. The places exist from eternity and people are born to occupy them.

This said, one can see that my wife takes even life itself very seriously indeed. She occupies her places one after the other with great seriousness. I think
that even as a baby she must have had a certain dignity. It goes without saying
that the task of a baby was to suckle, to cry at night, and to get ill. Her real duties
came later and as far as I know she learned very young the distinction between
clothes worn at home and clothes worn in town and that one should not show
oneself even at the garden gate in house clothes nor delay changing out of one's
town clothes the second one returns home.

In truth I think that this serious life has been exactly divided into various
periods each of which has its particular joys and sorrows. Thus when she sees
someone younger than she is she immediately recalls how she was in that period
and from this there results a supremely pleasurable sense of justice. She too at
that age had the pleasure of disputing the wishes no matter how just of whoever
commanded her, of breaking things to see how they worked, of jumping or
dancing or shouting. For my part I do not remember ever having been irrational
or, at least, if I were irrational, considering myself each day as a newborn animal,
I would never dream of recollecting and justifying my past lapses. That newborn
animal ought to have been punished then and those contemporaries of mine who
were irrational I would like to punish myself.

"When I was like that . . ." she says, often and never regretfully. Another
thing I do not understand is this lack of regret for the past. I have to think that she
accepts the justice of the present to such a degree as to be able to place it, without

excessive emotion, alongside the past and to look at them both as equivalents. It seems an indifference but instead I perceive that it is an absolute, inexplicable *joie de vivre*. At times I am filled with fear to watch her enjoying the things that exist about her or, even more, the things she possesses. What a capacity for happiness and unhappiness! For me the eternal doubt not only as to whether I do or do not exist but also as to what is yours and what is mine results in such a mortal indifference that whatever might befall me could sadden me or irritate me or even make me cry but never amaze me! At bottom, what is there to be amazed about? Stones rain down from the stars above, if we pierce the earth's crust we find there is fire below, the entire human race might be converted so that it consisted of saints or of assassins, and we would know it could happen in this way because some part of life has always been like this. She, on the other hand, hears every day of new things that amaze her and make her pensive. No *doubts,* of course! there is no place for them. Her prayers at the usual hour will be listened to on high, often they are not granted but after all we humans can be conscious of having done what was necessary and can remain unperturbed.

Each fashioned in this way, we have remained together; this must be the most amazing thing of all! Allow me to go further. I, made for rebellion, for indifference, for corruption, forever hankering after what might be and never respectful of what is, married in the conviction that we were in process of making an utterly novel sociological experiment, the union of two equal beings bound by an attraction that might be only momentary, a union from which jealousy would be banished by science (that is, a certain resignation to things as they are and to existing feelings), a union that imposed no change upon either of the two since fundamentally to remain together there was no need at all to resemble one another. I married certain that if one of us changed it would not be me! In fact I wished to change my wife a bit in the sense of giving her her freedom and teaching her to know herself. I assembled some books by Schopenhauer, Marx and Bebel [founder of the German Social-Democratic party and author of *Women and Socialism*], meaning not to impose them but to insinuate them little by little. We discussed my ideas only once and that apropos of Heine. Hard luck on that romantic poet whom once upon a time I had proclaimed to be my God! After that one time my ideas were left to be alone with me. Most astutely, most sweetly, she politicly avoided upsetting me by talking to me about them. For this bourgeois creature the essential thing is to live with everyone in decent peacefulness and to keep one's own ideas in one's own small head defended by such thick hair: it is not important to convince others of them. Everyone after all is the apostle of some idea or other, or of nothing!

I have to agree with her on this point and so saying I am not sure whether I feel admiration or anger. She may not care to convince anyone but my household seems to be more hers than mine. In it there is a high orderliness, as well as some beautiful object or other of which she is inordinately proud and I too, naturally, with her. Sometimes a sacrifice must be made in order to attain some other object of which she feels the need or else in order to substitute it for something else which fulfills its function very well indeed but is less than beautiful. I give my consent but sometimes I do worse than that—I discuss the matter and refuse. Several days ago she had an exquisite idea: she spoke of introducing gas stoves into the household. It is important to realize that where we live the cost of gas makes it seem as if it were extracted from gold rather than coal. I recalled the maxims of the prudent householder and refused to give my consent. Undoubtedly there is great pleasure in refusing something and doing it in the style of the lord and master and I was overwhelmingly amazed to note that my refusal, done to carry out an interesting experiment, was being taken seriously. Consequently I experienced some doubt and now as lord and master I am pondering whether it might not be opportune to introduce gas stoves into the household. Here I am, therefore, truly lord and master.

All in all my wife, my mother-in-law and my father-in-law and all my cousins male and female tell me that I am a good husband. The worst of it is that when they tell me so I don't get angry.

(*Epistolario,* pp. 65–69; August 12, 1897)

Two Trieste Poems by James Joyce with Italian Translations by
Eugenio Montale

1. *Watching the Needleboats at San Sabba*

I heard their young hearts crying
Loveward above the glancing oar
And heard the prairie grasses sighing:
No more, return no more!

O hearts, O sighing grasses,
Vainly your loveblown bannerets mourn!
No more will the wild wind that passes
Return, no more return.

September 7, 1913
Pomes Penyeach

San Sabba is in south Trieste and today is part of the industrial section of the port. It is chiefly famous for being the site of the only death camp in Italy, operated by the SS from 1943 to 1945. The refrain line echoes Puccini, *La fanciulla dell'ovest*. Needleboats are racing shells; that day Joyce's brother Stanislaus was in one of them.

1. Guardando i canottieri di San Sabba

Ho udito quei giovani cuori gridare
spinti da Amore sul guizzante remo,
l'erbe dei prati ho udito sospirare
     non torna, non torna più!

O cuori, o erbe anelanti, invano gemono
gonfiate dall'amore le vostre bandierine!
Mai più il vento gagliardo che trascorre
vi tornerà vicino.

Quaderno di traduzioni
(Montale, *L'opera in versi*, p. 729)

2. A Flower Given to My Daughter

Frail the white rose and frail are
Her hands that gave
Whose soul is sere and paler
Than time's wan wave.

Rosefrail and fair—yet frailest
A wonder wild
In gentle eyes thou veilest,
My blueveined child.

1913
Pomes Penyeach

From *Giacomo Joyce:* "A flower given by her to my daughter. Frail gift, frail giver, frail blue-veined child." The giver was one of Joyce's students, Amalia Popper, to whom for a while he felt himself in amorous thrall. *Giacomo Joyce* is his suave, gnomic account of this relationship.

2. Per un fiore dato alla mia bambina

Gracile rosa bianca e frali dita
di chi l'offerse, di lei
che had l'anima più pallida e appassita
dell'onda scialba del tempo.

Fragile e bella come rosa, e ancora
più fragile la strana meraviglia
che veli ne' tuoi occhi, o mia azzurro-
venata figlia.

Quaderno di traduzioni
(Montale, *L'opera in versi,* p. 730)

A Directory of Characters

Roberto ("Bobi") Bazlen (1902–65)

Bazlen's friend and admirer Montale describes him as "a man whom it pleased to live in the interstices of culture and history, exercising his influence upon those who could understand him but forever refusing the limelight." An enigma to those of us who can only read of him—what is one to make of his addiction to the sub rosa? of his obsessed reclusiveness?—Bazlen was born in Trieste of mixed parentage: a German (Lutheran) father who died the year following his birth and an Italian (Jewish) mother. He was raised by an adoring circle of "three mothers"—his own plus two aunts—and, after several years' attendance at German-language schools in town, was left free to conduct his own education at home and in the Biblioteca Civica. The result was formidable. By the age of eighteen he was well known in Triestine intellectual circles for his precocious knowledge of literature and modern philosophy as well as for his raking irony towards all established tastes and pieties.

In 1923, on the first of his many "flights" from his native city (he left for good in 1939), Bazlen took a job with Shell Oil in Genoa and there met the slightly older Montale, who remembered him forever after as a mentor, "for me a window thrown open on a new world." It was Bazlen who first spoke to Montale of Italo Svevo (as well as of Kafka and Musil and Central European literature in general), and who directed the bursting of *la bomba Svevo* in the fall of 1925. Montale's passion for the city of Trieste and its literature is directly attributable to his friendship with the much more skeptical Bazlen, who never believed in the existence of a Triestine "creative culture."

Perhaps inevitably, the intellectually voracious Bazlen was an early Freudian (psychoanalyzed for a time, like Saba, by Dr. Edoardo Weiss [see entry on Freud]); later his needs and appetite for the esoteric led him to studies in Jung and Gurdjieff, gnosticism and Zen. His favored persona seems to have been that of the sardonic *flâneur,* brother to Oblomov. Asked once by Montale for help in founding a review, he replied, "Are you mad? I am someone who passes almost all his time in bed, smoking and reading, who every so often goes out to pay a visit or to go to the movies. Above all I lack the didact's messianic spirit and have never felt the need of sharing my ideas with others, let alone with readers of reviews." The strain of arrogance mingled with the acedia is clear enough.

Bazlen earned his always solitary living as a reader for publishers in Rome and Milan; the backlist of his own publishing venture (Biblioteca Adelphi, Milan) shows the extraordinary range of his vanguard tastes and interests. His own sparse writings—reader's reports to Einaudi and Adelphi, letters to Montale, drafts and fragments of a novel in German on the Ulysses theme—were published by Adelphi in memoriam after his death. (Surely he would have hated this breach of privacy.) Once in a note to himself he wrote: "I believe that it is no longer possible to write books. Almost all books are really footnotes puffed out into volumes. . . . I only write footnotes." But whatever the gestalt or phase of "postmodernity" he perceived he lived in, the record shows that he tried to write a book and then stopped; upon what grounds—block or blankness or fear of failure or philosopher's decision—remains unknown. Yet there is an aura of sadness about the gifted, restless, probably tormented, Bobi Bazlen.

(Daniele Del Giudice has written a novel *about* him, or about the mystery of his "silence." It is called *Lo stadio di Wimbledon* [Wimbledon Stadium]).

Silvio Benco (1874–1949)

Surely "witness" is the mot juste for this intelligent, industrious, decent, generous man whose assembled articles and books add up to the best possible guide to historical and literary Trieste during the first half of this century. Called "our strongest writer" in 1909 by the very competitive Slataper, Benco is now remembered mainly as a superb journalist and essayist on the arts—music and painting as well as literature. From 1890 to 1903 he was editor of the irredentist *Indipendente;* from 1903 to 1945 (with time out for wars) of the *Piccolo*. His liberal political views frequently made him persona non grata with the authorities during his long writing life, whether in Franz Josef's time or in Mussolini's.

Benco knew everybody, and wrote about what he knew with insight and clarity. His early book-length essay on Trieste is of permanent value to anyone interested in that city. If his first two novels are classifiably D'Annunzian in manner (Benco wrongly believed that Joyce laughed at them, but Joyce was disposed to admire exercises in that exotic vein), the third and last remains an original and unduly neglected piece of work—a psychological study of a young woman's erotic obsession with a run-of-the-mill libertine. (It takes place in Milan.) His three-volume, firsthand account of the final years of Austro-Hungarian rule in Trieste from the time of Sarajevo to the climactic mooring of the torpedo boat *Audace* is an extraordinary feat of reportage. As Montale later commented, its narrator "knew how to vanish into the events narrated with the profound humility of a medieval chronicler." Such modesty is also evident in Benco's last testament, the *Contemplazione del disordine* [Contemplation of disorder] written at the close of World War II, in which he meditates upon the accelerating entropy of the Europe he has observed over his long lifetime. Although the book is in fact a deeply personal act of witness, the author appears in person only in the preface, where he relates how he came to write it as a search for pattern or meaning in a time of heightening violence.

His daughter's memory of a scene from her childhood, watching her father at table with the joking Joyce and his fantastical Berlitz colleague Alessandro Francini Bruni, seems to me to evoke something of the good man's *coscienza:*

> His blue eyes danced with pleasure, and now and then he uttered some pungent remark. But not even during this happy meeting with two friends could Benco renounce the *apartheid* typical of his temperament. It would be too easy to define it as simple shyness. If it was indeed timidity, it must also be considered a principle of his austere way of living: to be aware both of himself and of the world around him—as if a man, by conscious awareness, could preserve intact his dignity as a thinking being . . .

Captain Sir Richard F. Burton, K.C.M.G., F.R.G.S. (1821–90)

This swashbuckling explorer and orientalist died in Trieste, and was British consul there from 1872 until his death. He found the place a backwater inhabited by moneygrubbers. He felt, probably rightly, that his peculiar talents were wasted in Trieste and took pains to live (with his devoted wife the Lady Isabel) as far away from his clientele as possible: up 102 steps to the top floor of Palazzo Economo on the station square, for example, where the Scomparini murals are hidden away today, or up at the Danube Inn across from the Obelisk in Opicina, where, in the 1880s, he made his notorious translation of the *Arabian Nights*.

"John Bull to the bone," Sir Richard characterized himself, "with personal Austrian sympathies, and a strong leaning to all that is of Arab blood." If he found the city squalid and violent, he nevertheless admired its people, at least in the abstract. "It speaks highly for the independent Triestines that, with weak laws, and authorities that act as though they dreaded them, the worst crimes are only stabbing when drunk and suicide; and the latter is entirely owing to the excitability of the climate and the utter throwing off of religion . . ."

Sigmund Freud et al.

Freud (1856–1939) made his first and main personal contact with Trieste in 1876 when he arrived as a medical student with a research grant to do laboratory work in the newly founded marine biology station. His task over several months was to test the truth of an experiment recently conducted there claiming that male eels had testes and were therefore not, as traditionally assumed, hermaphroditic. In the course of this endeavor he dissected some four hundred eels (some "of the tenderer sex") and came to the cautious conclusion, published the next year, that the claim might be valid. Privately he observed that Triestine human males were "small, fat, and excessively bearded" and the females "not beautiful from our German point of view." But the seaside ambiance he found enchanting.

"Triest ist kein Wien," as Gottlob Frege has pointed out—Trieste is no Vienna—but Trieste's geographic and economic proximity to Vienna suggests why it became an early and active center for psychoanalytic activity and the dissemination of Freud's researches into Italy and Mediterranean Europe. (Trieste's own peculiar form of neurosis—its hypochondria, its obsessive self-scrutiny resulting from its vexed political identity and conflicting loyalties, its classically unstable ego—was surely also a factor.) A key figure in Freud's ascendancy in Trieste was Edoardo Weiss (1889–1971), a Triestine who had studied in Vienna under Paul Federn and Freud himself and who practiced in his native city from 1918 until 1931, when he transferred to Rome. (A Jew, Weiss emigrated permanently to the United States in 1939, first to the Menninger Clinic, then opening a private practice in Chicago.)

A cofounder of the Società analitica italiana and the author of an important book on Freudian method (*Elementi di psicanalisi*, 1931), Weiss was on friendly terms with most of the small band of Triestine intellectuals and writers. He numbered Bazlen and, famously, Saba among his patients; it was through his relation with Weiss that Saba came to understand that the absence of a father was at the root of his *dolore*. He dedicated a book of related poems (*Il piccolo Berto*) to his doctor in gratitude.

Svevo and Weiss were related by marriage. At one time it was rumored that Weiss had been parodied as the complacent "Dr. S." whose warning letter opens *La coscienza di Zeno*. Svevo presented his friend with a copy and later ironically reported that he had been disappointed to hear from Weiss that the novel had nothing to do with himself or with Freud. (The historical occasion for Zeno's "confessions" came from Svevo's quizzical attempt at autoanalysis while at loose ends during the war.) Svevo, in fact, was interested in but extremely skeptical about the claims of Freudianism and is only being "svevoesque" when he says he had half expected to receive a telegram from the Master thanking him for having "introduced psychoanalysis into Italian aesthetics." He consoled himself characteristically: "We novelists often play around with great philosophies but are certainly not equipped to clarify them; we falsify but humanize them."

Virgilio Giotti (1885–1957)

Although he was born in Trieste, the young Giotti lived and worked as a sales-man, married, and helped to raise a family in Italy, mainly near Florence; habitu-ally he spoke a very "pure" Tuscan Italian. A friend once asked him why he did not speak the dialect he used in his poems. "What?" he replied, "you want me to use the language of poetry for everyday matters?"

In Giotti's case the language of poetry was primarily *triestino,* although even this was not of an "everyday" or popular variety. Benco describes it as somewhat archaic, a speech sought out and gathered on the outskirts of the rap-idly changing city chiefly from older people, once *contadini* perhaps, who pre-served, in their manners and voices at any rate, something of the past. An idio-syncratic, formal *triestino,* therefore, carefully selected and shaped rather than casually inherited, conservative and even elegiacal in nature. A language fitted perfectly to Giotti's characteristically intense and narrow focus, evoked by Mon-tale as "the most impoverished and most human sense of fireside and family, the lucid intimacy of life reduced to its elemental daily truths: the struggle for bread, the wife, the children, the brief domestic horizon." In the last year of his life, Saba wrote Giotti of how he had attempted in vain to translate a few of his favor-ites into Italian: "Born within you in dialect, it was impossible for me to change or alter a single word."

For over half their lives, Giotti and Saba were close friends and even colleagues: Saba published a volume of Giotti's Italian verse and prose in his Libreria antica e moderna, while Giotti, who was talented as a visual artist, ed-ited and designed two of Saba's books of verse. Towards the end, for reasons that Saba himself called "impalpable," they grew apart and avoided meeting. Possibly Saba's own exacer-

San Giusto Cathedral, as drawn by Virgilio Giotti as trademark for Saba's Libreria antica e moderna

bated sense of being insufficiently "recognized," as well as of Giotti as a rival, had something to do with this. Possibly Giotti's own tragic circumstances—continuing economic insecurity, an ill and mentally deranged wife, two sons killed in the war, a fear of insanity from his father's side of the family, which led him, as a poet, to adopt his mother's maiden name (he had been born Virgilio Schönbeck)—augmented his customary proud reserve to a final self-isolation.

J. Joyce (floruit 1850)

In 1926 Svevo wrote a letter to James Joyce in Paris inquiring if he were related to the J. Joyce who in 1850 had had printed and published by Lloyd Austriaco in Trieste a book entitled *Recollections of Salzkammergut, Ischle, Salzburg, Bad Gastein, with a Sketch of Trieste*. James Joyce's reply is unknown. This is all that is known of the premier J. Joyce in Trieste.

James Joyce (1882–1941)

James and Nora Joyce first arrived in Trieste in 1904 to find that the post he thought had been offered him as a teacher in the Berlitz School of Languages there in fact did not exist. He stayed for ten days, trying to find work and "borrowing left right and centre," and then, thanks to the efforts of the school's director Almidano Artifoni—gratefully remembered in *Ulysses*—went on to Pola, 150 miles south on the Istrian coast, where a new Berlitz branch had just been started. Joyce was not impressed with Pola ("a naval Siberia") nor with Istria ("a long boring place wedged into the Adriatic peopled by ignorant Slavs who wear little red caps and colossal breeches") and was more or less content to return to Trieste in four months when a Berlitz placement opened up. From March 1905 to June 1915, the growing Joyce family (Giorgio born in the first year, Lucia in 1907) occupied eight different flats in and about the town's center. A small world. The first flat, on Via San Nicolò just beside the school, was situated several floors above the antiquarian bookstore owned by Giuseppe Mayländer, publisher of

Benco's *Trieste*. Later the store was bought and run by Umberto Saba, whom Joyce never met.

An amusing account of Joyce's several Berlitz years can be found in his colleague Alessandro Francini Bruni's 1922 pamphlet *Joyce intimo spogliato in piazza* [Joyce stripped bare in public]. In 1907 Joyce quit Berlitz to try to earn his living offering private lessons; Silvio Benco recalls him "running from house to house to give their hour of English to all the Triestines." Among Joyce's pupils were: Niccolò Vidacovich, head of the local literary society (Gabinetto Minerva); Attilio Tamaro, future historian of Trieste; Roberto Prezioso, editor of the *Piccolo della Sera* and admirer—with her husband's approval—of Nora Joyce (as well as model for the perfidious journalist Robert Hand in Joyce's play *Exiles*); Amalia Popper, "virgin most prudent," who figures as the erotic *she* in Joyce's voyeuristic Trieste notebook *Giacomo Joyce;* and, of course, Livia and Ettore Schmitz.

Joyce attempted other ways of raising funds in Trieste. He gave lectures in Italian on Irish topics at Trieste's center for adult education, the Università popolare. He taught part time at the Scuola Superiore di Commercio Revoltella, which was to become, at war's end, the nucleus of the University of Trieste. With three Triestine businessmen he tried to start a movie theater, the Volta, in Dublin. (Svevo wrote Joyce of the failure of this venture that "your surprise at being cheated proves that you are a pure literary man.") He wrote various articles and reviews for the *Piccolo* and in this way met Silvio Benco, who had been asked by Prezioso to vet the Irishman's Italian. "My collaboration didn't last long," Benco recalls. "The day we argued about a word and he, dictionary in hand, was right, it was clear to me that his manuscripts had no need of my inky slashes."

During the war the Joyces moved to Zurich, returning to Trieste for some nine months starting in 1919. But Trieste redeemed was no longer the Trieste he had missed in Zurich. The handwriting was on the wall. As Joyce liked to say, "Now that everyone knows English I shall have to move on" and, anyway, as he wrote to Pound on the eve of his departure in the summer of 1920, *de mortuis nil nisi bonum.*

Joyce wrote a great deal in Trieste: much of the false start *Stephen Hero,* most of *Dubliners*, all of *A Portrait of the Artist as a Young Man, Exiles, Giacomo Joyce,* over half of *Pomes Penyeach,* many of the lectures and reviews now collected in the *Critical Writings,* Italian translations of plays by Yeats and Synge with Vidacovich, as well as drafts of the Telemachaia section of *Ulysses* plus the Nausikaa and Oxen of the Sun episodes. He did not comply with Svevo's request ("When will you write an Italian work about our town? Why not?"). But as Richard Ellmann has shown, there are many Triestine touches—of Svevo most of all—in *Ulysses* and its hero.

Stanislaus Joyce (1884–1955)

The grave of Stanislaus, James's younger brother, lies in the Protestant section of the cemetery of Sant'Anna in Trieste. The inscription reads "Professor" because Stanislaus Joyce held the chair of English at the University of Trieste from 1921 to 1954, when he had to retire at the mandatory age of 70.

He followed his brother to Trieste in 1905 and like him taught at the Berlitz School, branching out later into private lessons. Ant to James's grasshopper (as James liked to say) and far more responsible than Cain (though quite as resentful at times), the exasperated and admiring and dependable Stanislaus was often his brother's keeper and, as Ellmann puts it, spent much of the ten Trieste years from 1905 until James's departure for Zurich in 1915 saving him from "dubious friends, from dissipation, and from the great danger of inertia." Stanislaus himself called it a "long struggle" from which he "retired" when James left Trieste for Paris in 1920.

Stanislaus Joyce spent World War I interned in an Austrian detention center west of Vienna. He married a Triestine in 1927 and had one son, named James. After 1920 he met his brother only three times. His final years were spent writing his invaluable memoir *My Brother's Keeper.* Left incomplete by his death, it covers James Joyce's first twenty-two years, breaking off in 1904 at the start of the Trieste venture.

About the time in Trieste Ellmann writes, "there seems to be no reason to deny that James spent the ten years getting into scrapes and that Stanislaus spent the ten years getting him out of them." Stanislaus himself was more modest. "I functioned as a second work horse in this rugged stretch of his life. He still had the same intemperate habits, and I diligently set about to cure them. I had no illusions that I could influence him; I wanted by some timely effort to straighten the rudder when the ship was heeling over." After his emeritus university lecture, "The Meeting of Svevo and Joyce," in May 1955, he spoke briefly to the librarian Stelio Crise of his work on *My Brother's Keeper:* "Now comes the hard part. One must find an order. I have to see clearly. Above all I must tell the truth. From 1904 to 1915 is the hardest part."

He never lived to write it. (Stanislaus's Trieste diary has never been published.)

Biagio Marin (1891–1985)

Marin came from the lagoon island of Grado, just south of Aquileia and about twenty miles west across the gulf from Trieste. Despite his cosmopolitan higher education (in Florence, where he was associated with the *Voce* group, with the Stuparich brothers, and, above all, with Slataper; in Vienna; and in Rome, where he studied philosophy with Gentile), he elected from the start to be identified with his tiny lido community of fishermen and artisans, connected to the mainland by a bridge only at the end of the last century. He lived most of his life either in Grado or Trieste, working chiefly as director of the Grado baths, as a teacher and librarian. He was a prolific writer of lyric poetry in the restricted language (far more restricted than Giotti's) of his birthplace.

His 1950 preface to his first collected poems offers his own view of his situation and calling.

> The Grado dialect is a Venetic dialect that has remained arrested in its development, so that it might be considered the final remnant of an ancient, almost medieval language. The isolation in which my people have lived for centuries has favored the

conservation of certain of its [syntactical] forms as well as its extreme poverty of lexicon. . . . A world that was, humanly speaking, poor, but of vast horizons of sea and sky. . . . To possess it meant for me to possess the word required to express it; thus the language of my people is fused and confused with that world, in one unique reality.

I knew very well what it would mean to stay within those limits—that little world of fishermen isolated on a small spine of sand between sea and lagoon, but my internal necessity, and my love, permitted me no choice. I shall have been the voice of my island, Grado, nothing less, even at the cost of not being read.

In Italy, at least, Marin has been read. Despite the frequent necessary crutch of a glossary, and an unaccustomed ear, he is considered—with his neighbor Giotti—one of this century's rarest lyric voices.

Carlo Michelstaedter (1887–1910)

Born in Gorizia (his father was an executive in the Assicurazioni Generali offices in nearby Trieste), Michelstaedter studied mathematics in Vienna and Greek philosophy in Florence before killing himself at home at the age of twenty-three, having just completed his doctoral thesis. That thesis, *La persuasione e la rettorica* [Persuasion and rhetoric] is an entirely unacademic essay of Schopenhauerian eloquence and haunting severity on one of literary Trieste's great preoccupations: the nature of—in Svevo's phrase—"perfect moral health." A posteriori and in the light of his thesis, his suicide seems a logical action.

Eugenio Montale (1896–1981)

Although born in Genoa and raised there and on the Ligurian Riviera to the east of that city, Montale liked to consider himself a *triestino* by elective affinity. He arrived there first as a young infantry officer about to be discharged from the Italian army ("with the soul of a pilgrim who had helped . . . to bring her back into the living body of our nation") but it was his friendship with Bobi Bazlen (see Bazlen entry) that helped make Trieste an important part of Montale's life both as a man and a writer. His crucial part in the *caso Svevo* is well known.

Montale's first Trieste poem was dedicated to Linuccia Saba, the poet's young daughter, who in the mid-1920s was tutored by Bazlen. Bazlen's photo, still extant, of the attractive legs of a woman Montale never met, gave rise to one of his great Trieste portraits, "Dora Markus." Montale regularly reviewed the poetic output of Saba and Giotti. His most important act as a critic, however, was his lifelong advocacy of the work of Svevo, culminating in the great centennial address he gave in 1963 in Trieste. The city, concluded Montale, "in honoring one of its most illustrious sons, once again shows itself worthy of him and of his difficult message." (One wonders if the ghost of the dead master did not smile its smile—ingenuous mixture of pleasure and irony—when the applause began.)

Anita Pittoni (d. 1982)

Born in Trieste c. 1900, by the 1930s Anita Pittoni had earned a wide reputation for her work in the decorative arts, winning international prizes for fabric designs, textiles, and tapestries. In 1948, encouraged by Giani Stuparich, she founded and acted single-handedly as editor and designer of a series of attractively produced books and pamphlets called *Lo Zibaldone* [The miscellany], which aimed, quoting from the prospectus,

> to counterpose to disorder [i.e., civil tensions resulting from the postwar partitioning of Trieste and Istria] the order of culture. Towards this end, nothing more convincing and concrete than publishing original works of various eras by Giulian writers who, by means of a variety of arguments, could give an objective picture of the physiognomy of Trieste and the formerly Austrian Giulian territories, so little and so badly known in Italy.

In the *Zibaldone* first appeared Livia Svevo's account of the life of her husband, certain of Svevo's letters and diaries, poems by Giotti and Saba, Saba's "Quella che resta da fare ai poeti," stories and reminiscences by Stuparich, plus a number of relevant older historical materials. Up through the 1960s, Anita Pittoni's Sat-

urday afternoons in her offices behind the Borsa provided a focal point for Triestine artists and writers.

Pierantonio Quarantotti Gambini (1910–65)

This richly named Istrian was first encouraged to write fiction by Richard
Hughes, who produced a masterpiece, *A High Wind in Jamaica,* while wintering
in Capodistria, now Koper, in 1926–27. Quarantotti Gambini's short stories and
novels focus on contemporary life in Trieste, and have been filmed and widely
translated. During the war he served as director of the Biblioteca Civica in Trieste. He has left a valuable account of the harsh days of Yugoslav occupation,
Primavera a Trieste [Spring in Trieste], that is comparable to Benco's history of the
city in World War I. He was particularly close—like a son—to Saba, who gave
Quarantotti Gambini's best novel its name *(L'onda dell'incrociatore:* The Cruiser's
Wave) and who wrote him just before it was published:

> Trieste has given Italy . . . its best novelist (Svevo), its best poet (Saba) . . . and now
> the most luminous and complex of its younger narrators (Pierantonio Quarantotti
> Gambini). Of all this Italy seems to have noticed very little, and with gritted teeth;
> Trieste, moreover, is the pathetic fool you already know about.

Pasquale Revoltella (1799–1869)

Revoltella means *revolver* in Italian, but this slightly shady self-made man from
Venice acquired his considerable fortune by subtler means. A banker and entrepreneur, he followed his friend, the Baron Bruck, to Trieste in the 1830s and soon
became a director of Lloyd Austriaco. An Austrophile, he was a frequent guest at
the various residences of the Archduke Maximilian up to and including Miramar,
a familiar presence at the Viennese court and in Parisian banking circles, a vice-
president of Ferdinand de Lessups's Suez Company, and a strong supporter of
that venture in the counsels of empire.

In death he was a benefactor, leaving his entire estate to his adopted city. His villa in the center is now the Museo Civico Revoltella, Trieste's museum of fine arts. His property near Piazza Oberdan became the site in 1876 of the Scuola Superiore di Commercio Revoltella, where at different periods both Svevo and Joyce taught, much later the nucleus of the present University of Trieste.

Domenico Rossetti (1774–1842)

Born into one of Trieste's patrician old families, soon to be replaced by the merchant princes of the mid-nineteenth century, Rossetti was a wealthy lawyer, scholar, and ardent patron of his city over the period of Napoleonic occupations at the turn of the century and the resumed Habsburg hegemony that followed. His philanthropies were many: the Winckelmann memorial, the Gabinetto Minerva, the Petrarchan and Piccolominian collections that are the nucleus of the Biblioteca Civica, much of the disposition of the thoroughfares and parks of the newer ("Theresan") parts of town are owing to him. His brimming energies first fostered local archaeological and historical studies.

Although never an irredentist (there was no Kingdom of Italy in his lifetime) Rossetti was a passionate believer in his city's essential *italianità*. Benco thought of him as Trieste's "piccolo Macchiavelli" and indeed he often played the Italian fox with the Viennese authorities who wished to "Germanize" their port. Others, such as Slataper, have found in Rossetti's tightrope tactics a spirit of accommodation very different from Oberdan's idealism: for Slataper, Rossetti was a practical man in a very practical city, basically a well-intentioned "good German." It is certainly true that Rossetti saw a hard fact about Trieste: that its prosperity depended entirely upon the self-interested support of Vienna and that, Vienna once lost (even if it were replaced by Rome), Trieste would be out of a job. In Trieste III this seems a sad but obvious truth.

Umberto Saba (1883–1957)

Saba is the nom de plume, legally adopted in 1928, of the oldest of Italy's three great modern poets. (The others are Ungaretti and Montale.) Since Umberto was the name of the reigning second king of Italy, there must have been many baby Umbertos in irredentist Trieste in the last decades of the nineteenth century, where Saba was born Umberto Poli. Since his father was an Italian from Venice, the baby was Italian.

Through the offices of a marriage broker, Ugo Poli, a forty-year-old widower and installment-plan furniture salesman, had married the Triestine Jewess Rachele Coen in 1882, demanding and getting a large dowry in exchange for his nominal adherence to the Jewish faith. A few months later, he abandoned his wife and unborn son forever. The hard-pressed Rachele took refuge in the flat of her older and unmarried sister, who had a secondhand goods shop in the Jewish quarter of the *città vecchia,* leaving much of the care of her infant to a nurse, Gioseffa Sabaz (but versions differ: Sabbaz, Saber, Sobar, Schebar), the Slovene and Catholic wife of a butcher who lived on Via del Monte near the edge of town.

Saba met his father only once, when he was twenty. In an autobiographical sonnet sequence written much later, he recalls him as being like "a child . . . gay and light" who had floated up and away from his mother's grip—she who "felt all of life's weights"—"like a balloon."

> "Don't," she warned me, "don't be like your father."
> And later on within myself I found the answer:
> They were two races locked in ancient quarrel.

The adult Saba was even inclined to believe that his father had suddenly left Trieste and his little family "for something related to Oberdan's attempted assassination" of the Emperor Franz Josef rather than the brutal caddishness Rachele ascribed to him (she called him "assassin" in a different sense).

Saba's first pseudonym, the "Umberto Chopin Poli" he used to sign poems sent to his friends in 1902, merely added a musical grace note to his given name.

The second, the D'Annunzian "Umberto da Montereale" employed during his Florentine *vagabondaggio* between 1905 and 1907, has been supposed to be an allusion to his father, whose family came from Montereale Valcellina in the province of Udine. (Saba felt, as he wrote in *Autobiografia,* "that the gift that I have I had from him.") A few years later, disenchanted with D'Annunzio, he experimented with "Umberto Lopi," an anagram of Ugo's surname.

"Saba" was discovered in 1910, just in time to be part of the title of his first book. Anna Fano, wife of the poet's closest friend during that period, the philosopher Giorgio Fano, has left an odd account of how he came by it.

> I believe it is little known that the paternity of this name *Saba* now known through all the world is owed to Giorgio Fano. The poet did not like his surname Poli. . . . One time my husband, in an article that appeared in some newspaper, adopted the pseudonym *Saba* which had mysteriously flashed into his mind. He then yielded it to his friend who had been singularly pleased with it.

Why was he attracted?

Saba may possibly be related to the Hebrew Sabbath, or to the Kingdom of Sheba with its famous queen, or to the southern suburb of Trieste (San Sabba) where Joyce watched the needleboats. I have been told that in Hebrew *saba* means "satiety, surfeit, or abundance"; I have also been told it means "grandfather." (The *Encyclopedia Judaica* suggests that the name is "a tribute to his great-grandfather, the scholar Samuel David Luzzato.") But conventional wisdom, supported by the poet's daughter Linuccia, says that Saba was attracted to the name because of its resemblance to that of his beloved nurse. In the variant of the family romance offered in the pages of the *Canzoniere,* Saba's complete poems, Peppa Sabaz (or Saber, etc.) fills the role of the warm and nurturing mama while the unfortunate Rachele Coen Poli is mainly relegated to negligent stepmother status.

Altogether, "Umberto Saba" offers a rich cluster of unstable emotional allusions: womblike security, rejection of the family, Jewishness, Catholicism, a Slovenian butcher's wife who was an Austrian subject, an Italian king . . . (Later, when it was entirely too late, Saba regretted that he had not called himself "Umberto Giuliano" after his native region.) But the compelling need to modify or to create one's own name suggests a need for self-definition, which might be added to the elements of diversity and dividedness first noted by Saba's contemporary and rival Slataper as common aspects of a Triestine "type."

In 1921 Saba began the practice of collecting his poems—often revised and rearranged—under the general title of *Il canzoniere* [Book of songs]. It is in this massive lyric autobiography, containing in its final form over four hundred poems written between 1900 and 1954, that the bulk of his generous, idiosyncratic genius resides. Saba used a variety of traditional closed forms, including sonnets and *canzonette;* only toward the end of his life did he begin to experiment with the freer patterns he associated with Ungaretti. Saba considered the *Canzoniere* to be "the history . . . of a life relatively poor in external events but rich in emotions and inner resonances, in the people whom the poet loved in the course of his long life." This description from his remarkable book-length autocommentary, *Storia e cronistoria del Canzoniere* [History and chronicle of the *Canzoniere*], is apt enough, for Saba's material follows his biography like a shadow. In poem after poem, sequence after sequence, his story unfolds: torments and secret joys of childhood and adolescence, the army, courtship and marriage, the servitude and grandeur of domesticity, erotic adventures real and fancied, vignettes of friends and strangers, the antiquarian bookshop that gave him his living, the liberating experience of his psychoanalysis, old age embittered by Fascist persecution, by the trials of Trieste, by what he felt to be critical neglect. It is the story of a lifetime lived almost entirely in one place, Trieste, and Saba is the poet of that city as Svevo is its novelist. Hills and harbor, streets and houses and shops, men and women and children—all are fused in the pages of the *Canzoniere* through Saba's unique sympathy and limpid language.

At the end of the *Canzoniere* Saba placed his projected epitaph:

> Parlavo vivo a un popolo di morti.
> Morto alloro rifiuto e chiedo oblio.

Alive I spoke to a dead people.
Dead I refuse the laurel and ask oblivion.

In fact he is buried, with his wife and daughter, in the Catholic section of the cemetery of Sant'Anna, not very far from Svevo. The actual epitaph, echoing a motto given in a poem of his old age, reads less bitterly: *Pianse e capì per tutti.* He wept and understood for all of us.

Elio Schmitz (1863–86)

The diary the future novelist's younger brother kept from 1880 until his premature death of Bright's disease constitutes the best available source of information about Svevo's early years. "Inferior to Ettore in intelligence," he wrote in its closing pages, "I confined myself to the humble task of being his bookkeeper and historian. . . . No historian ever admired Napoleon as much as I admired Ettore!" In Elio's *diario* we read of the glassmonger Francesco Schmitz's ambitious plans for his sons (one of the explanations of Ettore's less than fluent Italian):

> You must study hard and become good boys, presentable figures who can one day help me in my business. A decent businessman should know 4 languages at least superficially. A Trieste businessman should know 2 perfectly. For this to be possible, you all will study German in Germany, at a school there. You can learn Italian in Trieste. [The family, of course, spoke the dialect.]

We learn of their education in "an Israelite elementary school run by the best rabbi in Trieste" and in Segnitz, Germany, a hundred miles north of Swabia (Svevia). We learn of the father's sudden bankruptcy, of their poverty, of Ettore's clerkship at the Unionbank, his first writings, his literary admirations (Schiller, Shakespeare in German translation, Zola), his lack of opportunity to write and increasing frustration. We read of Elio's own pathetic three-year drift toward death, a clear-eyed and impotent self-witness.

Ettore Schmitz (1861–1928)

As "Italo Svevo," one of the greatest Italian novelists. Schmitz's first nom de plume (wise precaution for a young bank clerk) was "E. Samigli," used for a number of articles and two short stories published in the *Indipendente* in the 1880s. Its personal significance for the writer is unknown, except that it solved an aesthetic problem he had with Schmitz, which is close to the German for "punch" or "blow" (*Schmiss*) and which consists, as he said, of "one poor little *i* squeezed among six consonants." It also preserved his initials and had an Italian ring.

His daughter offers the best rationale I know for "Italo Svevo."

> This ought not be interpreted in the manner of a number of critics who urge that my father had in this way wanted to underline his German origins on the one hand (his grandfather being of Rhenish extraction) and Italian on the other. He wished, rather, to make explicit in "Svevo" his "Swabian"—i.e., German—culture, the enormous cultural debt he owed to German culture; and in "Italo" his Italian fidelity, his fervent, impassioned love for the literature, culture and civilization of Italy, his authentic and ideal fatherland. German culture and an *italianità* that was psychological and moral, ideological and literary—this is what the definitive pseudonym he adopted was meant to signify.

(A witty remark on Svevo's style made by one of his earliest reviewers must not be allowed to disappear. *Poco Italo e troppo Svevo:* too little Italian, too much Swabian.)

Here is the projected epitaph, an idealized *vita,* devised for Svevo by Umberto Saba in 1929 at the request of his widow, Livia.

FORTUNE AS MUCH AS IT CAN FOR ANY MAN
SMILED UPON HIM
HE HAD HIS STUDIES AND TRANQUILITY IN
CHILDHOOD IN HIS YOUTH HOPE AND LOVE
LOVE AND WEALTH IN HIS BUSY MATURITY
AND IN HIS OLD AGE GLORY

> HE MADE A USEFUL VAST DIFFICULT COMPLEX
> INDUSTRY PROSPER FROM HIS CONSCIOUSNESS
> OF HIS RACE FROM THE AMBIANCE THAT DIS–
> REGARDED HIM HE DREW THE MATERIAL OF
> THREE NOVELS AND A SWEET FLOWERING OF
> FABLES A LONG NOVELLA
> HE LIVED IN HIS LAST YEARS THE THOUSAND
> AND ONE DAYS AS IN A DREAM WITHIN A
> SUNSET ALL OF GOLD

Too long, probably, and possibly Saba, in the middle of his psychoanalysis, lets his envy show too much. Svevo's actual epitaph (written, I should like to think, by Montale) can be found on the threshold of the Veneziani vault, in the Catholic cemetery at Sant'Anna, not very far from Saba.

> ETTORE SCHMITZ . . . LIES HERE BY THE SIDE OF HIS
> BELOVED LIVIA   HE SMILES AT THE LIFE THAT
> PASSES AND AT THE GLORY THAT LATE CROWNED THE
> WORKS OF ITALO SVEVO   IN WHICH NAME WAS
> CONCEALED HIS GENIUS

Scipio Slataper (1888–1915)

"Trieste has a Triestine type . . ." If so, Slataper must be considered the consummate self-conscious example. Here is his own brief for the claim, as quoted by Biagio Marin in his memoir of his dead friend.

> You know that I am Slavic-German-Italian. From my Slav blood I have within me strange nostalgias, a desire for novelty, for abandoned forests, a sentimentality (or sensibility) that demands caresses, praises: an infinite limitless dreaming. From my German blood I have my mulish obstinacy, my dictatorial will and tone, the certainty of my plans, the boredom I feel at having to accept discussion, my desire for

domination, for exertion. These elements are fused in the Italian blood which seeks
to harmonize them, to equilibrate them, to make me become 'classical' . . .
Marin comments: "here they are, the drama and essence of his personality, drama
and essence identical with the whole human history of Venezia Giulia." A Triestine type . . .

Marin, Slataper's self-styled "shadow," remembers him as "our natural
leader, the strongest of us, the self-made man who had already arrived, the writer
for *La Voce* who was the first to have revealed the reality of Trieste to the Italians
and, by speaking bitter truths, had scandalized his fellow-citizens."

His masterpiece, his impassioned study of the type, is *Il mio Carso*.

Giani Stuparich (1891–1961)

Stuparich spent most of his lifetime in his native city, "I might say against my
will since many times I have longed to leave this much loved and most bitter place
in which life is a torment and continuous vigil . . ." He attended universities in
Prague and Florence, and in 1915 escaped across the border to Italy where, with
his brother Carlo and Scipio Slataper, he volunteered for military service. Of the
trio he alone survived. From 1919 to 1942 he taught Italian literature at the Liceo
Dante Alighieri in Trieste (Quarantotti Gambini was one of his students). In 1945
he founded Trieste's Circle of Culture and Arts, of which he served as president,
easing the way for the related work of Anita Pittoni.

Stuparich, the survivor, is a writer who may be characterized as *pius* in the
Virgilian sense, recognizant of the continuity of the past. "An easy maxim," he
has written,

> is that which exhorts man to walk ahead without turning back. Perhaps he is a brave
> one who can conform to this in reality; I myself have not found myself capable of
> following it—it would seem to me that I were moving ahead like a sleepwalker, with
> the unconscious fear of suddenly coming awake and losing my balance. From time
> to time I feel the need of remaking myself through renewing the experiences and acts
> that have penetrated my life most deeply.

His first action in the postwar years, preceding his own creative work, was to gather, edit, and publish the papers of his brother Carlo and of Scipio Slataper, whose biography he wrote. His own genre is the novella and short story, the mood quietly elegiac, the subject based on the personal past, schooldays in Habsburgic Trieste, Istrian summers. *Trieste nei miei ricordi* [Trieste in my memories] is a valuable memoir of literary Trieste between the two wars.

Attilio Tamaro (1884–1956)

This historian's ferocious irredentism is to be distinguished from, say, Slataper's by its imperious xenophobia. This means that Tamaro's Trieste—like D'Annunzio's or Mussolini's—is Roman-Italian; for him its Slav or German components are entirely products of Central European or Balkan propaganda. Born in Trieste and educated there, and, *faute de mieux,* at the University of Vienna, Tamaro was a leader in the battles for an Italian-language university in his city as well as an irredentist correspondent for the *Indipendente* and the *Piccolo.* His post as secretary for the Università popolare (Trieste's adult education center) enabled him to offer his English tutor, James Joyce, the opportunity to give lectures on Irish topics, with Triestine analogies, in the Borsa auditorium. When war came, Tamaro fled to Italy and fought against Austria-Hungary as an infantry lieutenant. He became a passionate recruit to Fascism after Trieste's absorption by Italy and served the regime as minister in Helsinki and Berne until recalled in 1943. His final years in the Republic of Italy were embittered ones.

The two-volume *Storia di Trieste,* first published in 1924, is still, despite its narrow nationalism, extremely useful—especially volume 1, before it arrives at the machinations of the wicked House of Austria in the late *trecento.*

Literary Trieste:
Evidence of Its Existence

Dates are dates of first publication. For Joyce's Trieste writings, see his entry in appendix entitled A Directory of Characters.

1892   Svevo, *Una vita* (A Life), novel.

1898   Svevo, *Senilità* (Senility. It was Joyce who suggested English-language alternatives, either *Adieu Deo Gratias* or *As a Man Grows Older*), novel.

1909   Slataper, *Lettere triestine* (Triestine letters), culture criticism.

1910   Benco, *Trieste,* historical guide.
        Saba, *Poesie di Umberto Saba* (Poems of Umberto Saba), preface by Benco.

1912   Slataper, *Il mio Carso* (My Carso), lyric autobiography.
        Saba, "Quello che resta da fare ai poeti" (What remains for poets to do), unpublished poetics.
        Saba, *Coi miei occhi: il mio secondo libro di versi* (With my own eyes: My second book of verse).
        Marin, *Fiuri de tapo* (Flowers afloat), poems in Grado dialect.

1913   Michelstaedter, *La persuasione e la rettorica* (Persuasion and rhetoric), philosophical dissertation.

1914   Giotti, *Piccolo canzoniere in dialetto triestino* (Little songbook in Trieste dialect), poems 1909–12.

1921   Saba, *Il canzoniere 1900–1921* (Songbook): poems revised and collected.
        Benco, *Nell'atmosfera del sole* (In the atmosphere of the sun), novel.

1922   Benco, *La corsa del tempo* (The passage of time), essays, preliminary selection by Saba.

1923   Svevo, *La coscienza di Zeno* (Consciousness and conscience of Zeno. Current English rendering: *The Confessions of Zeno*), novel.

1926   Cantoni, *Quasi una fantasia* (Almost a fantasy), novel.
        Saba, *Figure e canti* (Figures and songs), poems.

1927   Marin, *Cansone piccole* (Little songs), lyric poems in Grado dialect.

1928   Giotti, *Caprizzi, canzonete e storie* (Caprices, little songs and stories), poems in Triestine dialect 1921–28.

1929   Stuparich, *Racconti* (Tales).
        Svevo, *La novella del buon vecchio e della bella fanciulla* (Story of the nice old man and the pretty young girl), short stories, with preface by Montale.

1932   Stuparich, *Donne nella vita di Stefano Premuda* (Women in the life of Stefano Premuda), short stories.
        Quarantotti Gambini, *I nostri simili* (Our semblables), novel.

1933   Saba, *Tre composizioni* (Three compositions), poems.

1935   Stuparich, *Nuovi racconti (New tales).*

1939   Montale, *Le occasioni* (Occasions), poems, including three based on Triestine sources: "Carnevale di Gerti," "A Liuba che parte," "Dora Markus."

1942   Stuparich, *L'isola* (The island), novella.

1943   Giotti, *Colori* (Colors), collected poems in Triestine dialect.

1945   Saba, *Il canzoniere 1900–1945,* poems revised and collected.

1946   Saba, *Scorciatoie e raccontini* (Shortcuts and little tales), aphorisms and recollections.
        Benco, *Contemplazione del disordine* (Contemplation of disorder), postwar reflections on modern Europe.

1947   Quarantotti Gambini, *L'onda dell'incrociatore* (The cruiser's wave), novel.

1948   Saba, *Storia e cronistoria del Canzoniere* (History and chronicle of the *Canzoniere*), autobiographical account of his poems.

Stuparich, *Trieste nei miei ricordi* (Trieste in my memories), autobiography.

1949 Svevo, *Corto viaggio sentimentale* (Short sentimental journey), incomplete novella and unpublished short stories.

1951 Marin, *I canti de l'isola* (Songs of the island), collected poems to date in Grado dialect.

1961 Saba, *Il canzoniere 1900–1954,* complete collected poems overseen by Saba.

Anonimo triestino, *Il segreto* (Anonymous Triestine = Guido Voghera, The secret), biographical novel of an episode in his son's life.

1964 Saba, *Prose.*

Stuparich, *Ricordi istriani* (Istrian memories), recollections.

1968 Stuparich, *Sequenze per Trieste* (Sequences for Trieste), autobiographical short stories.

1970 Marin, *I canti de l'isola (1912–1969),* poems to date in Grado dialect.

1975 Saba, *Ernesto,* incomplete novel.

1981 Marin, *I canti de l'isola (1970–81).*

1984 Bazlen, *Scritti,* writings including sections of an unfinished novel in German, comments on Trieste and Svevo, letters to Montale.

1986 Giotti, *Opere,* complete works of poetry in dialect and Italian, prose.

1988 Saba, *Tutte le poesie* (Complete poems), *Canzoniere* plus poems excluded from the canon (*Canzoniere apocrifo*).

Endnotes and Acknowledgments

Initial pages and Preliminary

vii   "My animal his sorrafool!" Lines from *Finnegans Wake* (p. 301) by James Joyce, copyright renewed (c) 1967 by Giorgio Joyce and Lucia Joyce. Used by permission of Viking Penguin, a division of Penguin Books USA Inc.

      "It was Trieste." Marcel Proust, *À la recherche du temps perdu* [Pléiade ed.], 3 vols. (Paris, 1954), 2:1121.

x   "Trieste" by Umberto Saba, from *Tutte le poesie* (1988; ed. Arrigo Stara), is used by courtesy of Arnoldo Mondadori Editore.

2   Adolescent Parsifal. Slataper, letter 1, *Lettere triestine*, p. 9.

3   "Majestically covered with a rich robe." *Tre giorni a Trieste*, ed. S. Formiggini et al., pp. 44–45.

4   *calda vita.* Saba, "Il borgo," *Tutte le poesie*, pp. 324–26.

      "I expound Shakespeare." Joyce, *Giacomo Joyce*, p. 10.

      "The rocky highlands and the shining sea," See appendix entitled Translations: Saba, "I Had."

5   Its air was azure. Saba, *Prose*, p. 654.

      "Treacherous white wine." Dario di Tuoni, *Ricordo di Joyce a Trieste*, p. 57.

8   "There are passages in *Senilità.*" Stanislaus Joyce, *The Meeting of Svevo and Joyce*, p. 7.

      "I never crossed the soglia." Joyce, *Letters II and III*, p. 241.

      "Smile at one another without envy." Giani Stuparich, *Trieste nei miei ricordi*, p. 74.

9   "One day is sufficient to visit the town." Joseph Cary, *Three Modern Italian Poets: Saba, Ungaretti, Montale,* p. 31.

10   Joyce recites Verlaine. Di Tuoni, *Ricordo di Joyce a Trieste,* p. 60.

Miramars

14   "Panoramas are not what they used to be," from "Botanist on Alp (No. 1)," in *Collected Poems* by Wallace Stevens. Copyright 1954 by Wallace Stevens. Reprinted by permission of Alfred A. Knopf, Inc., and Faber and Faber, Ltd.

    "Right enough the harbours were there." From James Joyce's *Ulysses,* p. 522. (The Corrected Text; Vintage Books, 1986). Reprinted by permission of Random House, Inc.

16   "Pearled Miramar." Montale, "Buona Linuccia che ascendi . . . ," *L'opera in versi,* p. 780.

17   "Love nest built in vain." Carducci, "Miramar," *Odi barbare* XXII, in *Odi barbaree Rime e ritmi,* vol 4 of *Opere [Edizione nazionale].*

19   "What is coming?" See account by Princess Marie von Thurn und Taxis-Hohenlohe, cited in *Selected Poetry of Rainer Maria Rilke,* trans. and ed. Stephen Mitchell (New York, 1984), p. 315.

    "You travel for hours." *21 Autori: Impressioni su Trieste,* ed. Linda Gasparini, pp. 81–82.

20   "Now I suppose you will think." Brenda Maddox, *Nora, The Real Life of Molly Bloom,* p. 215.

23   A. J. P. Taylor. "Trieste or Trst?" *The New Statesman and Nation,* 9 Dec. 1944, p. 386. See also Taylor, *The Habsburg Monarchy 1809–1918,* p. 202.

    "Once the fourth port." Jan Morris, *Destinations,* p. 214.

    Italian psychoanalyst E. Jogan, cited in Elio Apih, *Trieste,* pp. 195, 199.

24 "Where the sea's azure dissolution." Laura Ruaro Loseri, *Guida di Trieste,* p. 124.

"De mortuis nil nisi bonum." Joyce, *Letters II,* p. 467.

25 Cartoon by José Kollmann published in *La Cittadella,* weekly supplement to *Il Piccolo* (1985).

Up

26 "And the strangers there were sad and double." Bazlen, *Scritti,* p. 97.

34 "This is Illyria, lady." Shakespeare, *Twelfth Night, or, What You Will,* act 1, sc. 2, ll. 2–3.

"O Vague Something behind Everything!" Joyce, *Letters II,* pp. 109–10.

Trieste "waking rawly." Joyce, *Giacomo Joyce,* p. 8. Transposed version ("Paris rawly waking") in *Ulysses* ["The Corrected Text"], pp. 35–36.

Three Triestes

39 "Viva San Giusto!" *Inno marziale* [militant hymn] from Sinico's patriotic opera *Marinella,* first performed in Trieste 26 Aug. 1854.

Marx on Trieste. Cited in Guido Botteri, *Il portofranco di Trieste,* p. 152.

40 Lines from Italo Svevo's *L'avventura di Maria* (*Commedie,* p. 277; 1969); used by courtesy of Dell'Oglio Editore.

41 *Il Dittamondo.* Cited in Attilio Tamaro, *Storia di Trieste,* 1:295.

Three Triestes. Benco, *Trieste tra '800 e '900,* p. 195.

42 The Adriatic "canal." Pietro Kandler, cited in Elio Apih, *Trieste,* p. 8.

Trieste and St. Petersburg. Angelo Ara and Claudio Magris, *Trieste, un identità di frontiera,* 2d ed., p. 4. See Fyodor Dostoevsky, *Notes from Underground,* trans. Jessie Coulson (New York and London, 1972), p. 17.

43   "They live in a sort of stupor." Benco, *Trieste tra '800 e '900*, p. 197.

43–44   Avienus and Priscian. Cited in Tamaro, *Storia di Trieste*, 1:85.

45   Rossetti's allegorical melodrama. *Il sogno di Corvo Bonomo.*

46   "Italian in a different way." Slataper, letter 4, *Lettere triestine*, p. 37.

"Irredentismo." Slataper, *Scritti politici*, pp. 62–63.

"slavo-tedesco-italiano." Slataper, *Lettere*, 3:140–41.

Prezzolini on Slataper. Cited in *Intellettuali di frontiera: Triestini a Firenze (1900–1950)*, ed. Marco Marchi et al., p. 157.

47   "A strange, exotic, heterogeneous new world." Tamaro, *Storia di Trieste*, 1:130.

Apollonius of Rhodes. *Argonautica*, bk 4., ll. 282–337.

Strabo. Cited in E. H. Warmington, *Greek Geography* (London, 1934), p. 218.

Pliny the Elder. *Natural History*, bk. 3, pt. 4; trans. H. Rackham (Cambridge, Mass., 1947), pp. 93–94.

48   Etymologies for Tergeste-Trieste. Laura Ruaro Loseri, *Guida di Trieste*, p. 11.

Joys of Mapwork

52   First story by "E. Samigli." "L'assassinio di Via Belpoggio," in Svevo, *Racconti-Saggi-Pagine sparse.*

"All towns are labyrinths." Frank Budgen, *James Joyce and the Making of Ulysses*, p. 123.

56   Saba's heartbroken poem. "Tre poesie a Linuccia," poem 2. See appendix entitled Translations.

59 "The maze none could untangle." Virgil, *Aeneid*, bk. 6, ll. 27–30, trans. Robert Fitzgerald.

The very first to read that book. See Svevo's letter (in English) to Joyce 8 Feb. 1909, in *Epistolario*, pp. 527–28.

Three Local Martyrs

60 "The air of the room." Joyce, "The Dead," *Dubliners*, p. 223.

Far di sé stesso fiamma. Carlo Michelstaedter, *La persuasione e la rettorica*, p. 197.

"Today is the feast." Joyce, *Letters I*, p. 86.

62 *Acta Sanctorum*. Cited in Mario Mirabella Roberti, *San Giusto*, pp. 16, 56–57.

63 Benedetto Carpaccio, *Madonna, Child, and Two Saints*. Photograph: Neva Gasparo. Courtesy of Cassa di Risparmio di Trieste.

65 Melon song. Alberto Spaini, "Borinetto," in *Scrittori triestini del Novecento*, ed. O. H. Bianchi et al., pp. 947–9.

66 Maugham story. From *Sheppey, Collected Plays of W. Somerset Maugham*, 3 vols. (London, 1931), 3:298.

67 Details of Winckelmann's last weeks. E. M. Butler, *The Tyranny of Greece over Germany* (Boston, 1958); Dominique Fernandez, *Signor Giovanni*; Wolfgang Leppman, *Winckelmann*.

68 Goethe's *Autobiography*, trans. John Oxenford, 1:356.

69 *"Prepare to meet your God."* Spoken by a sailor in the cabman's shelter about "a man killed in Trieste by an Italian chap." Joyce, *Ulysses* ["The Corrected Text"], p. 514.

70 Chronogram. Quoted in Henry C. Hatfield, *Winckelmann and His German Critics 1755–1781*, p. 103.

71   The neoclassic movement. Hugh Honour, *Neo-classicism*, p. 62.

      "As a defiled temple reconsecrates itself." Benco, *Trieste*, pp. 65–66.

      A notable *schmier*. Fulvio Anzellotti, *Il segreto di Svevo*, pp. 60–61, 66.

73   Lady Burton on the Exposition. Isabel Burton, *Life of Captain Sir Richard F. Burton*, 2:237–38, 244.

74   A poem by Carducci. Carducci, "Saluto italico." *Odi barbare* XX, in *Odi barbare e Rime e ritmi*, vol. 4 of *Opere [Edizione nazionale]*. See next chapter.

76   Carducci on Oberdan. Carducci, *Opere [Edizione nazionale]*, 9:191–95.

      Slataper on Oberdan. See Slataper, "L'irredentismo" and "Il valore d'un anniversario: Guglielmo Oberdan," *Scritti politici*, pp. 81–85, 245–52.

Faithfully Waiting

79   "I was born with Italy." Svevo, *Epistolario*, p. 609.

80   "Penetrate like a wedge." Carducci, *Opere*, 19:206, 196.

83   A ghostly possibility, nothing more. Unless there is information to the contrary in the unpublished Trieste diary of Stanislaus Joyce, Richard Ellmann has no grounds for saying Joyce "probably attended the important exhibition of futurism which was held in Trieste about 1908" (*James Joyce*, rev. ed., p. 430 n.); the date is wrong in any case. On no better grounds, Gianni Pinguentini asserts that Joyce "certamente assistava" at the 1910 soirée (*James Joyce in Italia*, p. 175).

84   Tricolor sea. Cited in Walter Vaccari, *Vita e tumulti di F. T. Marinetti*, p. 173.

85   Marinetti's memoir of the Trieste soirée. Cited in Francesco Cangiullo, *Le serate futuriste*, pp. 263–71. A slightly different version, which includes Marinetti's complete discourse to the Triestines, is in F. T. Marinetti, *Teoria e invenzione futurista*, pp. 210–16.

87   Marinetti drawing from *Futurismo and Futurismi,* ed. Pontus Hulten (Milan 1986), p. 192.

"You are the scarlet." Marinetti, *Teoria e invenzione futurista,* p. 247.

88   Cocteau on Marinetti. *Le rappel à l'ordre* (Paris, 1948), p. 83.

Testudoform. Joyce, *Giacomo Joyce,* p. 8.

"A man who writes too well to be sincere." Svevo, *Racconti-Saggi-Pagine sparse,* p. 820.

91   One witness of that mooring. Carlo Schiffrer, cited in Angelo Ara and Claudio Magris, *Trieste, un identità di frontiera,* 2d ed., p. 109.

Translation from Goethe, *Faust,* pt. I, by Louis MacNeice (New York, 1959), p. 59.

Tableaux morts

97   Contemporary judgments of the Borsa. *Il Palazzo della Borsa vecchia di Trieste 1800–1980,* ed. Franco Firmani, p. 29.

98   "To stir things up." Attilio Tamaro, *Storia di Trieste,* 2:459.

Joyce lecture. Trans. Ellsworth Mason in Joyce, *The Critical Writings,* pp. 153–74.

100–101   *Carlo VI concede Trieste le franchigie portuali* by Giuseppe Bernardino Bison, on the ceiling of the sala grande on the piano nobile of the Palazzo della Borsa Vecchia. Photograph: Neva Gasparo.

103   "Grandpa, do they know." Letizia Svevo Fonda Savio and Bruno Maier, *Iconografia sveviana,* pp. 132–33. Svevo uses a variant of this episode in his incomplete novella "Corto viaggio sentimentale," *Racconti-Saggi-Pagine sparse,* p. 175.

105   Franz Josef's letter. Cited in F. Fölkel and C. L. Cergoly, *Trieste provincia imperiale,* p. 41.

106   "A vast collection of Irelands." A. J. P. Taylor, *The Habsburg Monarchy 1809–1918*, p. 22.

110   "Jinns and Jinniyahs." Richard Burton, *The Book of the Thousand Nights and a Night*, 1:vii, 10:124–25.

111   Benco's ironic hindsight. Benco, *Trieste*, pp. 106–8.

112   Musil's "magic formula: '*Ass.*'" Robert Musil, *The Man without Qualities*, trans. Eithne Wilkins and Ernst Kaiser, 1:266.

       Benco on the railroad terminal. Benco, *Trieste*, p. 139.

114–115   *Il Commercio* (*Commerce*) and *L'Industria* (*Industry*), murals by Eugenio Scomparini, in the Galleria Nazionale d'Arte Antica in Trieste. Courtesy of Cassa di Risparmio di Trieste.

117   "literary" station caffè. Gîani Stuparich, *Trieste nei miei ricordi*, p. 194.

The Sloblands of Fairview

119   "In this city there shall dominate." Svevo, *Lettere a Svevo. Diario di Elio Schmitz*, p. 88.

120   "Palm trees don't grow on ice." Umberto Veruda, cited by Benco, *Trieste tra '800 e '900*, p. 244.

122   Stendhal in Trieste. Nora Franca Poliaghi, *Stendhal e Trieste*, pp. 51, 53, 113.

       Richard Burton's diary. Cited in Lesley Blanch, *The Wilder Shores of Love*, p. 88.

123   Elio Schmitz's diary. Svevo, *Lettere a Svevo*, p. 256.

       Svevo's own diary. Svevo, *Racconti-Saggi-Pagine sparse*, pp. 814–15.

123–25   Quotations and paraphrases from *Una vita*. Svevo, *Romanzi*, 1:199, 233, 237–39.

124   Schopenhauerian Q.E.D. Svevo, "Profilo autobiografico," *Racconti-Saggi-Pagine sparse,* p. 801.

125   "Operetta wisdom." Hermann Broch, *Hugo von Hofmannsthal and His Time,* trans. Michael P. Steinberg, p. 81.

        Kundera on Biedermeier. Milan Kundera, "Sixty-three Words," *The Art of the Novel,* trans. Linda Asher, p. 124.

        Svevo's "iron resolution." Svevo, *Racconti-Saggi-Pagine sparse,* p. 818.

126   "Signor Ettore Schmitz." In *Corriere di Gorizia,* 18 Oct. 1898.

        Review of *Una vita* in *Corriere della Sera.* Cited in Letizia Svevo Fonda Savio and Bruno Maier, *Iconografia sveviana,* p. 143. The reviewer was Domenico Oliva.

        Quotation from *Senilità.* Svevo, *Romanzi,* 1:433–34.

126–27 Benco's review of *Senilità.* Fonda Savio and Maier, *Iconografia sveviana,* pp. 143–45.

127   Svevo in Florence. Livia Veneziani Svevo, *Vita di mio marito,* p. 30.

        Benco on Triestine literature. Benco, *Trieste,* pp. 186–89.

128   Ziliotto on modern Triestine literature. Baccio Ziliotto, *Storia letteraria di Trieste e dell'Istria,* pp. 92–95.

131   "The growth of a soul in Trieste." Slataper, *Il mio Carso,* p. 105.

        Slataper as "pure Slav." Slataper, letter 1, *Lettere triestine.*

132   "To make me 'classical.'" Slataper, *Lettere,* 3:138.

        On the phrase *Vorrei dirvi.* See Angelo Ara and Claudio Magris, *Trieste, un identità di frontiera,* 2d ed., ch. 1.

        "Mixed and insecure Italianness." Slataper, "Irredentismo," *Scritti politici,* pp. 62–63.

133   "The golden thread." Saba, "Ai miei lettori," *Prose,* p. 665.

Saba as "timid." Slataper, "Perplessità crepuscolare," *Scritti letterari e e critici*, p. 182.

"Born in the shadow of San Giusto." Svevo, "Triestinità di un grande scrittore irlandese: James Joyce," *Scritti su Joyce*, p. 39.

133–34   Stephen's literary walk. Joyce, *A Portrait of the Artist as a Young Man*, p. 176.

134   Father Conmee's walk. Joyce, *Ulysses* ["The Corrected Text"], p. 182.

Apace apace on horseback. Joyce, *Giacomo Joyce*, p. 8. Compare the librarian Best in *Ulysses* ["The Corrected Text"], p. 151: "He came a step a sinkapace forward on neatsleather creaking and a step backward a sinkapace on the solemn floor."

"Easy now, Jamesy!" Joyce, *Giacomo Joyce*, p. 6. Compare Molly Bloom in *Ulysses* ["The Corrected Text"], p. 633: "O Jamesy let me up out of this pooh . . ."

"He walks in order to be left to himself." Svevo, "Mr James Joyce described by his faithful pupil Ettore Schmitz," [in English] *Racconti-Saggi-Pagine sparse*, p. 748.

135   Saba's noisy scapegoat. Saba, "La capra," *Tutte le poesie*, p. 78. See Joseph Cary, *Three Modern Italian Poets: Saba, Ungaretti, Montale*, pp. 64–65.

Trieste Trouvée

137   Passage from Roberto Bazlen interview is from *Scritti* (1984); used by courtesy of Adelphi Edizione S.p.A.

138   "There is something in this city." Giani Stuparich, *Trieste nei miei ricordi*, in *Cuore adolescente, Trieste nei miei ricordi* (Rome: Edizioni Riuniti, 1984), p. 81. © heirs of Stuparich.

"Trieste is perhaps the sole Italian city." From *Carteggio Svevo/Montale*, p. 120, © 1976 Arnoldo Mondadori. Published by courtesy of Arnoldo Mondadori Editore S.p.A.

139   Prezzolini's view of Slataper. Cited in *Intellettuali di frontiera*, ed. Marco Marchi et al., p. 157.

On *La Voce* and Slataper. Giuseppe Prezzolini, *La Voce 1908–1913. Cronaca, antologia e fortuna di una rivista*, pp. 44, 80–82, 94–95, 242.

142   Trieste's reactions to *Lettere triestine*. Summarized by Slataper in an unpublished ms. cited in Slataper, *Lettere triestine*, p. 53.

143   *Carsina*. Slataper, *Il mio Carso*, p. 147, and Roberto Damiani, "Introduzione," in ibid., p. 20.

Various schemes for *Il mio Carso*. Slataper, *Epistolario*, pp. 58, 209.

"Read *Il mio Carso*." Cited in Saba, *Prose*, p. 441.

Final tercet of an autobiographical sonnet. Saba, *Autobiografia*, sonnet 10, *Tutte le poesie*, p. 264.

144   Sabotage of *Coi miei occhi*. *Intellettuali di frontiera*, pp. 121–22, 129–30, 139; Saba, *La spada d'amore*, pp. 78–79, *Prose*, p. 441.

144–45   Benco's portrait of Saba. First published in *Solaria* [Saba issue] (May 1928), reprinted in *galleria* [Saba issue], p. 106.

145–46   Slataper's reviews of Saba. Slataper, "Perplessità crepuscolare" and "Poesie," *Scritti letterari e critici*, pp. 181–89, 239–42.

146   Slataper's Zarathustran standard. Slataper, *Epistolario*, p. 114.

147   Saba's response to Slataper. Alberto Spaini, "Umberto Saba e *La Voce*," *galleria* [Saba issue], pp. 163–66.

Saba's views of *Poesie di Umberto Saba*. Saba, *Prose*, p. 406; *Intellettuali di frontiera*, p. 116.

Saba's letters to Slataper. Saba, *La spada d'amore*, pp. 69–70; Saba, *Prose*, p. 406.

147–48   "Quella che resta da fare ai poeti." Saba, *Prose,* pp. 751–59.

148   "E così ha fatto il Pascoli." Stelio Mattioni, *Storia di Umberto Saba,* p. 57.

149   "No fortune." Saba, *Prose,* p. 441. On "Quella che resta," see Joseph Cary, *Three Modern Italian Poets: Saba, Ungaretti, Montale,* pp. 14–18, 45–46.

Slataper and *Sturm und Drang.* Stuparich, *Trieste nei miei ricordi,* p. 152.

149–50   "Mr James Joyce described." Richard Ellmann, *James Joyce,* rev. ed., pp. 272–73.

150–51   Joyce reads Svevo: Stanislaus Joyce, *The Meeting of Svevo and Joyce* (1965); reprinted by permission of Del Bianco Editore.

151   Svevo on *A Portrait.* Svevo, *Epistolario,* pp. 527–28.

"What my brother found in Italo Svevo." Stanislaus Joyce, "Introduction" to Svevo, *As a Man Grows Older,* trans. Beryl di Zoete.

Vidacovich on Svevo. Stanislaus Joyce, *The Meeting of Svevo and Joyce,* p. 8.

152   Why Svevo wrote *"so badly."* Benco, "Italo Svevo" *Pegaso* 1, no. 1 (Jan. 1929): 49.

On Svevo's Italian and German. Letizia Svevo Fonda Savio and Maier, *Iconografia sveviana,* pp. 41–43; Giorgio Voghera, "Considerazioni eretiche sulla 'scrittura' di Italo Svevo," *Gli anni di psicanalisi,* pp. 45–51.

153   On Svevo's laziness. Bazlen, *Scritti,* pp. 380–81; Pierantonio Quarantotti Gambini, *Il poeta innamorato,* pp. 31–32.

Joyce's Italian. Alessandro Francini Bruni, *Joyce intimo spogliato in piazza;* Benco, "Ricordi di Joyce," *Pegaso* 2, no. 8 (Aug. 1930): 152–53.

Both translated in *Portraits of the Artist in Exile: Recollections of James Joyce by Europeans,* ed. Willard Potts.

Montale's phrase. "Omaggio a Italo Svevo," in *Carteggio Svevo/Montale,* p. 77.

154   "Merchant of gerunds." Svevo, "Scritti su Joyce," *Racconti-Saggi-Pagine sparse,* p. 709.

Details of Svevo's wartime repose. Svevo, "Profilo autobiografico," *Racconti-Saggi-Pagine sparse,* pp. 807–8.

155   "My ancient phantasms." Svevo, *Epistolario,* pp. 824–25; a fuller, complete version in Bruno Maier, *Saggi sulla letteratura triestina del Novecento,* p. 74.

"If Italy had not come to me." Maier, *Saggi sulla letteratura triestina,* p. 74.

156   Benco's review of *La coscienza di Zeno.* Cited in Fonda Savio and Maier, *Iconografia sveviana,* pp. 145–47.

157   Joyce's letter of advice to Svevo. Joyce, *Letters III,* pp. 86–87.

Montale's first essay. "Omaggio a Italo Svevo," in *Carteggio Svevo/Montale,* pp. 71–82.

Stile tremendo! Bazlen, *Scritti,* p. 359.

La bomba Svevo. Ibid., p. 365.

158   "Reading him translated." Giulio Caprin, cited in *Leggere Svevo. Antologia della critica sveviana,* ed. Luciano Nanni, pp. 148–49.

"The three great . . . Triestine artists." Montale, "Umberto Saba," *Sulla poesia,* pp. 206–7.

158–59 Montale's discourse on the Svevo centenary. *Carteggio Svevo/Montale,* pp. 120–21.

159 "Married it to Italy forever with my song." Saba, "Avevo," *Tutte le poesie*, p. 510. See appendix entitled Translations.

160 "Today it is possible to affirm." Pietro Pancrazi, "Giani Stuparich triestino," *Scrittori d'oggi (serie seconda)*, pp. 103–4.

The Masters in the Public Garden

167 "Alas, we are so fashioned." Biagio Marin, *Strade e rive di Trieste*, pp. 210–11.

168 "The most beautiful book." Benco, "Su Scipio Slataper," *Scritti di critica letteraria e figurative*, p. 316.

Stuparich teased by Montale. Giani Stuparich, *Trieste nei miei ricordi*, p. 176.

169 *Triestino d'elezione.* Montale, "Ricordo di Roberto Bazlen," in *Carteggio Svevo/Montale*, p. 146.

Three Farewells

172 Maximilian and the fata morgana. Cited in Ville de Trieste/Institute Cultural Italien à Paris, *Portraits pour une ville: Fortunes d'un port adriatique*, p. 225.

174 *«Ulisse» ossia «Sua mare grega»* Livia Veneziani Svevo, *Vita di mio marito*, pp. 101–3. See also Joyce, *Selected Letters*, pp. 275–77, and Richard Ellmann's editor's notes. Brenda Maddox suggests that the bundle also contained "Nora's obscene letters of 1909" (*Nora, the Real Life of Molly Bloom*, p. 204).

175 In the gloom the gold. See Ezra Pound, canto XI, *The Cantos* (London, 1986), p. 51.

179   Seagulls in Trieste. Svevo, *Una vita, Romanzi*, 1:207–8.

Translations Appendix

184–207   These nine poems from Umberto Saba's *Tutte le poesie* (1988; ed. Arrigo Stara) are used by courtesy of Arnoldo Mondadori Editore.

212   Photograph in Letizia Fonda Savio and Bruno Meier, *Iconographia sveviana: scritti parole e immagini della vita privata di Italo Svevo* p. 67, © by Edizioni Studio Tesi S.r.L., 1981.

213–16   Passage from Italo Svevo's *Epistolario* (1966) used by permission of Dell'Oglio Editore S.r.L.

218, 220   "A Flower Given to My Daughter," "Watching the Needleboats at San Sabba," from James Joyce, *Collected Poems*. Copyright 1918 by B. W. Huebsch, Inc., 1927, 1936 by James Joyce, 1946 by Nora Joyce. Used by permission of Viking Penguin, a division of Penguin Books USA Inc.

219, 221   The two Montale translations of the Joyce poems are from *Quaderno di traduzioni* in *L'opera in versi*, 1980, and are used by courtesy of Arnoldo Mondadori Editore.

A Directory of Characters

224   Montale on Bazlen. "Ricordo di Roberto Bazlen," *Carteggio Svevo/Montale*, pp. 145–47.

"Are you mad?" Bazlen, *Scritti*, p. 363.

225   "No longer possible to write books." Ibid., p. 203.

226   "His blue eyes danced." Aurelia Gruber Benco, "Between Joyce and Benco," *James Joyce Quarterly* [Trieste issue] 9, no. 3 (Spring 1972): 328.

227   "John Bull to the bone." Isabel Burton, *Life of Captain Sir Richard F. Burton,* 2:512.

       Freud on the Triestines. "Che brutti, i triestini," *Il Piccolo,* 12 Dec. 1989 [excerpts from Freud's letters to Eduard Silberstein].

228   "Trieste is no Vienna." "On Concept and Object," *Translations from the Writings of Gottlob Frege,* ed. P. T. Geach and Max Black, Oxford 1970, p. 50.

       Svevo on Freud. Svevo, *Racconti-Saggi-Pagine sparse,* pp. 685–86, 807.

       On Weiss and Triestine intelligensia, see Giorgio Voghera, *Gli anni di psicanalisi,* pp. 3–42.

229   Giotti on the language of poetry. Pier Paolo Pasolini, "La lingua della poesia," in Giotti, *Opere,* pp. 30–31.

       Benco on Giotti's language. Benco, "Un giorno con Giotti," *Scritti di critica letteraria e figurative,* p. 343.

       Montale on Giotti's focus. *Sulla poesia,* p. 232.

229–30   Relations of Giotti and Saba. Giotti, "Appunti inutili," *Opere,* pp. 391–92; Stelio Mattioni, *Storia di Umberto Saba,* pp. 112, 159–60, 173–74; Giani Stuparich, *Trieste nei miei ricordi,* p. 75; Ettore Serra, *Il tascapame di Ungaretti. Il mio vero Saba,* p. 200; Pierantonio Quarantotti Gambini, *Il poeta inamorato,* pp. 72–77.

230   Joyce on Istria. Richard Ellmann, *James Joyce,* rev. ed., p. 186.

231   Benco on Joyce's Italian. Benco, "James Joyce a Trieste," *Trieste tra '800 e '900,* pp. 272–73.

232   "When will you write an Italian work." Svevo, *Epistolario,* p. 692.

232–33   Ellmann on the role of Stanislaus. Introduction to Stanislaus Joyce, *My Brother's Keeper,* p. 16.

233   "I functioned as a second work horse." *Recollections of James Joyce by His Brother Stanislaus,* trans. Ellsworth Mason, p. 24.

       "Now comes the hard part." Stelio Crise, *Epiphanies & Phadographs,* p. 12.

       On Stanislaus's Trieste diary, see Brenda Maddox, *Nora, the Real Life of Molly Bloom,* p. 411 n. 39.

233–34   Marin's 1950 preface. In Biagio Marin, *Parola e poesia,* p. 15.

234   "With the soul of a pilgrim." "Italo Svevo, nel centenario della nascita," in *Carteggio Svevo/Montale,* p. 143.

235   *Lo Zibaldone* prospectus. Anita Pittoni, *Catalogo generale dello Zibaldone 1949–1969,* p. 3.

236   Saba's letter. *Il vecchio e il giovane: Umberto Saba/Pierantonio Quarantotti Gambini, Carteggio 1930–1957,* pp. 38–39.

239   Fano on "Saba". Anna Fano, "L'amicizia tra gli scaffali della Libreria Antiquaria," *Il Piccolo,* 25 Aug. 1967, 3.

241   Elio's diary. Svevo, *Lettere a Svevo. Diario di Elio Schmitz,* pp. 199, 295.

242   Svevo's daughter on "Italo Svevo". Letizia Svevo Fonda Savio and Bruno Maier, *Iconografia sveviana,* p. 79.

       "*Poco Italo e troppo Svevo.*" Cited in Fulvio Anzellotti, *Il segreto di Svevo,* p. 178.

242–43   Saba's epitaph for Svevo. In Saba, *Tutte le poesie,* p. 970.

243–44   Marin on Slataper. Marin, *I delfini di Scipio Slataper,* pp. 13, 34, 59–60.

244   "An easy maxim." Stuparich, "Continuità," *Il ritorno del padre,* p. 125.

Bibliography

Guides to Trieste and Environs

Agapito, Girolamo. *Compiuta e distesa descrizione della fedelissima città e porto-franco di Trieste*. Vienna, 1824.

Baedeker, Karl. *Baedeker's Austria-Hungary, with Excursions to Cetinse, Belgrade, and Bucharest*. Leipzig, London, and New York, 1911.

Benco, Silvio. *Trieste*. Trieste, 1910.

Bevilacqua, Matteo di. *Descrizione della fedelissima imperiale regia città e portofranco di Trieste*. Venice, 1820; reprint Trieste, 1982.

Formiggini, S., et al., eds. *Tre giorni a Trieste*. Trieste, 1858; reprint Trieste, 1982.

Ruaro Loseri, Laura. *Guida di Trieste: La città nella storia, nella cultura e nell'arte*. Trieste, 1985.

Touring Club Italiano. *Friuli-Venezia Giulia*. Milan, 1982.

Weaver, William. "Trieste: Between the Two Europes," *New York Times,* 23 Jan. 1983, Sunday travel section.

Historical Studies of Trieste

Apih, Elio, with Giulio Sapelli and Elvio Guagnini. *Trieste*. Bari, 1988.

Bettiza, Enzo. *Mito e realtà di Trieste*. Milan, 1966.

Botteri, Guido. *Il portofranco di Trieste: Una storia europea di liberi commerci e traffici*. Trieste, 1988.

Cusin, Fabio. *Appunti alla storia di Trieste*. Milan, 1930.

Fölkel, F., and C. L. Cergoly. *Trieste provincia imperiale: Splendore e tramonto del porto degli Asburgo*. Milan, 1983.

Godoli, Ezio. *Trieste*. Rome and Bari, 1984.

Ireneo della Croce. *Historia antica e moderna, sacra e profana della città di Trieste fino a quest'anno 1698.* Venice, 1698.

Kandler, Pietro. *Storia del Consiglio dei patrizi di Trieste dall'anno MCCCLXXXII all'anno MDCCCIX.* Trieste, 1868.

Mihelić, Dusan. *The Political Element in the Port Geography of Trieste.* Chicago, 1969.

Novak, Bogdan C. *Trieste 1941–1954: The Ethnic, Political, and Ideological Struggle.* Chicago, 1970.

Powell, Nicolas. *Travellers to Trieste. The History of a City.* London, 1977.

Rossetti, Domenico. *Meditazione storica-analitica sulle franchigie della città e porto franco di Trieste.* Venice, 1815.

Rutteri, Silvio. *Trieste, spunti dal suo passato.* Trieste, 1950.

Tamaro, Attilio. *Storia di Trieste.* 2 vols. Trieste, 1924; reprint Trieste, 1976.

Vivante, Arturo. *Irredentismo adriatico. Contributo alla discussione.* Florence, 1912.

Related Historical Materials Pertaining to the Intellectual and Social History of Trieste, Italy, and Central Europe

Ara, Angelo, and Claudio Magris. *Trieste, un identità di frontiera.* 2d ed. Turin, 1987.

Ash, Timothy Garton. "Does Central Europe Exist?" *New York Review of Books,* 9 Oct. 1986, 45–52.

Broch, Hermann. *Hugo von Hofmannsthal and His Time: The European Imagination 1860–1920.* Trans. Michael P. Steinburg. Chicago, 1984.

———. *The Sleepwalkers. A Trilogy.* Trans. Willa and Edwin Muir. New York, 1947.

Caprin, Giuseppe. *I nostri nonni. Pagine della vita triestina dal 1800 al 1830.* Trieste, 1888.

Coons, Ronald E. *Steamships, Statesmen, and Bureaucrats: Austrian Policy towards the Steam Navigation Company of the Austrian Lloyd.* Weisbaden, 1975.

Crankshaw, Edward. *Maria Theresa.* New York, 1970.

———. *The Fall of the House of Habsburg.* New York, 1983.

David, Michael. *La psicanalisi nella cultura italiana.* Turin, 1966.

Gasparini, Linda, ed. *21 Autori: Impressioni su Trieste 1793–1887.* Trieste, 1951.

Goethe, Johann Wolfgang von. *Autobiography.* 2 vols. Trans. John Oxenford. Chicago, 1974.

Hatfield, Henry C. *Winckelmann and His German Critics 1755–1781.* New York, 1943.

Hofmannsthal, Hugo von. *Selected Prose.* Trans. Mary Hittinger and Tania and James Stern. New York, 1952.

Honour, Hugh. *Neo-classicism.* Harmondsworth, 1968.

Hughes, H. Stuart. *Prisoners of Hope: The Silver Age of the Italian Jews 1924–1974.* Cambridge, Mass., 1983.

Janck, Allan, and Stephen Toulmin. *Wittgenstein's Vienna.* New York, 1973.

Johnston, William M. *The Austrian Mind: An Intellectual and Social History 1848–1938.* Berkeley and Los Angeles, 1983.

Kundera, Milan. *The Art of the Novel.* Trans. Linda Asher. New York, 1988.

———. "The Tragedy of Central Europe," *New York Review of Books,* 24 Apr. 1984, 33–38.

Mack Smith, Denis. *Italy, a Modern History.* Ann Arbor, Mich. 1969.

Mann, Vivian B., ed. *Gardens and Ghettos: The Art of Jewish Life in Italy.* Berkeley and Los Angeles, 1989.

Moodie, A. E. *The Italo-Yugoslav Boundary. A Study in Political Geography.* London, 1945.

Morris, Jan. *Destinations.* New York, 1980.

Musil, Robert. *The Man without Qualities.* 3 vols. Trans. Eithne Wilkins and Ernst Kaiser. London, 1979.

———. *Precision and Soul. Essays and Addresses.* Trans. and ed. Burton Pike and David S. Luft. Chicago, 1990.

Pârvan, Vasile. *Dacia, an Outline of the Early Civilization of the Carpatho-Danubian Countries.* Cambridge, 1928.

Pater, Walter. *The Renaissance.* Cleveland and New York, 1961.

P.E.N. Club International. *Scrittori e letterature di frontiera*. Lugano, 1987.

Quarantotti Gambini, Pierantonio. *Primavera a Trieste*. Milan, 1967.

Roberti, Mario Mirabella. *San Giusto*. Trieste, 1970.

Rossetti, Domenico. *Il sogno di Corvo Bonomo*. Trieste [1814], 1882.

Roth, Joseph. *The Radetzky March*. Trans. Eva Tucker and Geoffrey Dunlop. Woodstock, N.Y., 1983.

Schorske, Carl E. *Fin-de-Siècle Vienna, Politics and Culture*. New York, 1981.

Seri, Alfieri. *Trieste nelle sue stampe*. Trieste, 1980.

Taylor, A. J. P. *The Habsburg Monarchy 1809–1918. A History of the Austrian Empire and Austria-Hungary*. Chicago, 1976.

———. "Trieste or Trst?" *The New Statesman and Nation*, 9 Dec. 1944, 386.

Varnadoe, Kirk. *Vienna 1900: Art, Architecture and Design*. New York, 1986.

Ville de Trieste/Institute Cultural Italien à Paris. *Le Bateau blanc. Science technique, design: La construction navale à Trieste*. Trieste, 1985.

Ville de Trieste/Institute Cultural Italien à Paris. *Portraits pour une ville: Fortunes d'un port adriatique*. Trieste, 1985.

Ville de Trieste/Institute Cultural Italien à Paris. *Un Regard retrouvé: Auteurs et acteurs du cinéma de Trieste*. Trieste, 1985.

Zuccotti, Susan. *The Italians and the Holocaust: Persecution, Rescue and Survival*. New York, 1987.

Literary and Cultural Trieste
(work specifically by and on Benco, Joyce, Saba, Slataper, and Svevo follows this section)

Anonimo triestino [Guido Voghera]. *Il segreto*. Turin, 1961.

Anonymous. *Eugenio Scomparini. Pittura ed altro da Sedan a Sarajevo*. Trieste, 1984.

Bazlen, Roberto. *Scritti*. Milan, 1984.

Bettiza, Enzo. *Il fantasma di Trieste*. Milan, 1958.

Bianchi, O. H., et al., eds. *Scrittori triestini del Novecento*. Trieste, 1968.

Blanch, Lesley. *The Wilder Shores of Love*. London, 1954.

Burton, Isabel. *Life of Captain Sir Richard F. Burton, K.C.M.G., F.R.G.S.* 2 vols. London, 1893.

Burton, Richard. *The Book of the Thousand Nights and a Night.* 10 vols. London, n.d.

Cangiullo, Francesco. *Le serate futuriste. Romanzo storico vissuto.* Milan, 1961.

Cantoni, Ettore. *Quasi una fantasia.* Milan, 1926.

Carducci, Giosuè. *Opere [Edizione nazionale].* 20 vols. Ed. Luigi Federini et al. Rome, 1889–1909.

Critique [special issue, *Le Mystère de Trieste*] 39, no. 435–36 (Aug.–Sept. 1983).

Del Giudice, Daniele. *Lo stadio di Wimbledon.* Turin, 1983.

Fernandez, Dominique. *Signor Giovanni.* Paris, 1981.

Firmiani, Franco, ed. *Il palazzo della Borsa vecchia di Trieste 1800–1980. Arte e storia.* Trieste, 1981.

Giotti, Virgilio. *Opere: Colori-Altre Poesie-Prose.* Trieste, 1986.

Haller, Hermann W. *The Hidden Italy: A Bilingual Edition of Italian Dialect Poetry.* Detroit, 1986.

Hulton, Pontus, ed. *Futurismo e futurismi.* Milan, 1986.

Larbaud, Valery. *Journal intime de A. O. Barnabooth.* Paris, 1913.

Leppmann, Walter. *Winckelmann.* New York, 1970.

Maier, Bruno. "La letteratura triestina del Novecento," introductory essay to *Scrittori triestini del Novecento.* See Bianchi, O. H., et al.

———. *Saggi sulla letteratura triestina del Novecento.* Milan, 1972.

Marchi, Marco, et al., eds. *Intellettuali di frontiera: Triestini a Firenze (1900–1950).* Florence, 1983.

Marin, Biagio. *I delfini di Scipio Slataper.* Milan, 1965.

———. *Parola e poesia.* Genoa, 1984.

———. *Poesie.* Ed. Claudio Magris and Edda Serra. Milan, 1981.

———. *Strade e rive di Trieste.* Milan, 1987.

Marinetti, F. T. *Teoria e invenzione futurista.* Milan, 1968.

Masiero, Roberto, ed. *Il mito sottile: Pittura e scultura nella città di Svevo e Saba.* Trieste, 1991.

Michelstaedter, Carlo. *Il dialogo della salute e altri dialoghi*. Milan, 1988.

———. *La persuasione e la rettorica*. Milan, 1982.

Montale, Eugenio. *L'opera in versi*. Turin, 1980.

———. *Sulla poesia*. Milan, 1976.

Pancrazi, Pietro. "Giani Stuparich triestino," *Scrittori d'oggi (serie seconda)*. Bari, 1946.

———. "Giotti poeta triestino," *Scrittori d'oggi (serie quarta)*. Bari, 1946.

Pellegrini, Ernestina. *La Trieste di carta. Aspetti della letteratura triestina del Novecento*. Bergamo, 1987.

Pittoni, Anita. *Catalogo generale dello Zibaldone 1949–1969*. Trieste, 1969.

Poliaghi, Nora Franca. *Stendhal e Trieste*. Florence, 1984.

Prezzolini, Giuseppe. *La Voce 1908–1913. Cronaca, antologia e fortuna di una rivista*. Milan, 1974.

Quarantotti Gambini, Pierantonio. *Il poeta innamorato. Ricordi*. Pordenone, 1984.

———. *L'onda dell'incrociatore*. Turin, 1947.

———. *Luce di Trieste*. Turin, 1964.

Rocco-Bergera, Niny, with Carlina Rebecchi-Piperata. *Itinerary of Joyce and Svevo through Artistic Trieste*. Trieste, 1971.

Stuparich, Giani. *Cuore adolescente. Trieste nei miei ricordi*. Rome, 1984.

———. *Il ritorno del padre*. Turin, 1961.

———. *Ricordi istriani*. Trieste, 1964.

———. *Sequenze per Trieste*. Trieste, 1968.

Tomizza, Fulvio. *Trilogia istriana*. Milan, 1968.

Vaccari, Walter. *Vita e tumulti di F. T. Marinetti*. Milan, 1959.

Verne, Jules. *Mathias Sandorf*. Paris, 1885.

Voghera, Giorgio. *Gli anni di psicanalisi*. Pordenone, 1980.

Wostry, Carlo. *Storia del Circolo artistico di Trieste*. Udine, 1934.

Ziliotto, Baccio. *Storia letteraria di Trieste e dell'Istria*. Trieste, 1924.

SILVIO BENCO

Novels

> *Il castello dei desideri.* Milan, 1906.
> *La fiamma fredda.* Milan, 1904.
> *Nell'atmosfera del sole.* Milan, 1921.

Historical Essays

> *Contemplazione del disordine.* Udine, 1946.
> *Gli ultimi giorni della dominazione austriaca a Trieste.* 3 vols. Rome, Milan, and Trieste, 1919.
> *Trieste.* Trieste, 1910.

Criticism

> *La corsa del tempo.* Trieste, 1922.
> "*La coscienza di Zeno,* romanzo di Italo Svevo," in *Iconografia sveviana.* See Fonda Savio, Letizia Svevo, and Bruno Maier (under Svevo).
> "Italo Svevo," *Pegaso* 1, no. 1 (Jan. 1929): 48–57.
> "Prefazione," *Poesie di Umberto Saba.* Florence, 1910.
> "Ricordi di Joyce," *Pegaso* 2, no. 8 (Aug. 1930): 150–65.
> *Scritti di critica letteraria e figurative.* Ed. O. H. Bianchi, B. Maier, and S. Pesante. Trieste, 1977.
> "*Senilità* di Italo Svevo," in *Iconografia sveviana.* See Fonda Savio, Letizia Svevo, and Bruno Maier (under Svevo).
> "*Senilità* di Italo Svevo dopo trent'anni," *Piccolo della Sera,* 6 Sept. 1926, reprinted in *Scritti di critica,* 324–28.
> *Trieste tra '800 e '900: una città tra due secoli.* Bologna, 1988.
> "L'*Ulisse* di James Joyce," *La Nazione,* 1 Apr. 1922.
> "Un 'Ulisse' irlandese," *Il Secolo,* 18 Nov. 1921.
> "*Umberto Veruda.* Trieste, 1907.

JAMES JOYCE

Works

Collected Poems. New York, 1965.

The Critical Writings. Ed. Ellsworth Mason and Richard Ellmann. New York, 1959.

Dubliners. New York, 1962.

Exiles. New York, 1945.

Finnegans Wake. New York, 1966.

Giacomo Joyce. Ed. Richard Ellmann. New York, 1968.

Letters I. Ed. Stuart Gilbert. New York, 1966.

Letters II and III. (2 vols.). Ed. Richard Ellmann. New York, 1966.

A Portrait of the Artist as a Young Man. New York, 1966.

Selected Letters. Ed. Richard Ellmann. New York, 1975.

Stephen Hero. New York, 1944.

Ulysses ["The Corrected Text"]. New York, 1986.

Critical/Biographical

Bollettieri, Rosa Maria Bosinelli. "The Importance of Trieste in Joyce's Work, with Reference to His Knowledge of Psychoanalysis," *James Joyce Quarterly* 7, no. 3 (spring 1970): 177–85.

Budgen, Frank. *James Joyce and the Making of Ulysses.* Bloomington, Ind., 1961.

Crise, Stelio. *Epiphanies & Phadographs. James Joyce e Trieste.* Milan, 1967.

Ellmann, Richard. *James Joyce.* Rev. ed. Oxford and New York, 1972.

Francini Bruni, Alessandro. *Joyce intimo spogliato nel piazza.* Trieste, 1922.

James Joyce Quarterly [Joyce and Trieste Issue] 9, no. 3 (spring 1972).

Joyce, Stanislaus. "Introduction" to Svevo, *As a Man Grows Older.* Trans. Beryl de Zoete. New York, 1968.

———. *My Brother's Keeper.* London, 1958.

———. *Recollections of James Joyce by His Brother Stanislaus.* Trans. Ellsworth Mason. New York, 1950.

————. *The Meeting of Svevo and Joyce*. Udine, 1965.

Maddox, Brenda. *Nora, the Real Life of Molly Bloom*. Boston, 1988.

Melchiori, Giorgio, ed. *Joyce in Rome: The Genesis of Ulysses*. Rome, n.d.

Mottola, Alfonso. *Immagini triestine per Giacomo Joyce*. Supplement to *James Joyce Quarterly* 28, no. 3 (Spring 1991).

Pinguentini, Gianni. *James Joyce in Italia*. Florence, 1963.

Potts, Willard, ed. *Portraits of the Artist in Exile: Recollections of James Joyce by Europeans*. San Diego and New York, 1986.

Scholes, Robert, and Richard M. Kain, eds. *The Workshop of Daedalus: James Joyce and the Raw Materials of a Portrait of the Artist as a Young Man* [contains Joyce's "Trieste Notebook"]. Evanston, Ill., 1965.

Staley, Thomas. "James Joyce in Trieste," *Georgia Review* 16 (Winter 1972): 446–49.

Tuoni, Dario di. *Ricordo di Joyce a Trieste*. Milan, 1966.

UMBERTO SABA

Works

Il canzoniere 1900–1954. Turin, 1965.

Ernesto. Turin, 1975.

Prose. Ed. Linuccia Saba. Milan, 1964.

Tutte le poesie. Ed. Arrigo Stara. Milan, 1988.

L'adolescenza del Canzoniere e undici lettere. Ed. Folco Portinari. Turin, 1975.

Amicizia. Storia di un vecchio poeta e di un giovine canarino. Ed. Carlo Levi. Milan, 1976.

Il canzoniere 1921. Ed. Giordano Castellani. Milan, 1981.

Coi miei occhi. Ed. Claudio Milanini. Milan, 1981.

Poesie di Umberto Saba. Pref. by Benco. Florence, 1910.

Letters (the complete *Epistolario,* as edited by the poet's late daughter Linuccia, remains unpublished to date)

Atroce paese che amo. Lettere famigliari (1945–1953). Ed. Gianfranca Lavezzi and
    Rossana Sacconi. Milan, 1987.

Lettere a un'amica (74 lettere a Nora Baldi). Turin, 1966.

Lettere a un amico vescovo. Vicenza, 1980.

Lettere sulla psicanalisi. Carteggio con Joachim Flescher 1946–1949. Ed. Arrigo
    Stara. Turin, 1991.

Saba Svevo Comisso (lettere inedite). Ed. Mario Sutor. Padua, 1967.

Serra, Ettore. *Il tascapane di Ungaretti. Il mio vero Saba*. Rome, 1983.

La spada d'amore. Lettere scelte 1902–1957. Ed. Aldo Marcovecchio. Milan,
    1983.

*Il vecchio e il giovane: Umberto Saba/Pierantonio Quarantotti Gambini, Carteggio
    1930–1957*. Ed. Linuccia Saba. Milan, 1965.

See also Lavagetto, Mario, ed. *Per Conoscere Saba*.

Critical/Biographical

Atti del Convegno Internazionale. *Il punto su Saba*. Trieste, 1985.

Baldi, Nora. *Il paradiso di Saba*. Milan, 1958.

———, and Alfonso Mottola. *Immagini per Saba*. Trieste, 1983.

Cary, Joseph. *Three Modern Italian Poets: Saba, Ungaretti, Montale*, 2d ed., re-
    vised and enlarged. Chicago and London, 1993.

Cecchi, Ottavio. *L'aspro vino (Ricordi di Saba a Firenze '43–44)*. Milan, 1967.

Debenedetti, Giacomo. *Saggi critici*. Milan, 1952.

———. "Ultime cose su Saba," *Intermezzo*. Milan, 1963.

Fano, Anna. "L'amicizia tra gli scaffali della Libreria Antiquaria," *Il Piccolo*,
    25 Aug. 1967, 3.

galleria [fasciolo dedicato ad Umberto Saba] (Jan.–April 1960).

Lavagetto, Mario. *La gallina di Saba*. Turin, 1974.

———. "Nascere a Trieste nel 1883," *Paragone* (June 1972): 4–32.

———, ed. *Per Conoscere Saba*. Milan, 1981.

Mattioni, Stelio. *Storia di Umberto Saba*. Milan, 1989.

"Omaggio a Saba," *Nuovi argomenti (nuova serie)* no. 57 (Jan.–Mar. 1978): 9–93.

Pittoni, Anita. *Caro Saba*. Trieste, 1977.

Solaria [Saba issue] (May 1928).

Zorn Giorni, Lionello. *Saba e il cinese e altri racconti*. Gorizia, 1987.

SCIPIO SLATAPER

Alle tre amiche. Milan, 1958.

Epistolario. Ed. Giani Stuparich. Milan, 1950.

Il mio Carso. Ed. Roberto Damiani. Trieste, 1988.

Lettere. 3 vols. Ed. Giani Stuparich. Turin, 1931.

Lettere triestine. Ed. Elvio Guagnini. Trieste, 1988.

Scritti letterari e critici. Ed. Giani Stuparich. Rome, 1920.

Scritti politici [includes *Lettere triestine*]. Ed. Giani Stuparich. Milan, 1954.

Stuparich, Giani. *Scipio Slataper*. Florence, 1922.

ITALO SVEVO

Works

Opera omnia

1. *Epistolario*. Ed. Bruno Maier. Milan, 1966.

2. *Romanzi*. 2 vols. Ed. Bruno Maier. Milan, 1969.

3. *Racconti-Saggi-Pagine sparse*. Ed. Bruno Maier. Milan, 1968.

4. *Commedie*. Ed. Ugo Apollonio. Milan, 1969.

5. *Lettere a Svevo. Diario di Elio Schmitz*. Ed. Bruno Maier. Milan, 1973.

6. *Carteggio con James Joyce, Valery Larbaud, Benjamin Crémieux, Marie Anne Comène, Eugenio Montale, Valerio Jahier*. Ed. Bruno Maier. Milan, 1965.

Carteggio Svevo/Montale con gli scritti di Montale su Svevo. Ed. Giorgio Zampa. Milan, 1976.

Samigli E. [pseud. Svevo], "Una lotta," *Paragone* 30 (1970): 61–72.

Scritti su Joyce. Ed. Giancario Mazzacurati. Parma, 1986.

Critical/Biographical

Anzellotti, Fulvio. *Il segreto di Svevo*. Pordenone, 1985.

Cahiers pour un temps: Italo Svevo et Trieste. Paris, 1987.

Debenedetti, Giacomo. *Saggi critici (seconda serie)*. Milan, 1971.

Fonda Savio, Letizia Svevo, and Bruno Maier. *Iconografia sveviana*. Pordenone, 1984.

Furbank, P. N. *Italo Svevo, the Man and the Writer*. London, 1966.

Gatt-Rutter, John. *Italo Svevo: A Double Life*. Oxford, 1988.

Kezich, Tullio. *Svevo e Zeno, vite parallele*. Milan, 1970.

Lavagetto, Mario. *L'impiegato Schmitz e altri saggi su Svevo*. Turin, 1975.

Modern Fiction Studies [Italo Svevo issue] 18, no. 1 (spring 1972).

Nanni, Luciano, ed. *Leggere Svevo. Antologia della critica sveviana*. Bologna, 1974.

Russell, Charles C. *Italo Svevo, the Writer from Trieste. Reflections on His Background and His Work*. Ravenna, 1978.

Veneziani Svevo, Livia. *Vita di mio marito*. Ed. Lina Galli. Milan, 1976.

Index

Alaric, 57

Alboin, 57, 131, 132

Angelis, Francesco. *See* Arcangeli,
Francesco

anima patria, 129, 133, 143, 169

Apollonius of Rhodes, 47

Aquileia, 43, 81, 233

Arabian nights, atmosphere of, 2, 42,
94, 96, 102, 110, 116, 243

Arabian Nights, book. *See* Burton,
Richard

Arcangeli, Francesco, 69–70

Artifoni, Almidano, 230

Attila, 43, 57

Audace, 22, 56, 85, 91, 226

Austria (Austria-Hungary 1867–
1918), 2, 3, 4, 11, 12, 15, 16–22,
39, 42–8, 52, 57, 68–9, 72–6, 78–
80, 82–3, 85, 93, 94, 96, 98, 106,
111, 116, 129, 140, 176, 179, 226,
227, 235, 239, 245

Avienus, Rufus Festus, 43

azure (*azzurro,* color of poetry), 5, 6,
18, 19, 53, 56, 58, 112, 113, 172,
180

Bartoli, Gianni, 164, 169

Bazlen, Roberto, 6, 26, 137, 153,
157–8, 160, 224–5, 228, 234–5, 250

Benco, Silvio, 6, 27, 41–6, 48, 71, 83,
111, 112, 113, 125–30, 141, 144–5,
147, 152, 153, 155, 156–7, 158,
159, 164, 168, 169, 225–6, 229,
231, 236, 237, 248, 249

Berlitz School ("Cul"), 35, 153, 177,
230–1, 232

Bezzecca, 79, 81

Biblioteca Civica, 1, 9, 224, 236, 237

Biedermeier (style), 3, 125, 142

Bison, Giuseppe Bernardino, 99–103

Boccardi, Alberto, 127–9

bomba Svevo, 157, 224

bora, 3, 16, 29, 34, 53, 56, 178

Borgo Teresiano, 5, 12, 53, 97, 124,
237

Borsa Vecchia, 2, 27, 29, 35, 97–105,
112, 121, 198–9, 236, 245

Broch, Hermann, 125

Bronzetti, Narciso (Garibaldian, d.
1859), 81

Bruck, Karl Ludwig von, 105–6, 236

Budgen, Frank, 53
Burton, Isabel, 73, 122, 227
Burton, Richard, 34, 73, 93, 110, 122, 227

Caesar, Octavian, 11, 43, 57, 66
caffès, 1, 6, 8, 16, 67, 83, 85, 113, 117, 196–9
calda vita, 4, 6, 10, 36, 165, 167
Canal Grande, 5–6, 7, 53, 124, 175
Cantoni, Ettore, 249
Carducci, Giosuè, 6, 17–18, 22, 74–6, 80–6, 89, 91, 111, 128, 129, 143, 146, 168
Carlota, Archduchess, Empress of Mexico, 6, 17–21, 110
Carpaccio, Benedetto, 62–4
Carso, 1, 11, 12, 15, 16, 19–23, 29, 35, 42, 46–7, 51, 57, 69, 95, 131, 132, 135, 145, 149, 154, 176
caso Svevo, 123, 128, 150, 152, 157, 235
Cavaceppi, Bartolommeo, 68
cavatappi (corkscrew), 9
Charles VI, Emperor, 12, 16, 67, 93, 95–7, 99–103, 106
Cinema Eden, 9
Cinema Sexy, 28, 59
Circle of Culture and Arts, 138, 158–9, 244

città vecchia, 35, 52, 53, 97, 178, 184–5, 209–10, 238
Cocteau, Jean, 88
Corazzini, Sergio, 146
coscienza, 139, 148, 160, 167, 226
Crémieux, Benjamin, 153, 157–8
crepuscolarismo, 146–7
Crise, Stelio, 233
Croats, 47, 208

Dalmatia, 9, 47, 79, 194–5
D'Annunzio, Gabriele, 34, 84, 88–91, 113, 128, 140, 141, 144, 146, 152, 153, 177, 226, 239, 245
Dante, 18–19, 41, 44, 66, 78, 133, 141
Davis, Bette, 17, 20
dedalo. See maze
dedizione (1382), 11, 12, 44–5, 47, 72, 93
Del Giudice, Daniele, 225
Dellaberrenga, Tito, 128
Dias, Willy, 127–8
Diocletian, Emperor, 62
Dostoevsky, Fyodor, 42
Duino, 3, 15, 18–19, 43, 177

Eliot, T. S., 157
Ellmann, Richard, 232, 233

Faa di Bruno, Emilio, 89–90
Faltus, F., 107–10

Fano, Giorgio, 239

Fascism, 2, 23, 28, 43, 91, 200–5, 240, 245

fata morgana, 34, 172, 180

Fazio degli Uberti, 41, 43, 66

Fittke, Arturo, 158, 169

Fiume (Rijeka), 23, 34, 44, 80, 88, 177

Flaubert, Gustave, 124

Fonda Savio, Letizia Svevo, 152, 213, 242

Ford, Ford Madox, 157

France, Anatole, 8, 151

Francini Bruni, Alessandro, 153, 226, 231

Franz Ferdinand, Archduke, 4

Franz Josef, Emperor, 16, 17, 42, 48, 73, 75–6, 105–10, 112, 129, 168, 177, 225, 238

Free Territory of Trieste, 12

Frege, Gottlob, 228

Freud, Sigmund, 6, 8, 154, 224, 227–8

Friuli-Venezia Giulia, 28, 45, 47, 80, 103, 117, 126, 127, 128, 131, 235, 240, 244

futurismo, 83–9, 116, 139

Gabinetto Minerva, 122, 141, 151–2, 153, 231, 237

Garibaldi, Giuseppe, 72, 74, 79

ghost(s), 7, 8–10, 23, 24, 35, 37, 52, 61, 66, 71, 82, 83, 88, 107, 135, 161, 169, 178, 180, 235

Giocare, Giuseppe (projects of), 4–10, 107, 135, 164, 174–5, 179–80; *Vocabolario esoterico,* vii

Giotti, Virgilio, 6, 117, 130, 138, 140, 155, 158, 159, 160, 164, 169, 229–30, 233, 234, 235, 248, 249, 250

Goethe, Johann Wolfgang von, 67–8, 70, 91

Gozzano, Guido, 146

Grado, 233–4

Grand Hotel. *See* Locanda Grande

Grand International Exposition of Trieste, 71–5

grappa, 51–9

grey (*grigio,* color of prose), 1, 6, 9, 16, 23, 29–37, 48, 104, 123–6, 151, 153, 174–5, 178, 179, 180

Guida di Trieste. See Ruaro Loseri, Laura

Habsburgs. *See* Charles VI, Franz Josef, Maria Theresa, etc.

Haydèe (Ida Finzi), 127–8

Honour, Hugh, 70–1

Hotel Al Teatro, 9, 27, 35, 36, 51, 56, 98, 178

Hughes, Richard, 236

Hugo, Victor, 75–6

Ibsen, Henrik, 34, 134
Illyria, 11, 34, 35
Indipendente (newspaper), 71, 225, 242, 245
Ireneo della Croce, 1
irredentism, 16, 22, 40, 42–7, 61, 66, 72–6, 78–91, 98, 107, 116, 129, 131, 142, 168, 169, 225, 237, 238, 245
Istria, 11, 12, 23, 28, 34, 35, 42, 44, 47, 65, 69, 80, 82, 111, 128, 129, 177, 230, 245

Joseph II, Emperor, 67, 96–7
Joyce, J., 230
Joyce, James, 4, 5, 6, 8, 10, 24, 27, 34, 35, 52, 53, 61, 71, 83, 88, 98, 103–4, 111, 127, 130, 134, 135, 149–54, 156, 164, 167, 168, 169–71, 173–4, 177, 226, 230–2, 237, 239, 245, 248; "The Dead," 7, 60, 150; *Dubliners,* 153, 168, 232; *Finnegans Wake,* vii, 10; *Giacomo Joyce,* 6, 34, 88, 220, 231, 232; *Pomes Penyeach,* 6, 183, 218–21, 232; *A Portrait of the Artist as a Young Man,* 59, 133–4, 151, 232; *Ulysses,* 7, 14, 34, 53, 69, 120, 134, 174–5, 179, 230, 232
Joyce, Nora, 8, 20, 154, 230, 231

Joyce, Stanislaus, 8, 127, 150–1, 154, 173, 218–19, 232–3
Juarez (film), 17, 20, 24

Kafka, Franz, 112, 224
Kakania. *See* Musil, Robert
Karst. *See* Carso
Kingdom of Italy (*Regno*), 12, 21–2, 42, 44, 56, 79–80, 84, 88, 91, 116, 129, 132, 133, 140, 237, 239
krš (karst), 15, 131, 208–9
Kundera, Milan, 125

labyrinth. *See* maze
Larbaud, Valery, 94, 153, 157–8
Lechner de Lechfeld, Giovanni Antonio, 52–8, 95, 97, 107
Leopardi, Giacomo, 133, 142, 145, 147, 152
Levi, Carlo, 149
Libreria antica e moderna (Libreria antiquaria Umberto Saba), 35, 131, 155–6, 202–3, 229, 230–1, 240
Libreria Italo Svevo, 28, 36, 51, 59, 106, 173
Lissa (Vis), 5, 79, 89–90, 194–5
Ljubljana (Laibach), 12, 69, 97, 105–6, 177
Lloyd Adriatico, 166

Lloyd Austriaco, 5, 12, 105, 107, 110, 122, 236

Lloyd Triestino, 16

Locanda Grande, 21, 67–9

Luzzato, Emma, 127

Luzzato, Samuel David, 239

mangiare il fegato, vii, 10

Manzoni, Alessandro, 127

maps, 5, 8, 9, 13, 27–8, 50–9, 164, 166–7, 170, 174, 176–7

Maria Theresa, Empress, 2, 12, 58, 67–9, 95, 96–7

Marin, Biagio, 6, 130, 140, 159, 167, 169, 233–4, 243–4, 248, 249, 250

Marinetti, Filippo Tommaso, 6, 83–9, 112, 116

Marx, Karl, 39, 86

Master of San Giusto, 62–4

Maugham, Somerset, 66

Maximilian, Archduke, Emperor of Mexico, 6, 17–21, 23, 35, 79, 107, 110–11, 121, 172, 236

maze, 50, 52–3, 57, 134, 135, 166

Mercury, 97, 113, 117, 119, 120, 122, 123, 128, 140, 175

meridiana (noon mark), 99, 104

Michelstaedter, Carlo, 6, 60, 234, 248

Miramar (castle), 16–23, 29, 34, 35, 42, 110, 121, 176, 236

miramar (strong verb and act), 15, 18–23, 27, 29, 35, 67

Mitteleuropa, 20, 23, 105–6, 110, 176, 224, 245

moles, 1, 5, 9, 15, 22, 23, 35, 53, 56, 67, 85, 91, 94, 97, 175, 192–3

Montale, Eugenio, 6, 16, 138, 153, 157–61, 168, 169, 183, 218–21, 224–5, 226, 229, 234–5, 238, 243, 249, 250

Montereale, Umberto da. *See* Saba, Umberto

Morpurgo, Mario, 20, 73, 121

Musil, Robert, 111–12, 224

Mussolini, 23, 43, 91, 139, 225, 245

Napoleon I, 2, 12, 22, 36, 45, 53, 58, 97, 103, 122, 175, 237, 241

Napoleon III. *See* Rains, Claude

neoclassicism, 71, 97, 99, 102, 175

Nietzsche, Friedrich, 131, 132, 146, 152

Obelisk, 1, 5, 19, 21, 22, 26, 27, 28, 33–7, 97, 107, 110, 122, 174, 227

Oberdan, Guglielmo, 12, 27, 30, 52, 61, 71–6, 83, 91, 237, 238

Opicina, 19–20, 23, 26–9, 84, 110, 134, 174, 227

Palazzeschi, Aldo, 146

Pancrazi, Pietro, 160

Papini, Giovanni, 139, 143, 144, 147

Pascoli, Giovanni, 146, 147, 148

Pater, Walter, 70, 157

Pennadoro. *See* Slataper, Scipio

Petrarch, Francesco, 122, 133, 142, 237

Piccolo (newspaper), 9, 24, 31, 33, 141, 153, 155, 176, 177, 225, 231, 245

Piccolomini, Enea Silvio, 122, 237

pigeons, 59, 94, 166, 167, 171, 177–8

Pitteri, Riccardo, 128, 164, 168

Pittoni, Anita, 149, 235, 244

Pliny the Elder, 47

Pola (Pula), 44, 78, 80, 82, 177, 230

Poli, Ugo, 72, 238

Poli, Umberto. *See* Saba, Umberto

Popper, Amalia, 220–1, 231

porta orientale, 16, 21, 91

portofranco, 52, 53, 56, 67, 72, 93, 95–7, 99–103, 117, 209

Pound, Ezra, 24, 175, 231

Prezioso, Roberto, 231

Prezzolini, Giuseppe, 46, 139–40, 144

Princip, Gavrilo, 4, 76

Priscian, 44

Proust, Marcel, vii, 24

Public Garden, 2–3, 9, 51, 134, 161, 164–71

Puccini, Giacomo, 5, 218–19

puntofranco, 117

Quarantotti Gambini, Pierantonio, 117, 153, 236, 244, 249

Quarnero, 44, 78, 88

railroads, 12, 93, 175–7

railroad station, 35, 51, 105–17, 121, 175–7

Rains, Claude, 17

Regio X (Roman Tenth District), 11, 43–4, 57

Republic of Italy, 11, 12, 15, 42, 245

Revoltella, Pasquale, 3, 6, 20–1, 111, 121, 122, 124, 236–7

Rex (bar, dog), 27, 29, 36, 37, 58, 174

Rilke, Rainer Maria, 19

risorgimento, 3, 22, 84

Roman Empire, 1–2, 11, 42–8, 57, 62, 66, 82

Rossetti, Domenico, 2, 45–6, 58, 71, 83, 122, 166, 167, 237

Ruaro Loseri, Laura, 2, 9, 24, 28–33, 36, 48, 135, 175

Saba, Lina, 135, 192–3, 202–3

Saba, Linuccia, 6, 56, 149, 158, 202–3, 204–7, 235, 239

Saba, Umberto, x–xi, 1, 2, 4, 5, 8, 27, 34, 52, 56, 72, 83, 134–5, 140,

142, 144–5, 152, 155, 158, 159, 160, 161, 164, 170–1, 209, 228, 229–30, 231, 235, 236, 238–41, 242–3; *Il canzoniere*, 5, 131, 135, 149, 156, 183–207, 239, 240–1, 248, 249, 250; *Coi miei occhi (Trieste e una donna)*, 6, 130, 144, 147, 148, 149, 248; *Poesie di Umberto Saba*, 130, 143, 145–7, 248; "Quello che resta da fare ai poeti," 147–9, 235, 248; *Storia e cronistoria del Canzoniere*, 240, 249

Sabaz, Peppa, 238, 239

Salieri, Antonio, 121

Samigli, E. *See* Svevo, Italo

San Giusto (cathedral), 3, 16, 35, 62–7, 71, 229

San Giusto (hill), 1, 16, 35, 39, 53, 62, 64, 71, 80–2, 97, 133, 206–7

San Giusto (hymn), 39, 167, 168

San Giusto (saint and martyr), 61–6

San Sabba, 5, 7, 218–19, 239

San Sergio/Servolo, 62–4

saracinesche, 178

Sartorio, Giovanni Guglielmo, 20, 121

Sbisà, Carlo, 3

Schmitz, Elio, 119, 123, 241

Schmitz, Ettore. *See* Svevo, Italo

Schmitz, Francesco, 241

Schönbeck, Virgilio. *See* Giotti, Virgilio

Scomparini, Eugenio, 113–17, 227

Scussa, Vittorio, 65

seagulls, 89, 177–9

Seldes, Gilbert, 157

Shakespeare, William, 4, 34, 35, 120, 122, 241

Signor Giovanni. *See* Winckelmann, Johann

Sinico, Giuseppe, 39, 164, 167, 168

Slataper, Scipio, 2, 6, 46, 48, 74, 76, 139, 144–9, 155, 159, 160, 164, 168, 169, 172, 225, 233, 237, 243–4, 245; *Lettere triestine*, 46, 120, 137, 140–3, 146, 152, 243, 248; *Il mio Carso*, 128, 130, 131–3, 143–4, 183, 208–210, 244, 248

Slavs, 11, 15, 23, 46, 47, 48, 74, 91, 94, 106, 131, 132, 160, 168, 196–7, 208–9, 230, 243, 245

Slovenes, 9, 15, 23, 46, 47, 91, 131, 139, 143, 238

Soffici, Ardengo, 139

Solaria, 158

souvenirs, 16, 17, 95, 106

Stendhal, 122

Stevens, Wallace, 14

Strabo, 47

Stuparich, Carlo, 140, 233, 244, 245

Stuparich, Giani, 6, 8, 117, 138, 140, 149, 155, 158, 160, 164, 168, 169, 233, 235, 244–5, 249, 250
sua mare grega, 34, 173–5, 179
Südbahn (T.-Vienna railway), 12, 19, 20, 93, 105–11, 177
Suez Canal, 12, 21, 236
Svevo, Italo, 4, 5, 7, 8, 27–8, 52, 58, 59, 71, 79, 83, 85, 88, 103–4, 113, 116, 119, 123–8, 133, 134–5, 138, 141, 149–61, 164, 168, 169–71, 173, 224, 228, 231, 232, 233, 234, 235, 236, 237, 240, 241, 242–3, 249, 250; *L'avventura di Maria,* 40; *La coscienza di Zeno,* 5, 6, 28, 34, 126, 128, 131, 154–7, 160, 228, 248; "Cronaca della famiglia," 183, 212–16; "Mr James Joyce described by his faithful pupil Ettore Schmitz," 135, 149–50; *Senilità,* 5, 6, 8, 125–7, 130, 145, 151, 153–4, 157, 160, 168, 248; *Una vita,* 8, 104, 123–6, 130, 151, 153, 179, 248
Svevo, Livia Veneziani, 6, 7, 150–1, 173, 212–16, 231, 235, 242–3

Tamaro, Attilio, 44–7, 72, 98, 132, 142, 231, 245
Taylor, A. J. P., 23, 106, 110
Tergeste, 41, 43–4, 47–8, 63, 70, 179, 196–7
Tiepolo, Giovanni Battista, 102
Timavo (river), 11, 15, 18, 47
Touring Club Italiano, 9, 18
Trajan, Emperor, 43, 66
tram (T.-Opicina), 1, 9, 26–34, 36–7, 52
tram (T.-Servola), 155
Tre giorni a Trieste, 20–1, 110–111, 118, 121–2, 140
Trentino (and Trento), 46, 80, 81, 139
triangle(s), 5, 7, 8, 83, 107, 129, 130, 169–70
Trieste (guidebook by Benco), 111, 112, 141, 226, 248
Trieste, identity crisis of, 23, 46, 132, 142, 160, 172, 228, 240
Trieste, literary, 4–6, 27, 35, 83, 88, 91, 122, 127, 129, 130, 133–5, 142, 158–63, 169, 175, 179, 234, 245, 247–50
Trieste, personifications of, 1–3, 45, 58, 97, 121, 140–1, 166, 236
Trieste (III, II, I), 41–8, 79, 82, 91, 95, 113, 125, 128, 129, 131, 159, 160–1, 168, 169, 237
"triestinitis," vii
triestino (dialect), 9, 29–33, 152, 158, 159, 174, 178, 179, 229, 241
triste Trieste (joke), vii, 7, 10, 23, 179
"Trouver Trieste" (Paris exhibition,